CATHAY
AND THE WAY THITHER

CATHAY
AND THE WAY THITHER

BEING A COLLECTION OF
MEDIEVAL NOTICES OF CHINA

TRANSLATED AND EDITED

BY

COLONEL SIR HENRY YULE, R.E., C.B.,
K.C.S.I.

CORR. INST. FRANCE

WITH A
PRELIMINARY ESSAY

ON THE INTERCOURSE BETWEEN CHINA AND THE WESTERN NATIONS PREVIOUS TO THE DISCOVERY OF THE CAPE ROUTE

NEW EDITION, REVISED THROUGHOUT IN THE LIGHT OF RECENT DISCOVERIES

BY

HENRI CORDIER, D. LITT., HON. M.R.A.S.,
HON. COR. M.R.G.S., HON. F.R.S.L.

MEMBER OF THE INSTITUT DE FRANCE
PROFESSOR AT THE ECOLE DES LANGUES ORIENTALES VIVANTES, PARIS

VOL. III

MISSIONARY FRIARS—RASHIDUDDIN—PEGOLOTTI—
MARIGNOLLI

GYAN

Published by

Gyan Publishing House
5, Ansari Road
Daryaganj, New Delhi-110002
Phone: 011-47034999, 9811692060
E-mail: books@gyanbooks.com

Distribution Network
gyanbooks.com
India, USA, Canada, UK, Australia, France

ISBN : 978-81-212-3198-5 (Set)
ISBN : 978-81-212-4819-8 (HB)
First Published, London, 1914

2nd Impression 2020

Printed at: Gyan Press, Delhi.

Cathay and the Way Thither Vol. III
Author: Colonel Sir Henry Yule

CATHAY
AND THE WAY THITHER

BEING A COLLECTION OF
MEDIEVAL NOTICES OF CHINA

TRANSLATED AND EDITED

BY

COLONEL SIR HENRY YULE, R.E., C.B., K.C.S.I.
CORR. INST. FRANCE

WITH A
PRELIMINARY ESSAY
ON THE INTERCOURSE BETWEEN CHINA AND THE WESTERN
NATIONS PREVIOUS TO THE DISCOVERY OF THE CAPE ROUTE

NEW EDITION, REVISED THROUGHOUT IN THE LIGHT
OF RECENT DISCOVERIES

BY

HENRI CORDIER, D.LITT., HON. M.R.A.S.,
HON. COR. M.R.G.S., HON. F.R.S.L.
MEMBER OF THE INSTITUT DE FRANCE
PROFESSOR AT THE ÉCOLE DES LANGUES ORIENTALES VIVANTES, PARIS

VOL. III

MISSIONARY FRIARS—RASHÍDUDDÍN—PEGOLOTTI—
MARIGNOLLI

LONDON:
PRINTED FOR THE HAKLUYT SOCIETY
MDCCCCXIV

TABLE OF CONTENTS

CATHAY AND THE WAY THITHER

II. LETTERS AND REPORTS OF MISSIONARY FRIARS FROM CATHAY AND INDIA (1292—1338)

ILLUSTRATION

II

LETTERS AND REPORTS OF MISSIONARY FRIARS FROM CATHAY AND INDIA

II

LETTERS AND REPORTS OF MISSIONARY FRIARS FROM CATHAY AND INDIA

INTRODUCTORY NOTICES

THE first two letters in this part of our collection are from the pen of John of MONTE CORVINO, the founder of those Catholic missions in China which enjoyed so much apparent prosperity during the continuance of the Mongol dynasty, and also the first Archbishop of Cambalec or Peking. They are transcribed by Wadding from an old chronicle which he assigns to Odoric of Pordenone, erroneously as we have seen[1].

The third document also, I believe to contain, for reasons which will be given, a letter from the same ecclesiastic, of earlier date than the two preceding.

The birth of this John is fixed to about the year 1247, by an incidental allusion in the first of these letters. The place of his birth is doubtful, as the honour has been claimed by two towns or villages of the name; one in the Capitanata near Lucera, and the other about fifteen miles east of Salerno in the Principato Citra[2].

[1] *Ante*, p. 22.

[2] Wadding (vi, p. 94) mentions the double claim. The former village is marked in Murray's map as Pietra Montecorvine, about twenty-two miles west of Foggia.

["Joannem hunc ab oppido nativo, de Monte Corvino cognominatum diximus, idque in Apulia Daunia situm: sed alii non hoc sed altero ejusdem nominis majori, & nobiliori oppido Montis Corvini non longe a Salerno, & flumine Silario inter Picentenos in Principatu citeriori, natum contendunt: quorum pio studio facile cedo, dum apud se ortum ostenderint; neque enim tantum virum Apulis eripere,

The first mention of him that I have found is on the occasion of his being sent in 1272, already a Franciscan, by the Emperor Michael Palæologus to Pope Gregory X, with a communication on the subject of that union of the Greek Church with Rome, which the Emperor, in his own supposed interest, professed to promote, though his efforts ended only in his being excommunicated by one of Gregory's successors, and denied Christian burial by his own.

John was sent back to the east with several companions, probably soon afterwards, and appears to have remained abroad till 1289, when he returned to the Papal Court bringing intelligence of the wide reception of the Faith in Western Asia, and of the desire of the princes and people for the preaching of the Word, the favourable dispositions of Arghún, the reigning Khan of the House of Húlakú[1], being especially eulogised. The Pope [Nicholas IV] thought it well to send back to the field of labour with additional aid a missionary so experienced as John now was, giving him letters of commendation to Arghún, to the King and Queen of (Lesser) Armenia, to the Patriarch of the Jacobites and Bishop of Tauris, and also to the great Kúblái himself, and to Kúblái's rival, Kaidu of Turkestan.

John remained at Tabriz till 1291, and then proceeded to the Far East in order to fulfil his mission to Kúblái, travelling by the way of India as he tells us in the first

neque Licentinis adjudicare velim sine gravi aliqua ratione aut auctoritate." *Wadding*, vi, p. 94.]

[There are two *comuni* of this name in the Province of Salerno: Montecorvino Pugliano and Montecorvino Rovella.—"Due sono i Montecorvino nella provincia di Salerno, oltre il Pietra Montecorvino nella provincia di Foggia. In uno dei detti comuni (propendendo lo Yule ed il Da Civezza per quest' ultimo), nacque nel 1247 Giovanni che trovo talvolta ricordato col nome di Giovanni Valente; indagini da me fatte non mi permettono di affermare se questo sia casato di famiglia." Amat di S. Filippo, *Studi biog. e bibliog.*, 2ª ed., 1882, I, p. 79.]

[1] Reigned 1284–1291.

of the following letters. It is not likely that he reached Cambalec in the lifetime of the old Khan, who died in the beginning of 1294, for voyages were slow, and he stayed long at St Thomas's and other places on the coast of Maabar or Coromandel[1].

It will be well here to say something of the third letter in the collection, which purports to be written from that coast. This is derived from a MS. in the Laurentian Library, of which I found the indication in Quétif's *Script. Ord. Prædicatorum*[2]. The transcriber Friar Menentillus of

[1] A party of friars had already been dispatched in April 1278 by Pope Nicholas III [successor of John XXI] on a mission to Cathay and with a very long letter from the Pope to Kúblái Khan, who was then alleged to have been baptised. He is addressed "*Quolibey, Magnus Cham, Imperator et Moderator Omnium Tartarorum Illustris.*" The members of the mission were Gerard of Prato, Antony of Parma, John of St Agatha, Andrew of Florence, and Matthew of Arezzo, all Minorites. There seems to be no further knowledge of them. The words of John of Montecorvino in the first of his letters seem to make it pretty certain that they did not reach Cambalec. (See *Mosheim*, p. 68, and *Append.*, Nos. xxii, xxiii.)

[It is rather difficult to give an exact date to the arrival of Monte Corvino in China: in one of his letters "data in civitate Cambaliech regni Catan, anno Domini MCCCV, die VIII mensis Januarii," see *infra*, John says that he had been alone in Cathay during eleven years, but that two years before this letter, a brother Arnold, of Cologne, joined him; thus he arrived thirteen years before 1305, viz. 1292; he might have known Kúblái, who died in 1294, after his expedition to Java in 1293; but these figures scarcely agree with another part of the same letter, when John says that he left Tauris in 1291, proceeded to India where he remained thirteen months, where he lost his companion, Nicholas of Pistoia; though, if his departure from Tauris were at the beginning of the year 1291, thirteen months would carry John to January or February 1292, and there is then a possibility of his having reached Cathay this very year 1292 or in 1293, always before the death of Kúblái.]

[2] The original, which is in quaint Italian, was published by Professor Kunstmann of Munich, in *Münchener Gelehrte Anzeigen*, 1855, Nos. 21 and 22, and I am indebted to his kindness for a copy which I had failed to procure otherwise. There is also a brief notice by the same author in one of his papers already referred to. (*Phillips* and *Görres*, Bd. 37, p. 26–7.) Before I obtained the papers from Professor Kunstmann I had got a transcript of the MS. from Florence, from which the translation was made. I have now been able to correct some passages of this by comparison with Professor Kunstmann's edition. [Marcellino da Civezza, *Saggio di Bibliografia Sanfrancescana*, 1879, p. 410, says that a copy of this letter, which he believes to be unpublished, is kept in the Biblioteca Laurenziana at Florence.]

Spoleto, in sending a copy or abstract of this letter to gratify the curiosity of an inquiring friend, informs him that it was written by a certain Franciscan missionary proceeding to the court of the Sovereign of all India, and who had been in company with their friend and brother Dominican Nicholas of Pistoia, when the latter died in India. Now we know from one of Montecorvino's authenticated letters that *he* was the Franciscan who was in company with Nicholas of Pistoia, when he died at St Thomas's, or the modern Madras. And moreover this very document, which we have here in an anonymous form, is quoted as "a letter of Friar John the Cordelier," or Franciscan, by a contemporary author, the celebrated physician and reputed sorcerer Pietro of Abano[1]. The document itself, as given by Friar Menentillus, is none of the most lucid, and reads like a translation by a not very intelligent person, rather than like a transcript of the original.

Besides these letters of Montecorvino's already spoken of, Wadding has handed down the fragment of another, written on Quinquagesima Sunday, 1306 (13th February). In this John mentions that a solemn deputation had come to him from a certain part of Ethiopia, begging him to go or to send preachers thither, for they had had no preachers since the time of St. Matthew the Evangelist, etc. (see below at the end of John's second letter this fragment in full)[2].

[1] "Moreover, almost quite recently hath Friar John the Cordelier written a letter respecting the inhabitants of the climate in question from the territory of Mohabar in India, in the coast where lieth the body of the Apostle Thomas. And in this he saith that you find it ever summer and never simmer (*semper æstas et non æstus*), because there be continually breezes which moderate the heat"—and so on, quoting several periods out of this very letter. (*Petri Aponensis*, etc., *Conciliator.*, Venet., 1521, f. 97; see note on Introductory Notices of Marignolli, *infra.*) [See *Marco Polo*, i, p. *119*, note on Pietro of Abano.]

[2] Wadding under 1307, § vi.

[P. 92. "Data dicebat littera ipsa in Cambaliech civitate regni Kathag, anno Domini MCCCVI, in Dominica Quinquagesimae mensis Februarii."]

This is a singular circumstance, and difficult to elucidate, even supposing that the deputation consisted only of some whom accident or trade had brought to such a centre of attraction as Cambalec. For even this is so improbable that I think we may adopt the suggestion of Professor Kunstmann that this fragment is really only the end of John's second letter from Cambalec, from which it had been accidentally separated. The date, which is absent from the second letter, fits in perfectly; and as it will be seen that in the end of that letter the writer was recurring to his experiences in Southern India, we should then see that he is speaking of the Ethiopian party as having visited him in that country, and not in China[1]. There is an old legend that St. Matthew preached in Ethiopia, which is referred to Nubia by Ludolf, as the Abyssinians have no tradition of his visiting them[2]. On the whole, however, perhaps no place to which the name of Ethiopia could be applied is more likely to have been the country of these people than Socotra, an island in which the traces of a debased Christianity still faintly lingered in the 17th century[3].

[1] *Kunstmann* in *Phillips* and *Görres*, Bd. 37, p. 236.

[2] The monk Burchard in the middle of the thirteenth century also speaks of *Æthiopia quæ hodie Nubia dicitur* as the field of St. Matthew's preaching.

[3] This is suggested by Assemani (p. 516).

The Christianity of the people of Socotra is mentioned by the Arab voyagers edited by Renaudot and again by Reinaud. That work alleges that Socotra was colonised with Greeks by Alexander the Great in order to promote the cultivation of the Socotrine aloes, and that after the advent of our Lord, when the other Greeks had embraced Christianity, these colonists also adopted it, and had retained the profession till that day (the ninth century). Edrisi tells the same story. Marco Polo tells us that the people of Socotra, though greatly addicted to incantations, were baptised Christians and had an Archbishop subject to a patriarch at Bagdad. [II, p. 406.] The next notice of the subject that I am aware of is found among the curious extracts given by Quétif, I, pp. 572–3, from a MS. in the Colbertian library, of which some account will be given further on. The author, writing about 1330, seems to speak of Socotra in the following extract: ["Ultra versus meridiem procedendo est quaedam insula in mari Indico satis

The letter in question was brought home from Tartary by Friar Thomas of Tolentino, who had already for some

magna, ubi populus circumcisionem obtinet pariter & baptismum. De qua quidem insula dicere quomodo aut qualiter illuc pervenerim, & de conditione illius gentis, & de moribus ac modo vivendi & de consuetudinibus & legibus & modo extraneo dominandi, si ad nostrum propositum conveniret, esset audientibus curiosum." The editor adds: "Quae sit illa insula geographis permitto inquirendum."]:—"As you proceed further to the south there is a certain island in the Indian Ocean of considerable size, where the people use both circumcision and baptism. And if it were but more pertinent to our subject it would be a very curious story to tell about that island, how I got there, as well as about the circumstances of the people, their manners and mode of living, their customs and laws and strange system of government." That the Socotran Christians practised circumcision is alleged also by Maffei, in his Indian History, in noticing the transactions of Albuquerque at Socotra, and this with others of their practices leads him to connect them distinctly with the Abyssinian church, in which a kind of circumcision is well known to have been maintained. They had sunk into an almost savage state; but retained the practice of annual fasts, daily prayers (which he alleges were in Hebrew?), and veneration for the cross, which they all wore round the neck. Marco Polo perhaps considered them as Nestorians, and this also is asserted by Nicolo Conti, who spent two months on the island in the first half of the fifteenth century. In the beginning of the sixteenth Barbosa speaks of their nominal profession of Christianity as still maintained, though in great ignorance and without baptism. That some faint traces of their former Christianity lingered even to the middle of the seventeenth century we learn from the Travels of Father Vincenzo Maria, who was sent from Rome in that age to reconcile the differences of the Malabar Christians with the Roman hierarchy, a work containing many interesting particulars, and which might be worth the attention of the Hakluyt Society were it not so lengthy. He says the people still retained a Christian profession, though having no true knowledge of the faith. They had in his day but a jumble of doctrines and observances; worshipping and sacrificing to the moon; *circumcising*, abominating wine and pork. They had churches which they called *Moquame* [Ar. *Maqâm* "locus statio"], dark, low, and dirty, the walls of which they anointed daily with butter. On the altar they had a cross, and one candle in a candlestick. For the cross they retained a singular but ignorant reverence, carrying it in their processions. Three times in the day and three times in the night they were assembled in their churches by the striking on a piece of timber in lieu of a bell, and in their worship burned much incense and fragrant wood. The priests were called *Odambo*, were elected and consecrated by the people, and were changed every year. They dressed like the rest of the people, being distinguished only by a cross full of eyes, upon the breast. These priests were also the judges of the people. There was a fast of sixty days observed annually, beginning with the new moon of April, during which they abstained from meat, milk, and fish, eating only raw vegetables and dried dates. Of baptism and the other sacraments they had lost all knowledge, and their marriages were very lax. There were two apparently distinct races on the

years been preaching among the heathen in Asia; and the reports which he made at the Papal Court of John's great devotion and success probably led to the creation of the metropolitan see of Cambalec in the latter's favour.

This seems to have taken place in the spring of 1307[1], and was accompanied or immediately followed by the appointment of seven other Franciscans to be suffragan Bishops under the new metropolitan. The powers conferred on the Archbishop were unusually ample, empowering him to rule like a Patriarch over all bishops and prelates of those parts, subject only to his recognition of the superiority of the Roman see, and to the reception of the pallium from it by himself and his successors.

The suffragan bishops thus nominated for Cathay were

island, one of negroes with crisp hair; the other less black, of better aspect, and with straight hair;—the first living on dates, butter, and flesh; the others on fish. All used sour milk. They never shaved any part of the body, so that many of them looked like absolute satyrs (compare in *Photii Bibliotheca* the notice from the Embassies of Nonnosus of a remote island in the Indian Sea inhabited by black hairy dwarfs who lived on fish and shell-fish). They had no houses, but lived in caves and holes. Their only art was that of weaving a coarse camlet of goat's hair. They cultivated a few palms and kept flocks; had no money, no writing, kept count of their flocks by bags of stones. Each family had a cave in which they deposited their dead without covering the bodies. They often put themselves to death when old or sick or vanquished. They had no remedies for disease except the aloe. When rain failed they selected a victim by lot, and placing him within a circle addressed their prayers to the moon, and if without success they cut off the poor wretch's hands. They had many who practised sorcery, and being very shy of communication with strangers, shut themselves out from better knowledge. The women were all called *Maria*, which the author regarded as one of the relics of their Christianity. The mountains abounded in wild hogs, *wild asses*, and partridges. The whole account is very curious. (*Anciennes Relations*, etc., of Renaudot, p. 113; *Jaubert's Edrisi*, i, 47; *Maffei, Hist. Indic.*, lib. iii; *Ludolf, Comment.*, p. 268; *Quétif, Scriptores Ord. Præd.*, i, pp. 572–3; *Livro de Duarte Barbosa*, p. 252; *Marco Polo*, ii, p. 406, and long note, pp. 408–410; *India in the Fifteenth Century, Conti*, p. 20; *Viaggio all' Indie Orientali del P. F. Vincenzo Maria*, etc., Roma, 1672, pp. 132 and 442.)

[1] Only a fragment without date remains of the bull of appointment. But the letter nominating William de Villa Nova to be one of the Suffragans is dated from Poitiers, 1st May, 1307. (*Wadding*, vi pp. 93, 147-8.) ["Datum Pitavis Kalen. Maji an. III."]

Gerard, Peregrine of Castello, Andrew of Perugia, Reader in Theology, Nicholas of Bantra or of Apulia, Minister (in the order) of the Province of St. Francis, Andrutius of Assisi, Ulrich Sayfustordt, and William of Villeneuve[1]. Of these, as we learn from the fourth letter in the present collection, only Gerard, Peregrine and Andrew ever reached their destination. They consecrated the Archbishop, and in course of time all three in succession officiated as Bishops at Zaitún. The next three in the list were killed by their first experience of Indian climate, and William either never started or did not prosecute his journey, for he certainly did not reach Cathay, and sixteen years later he is found holding episcopal office in Europe[2].

According to a story related by Wadding, the Emperor then reigning in Cambalec, and his mother, were eventually converted and baptized by John. Shortly afterwards the Khan died, and was buried with imperial solemnity in the Convent church. When the troubles broke out thirty (fifty?) years later, and the friars had to quit Cathay, they removed this imperial body with them to Saray, and when taken up it was found all fresh as when just buried. If the story of conversion were true the Emperor in question would probably be Ayur Balibatra, grandson of Kúblái, who died in 1311. But unfortunately there was scarcely a single Khan of the dynasty regarding whose conversion some story did not reach Europe; all probably alike baseless[3].

[1] There are some differences in regard to this list of bishops among the annalists. It is not worth while to go into detail, and I have followed the list adopted by Dr. Kunstmann.

[Nicholas of Bantra, Pietro de Castello and Andruzio of Assisi died in India. See my edition of Odoric, pp. xviii–xix.]

[2] Nominated to the diocese of Sagone in Corsica [on the 19th Feb.] 1323, and translated in 1327 to Trieste, where [he died in 1331], and where his tomb existed in the seventeenth century. (*Ughelli, Italia Sacra*, quoted by *Mosheim*, p. 98.) A certain Tuscan saintess is said to have prognosticated from the face of one of the bishops that he would not persevere in his mission. (*Mosheim, ib.*)

[3] Misled by such stories in relation to the Persian branch of the Mongol House, Edward II writes to Oljaïtu proposing that they

In 1311 the same Pope Clement V nominated three more bishops to serve under John of Montecorvino, by name Thomas, Jerome, and Peter of Florence[1]. This last we hear of, in *the Book of the Great Caan*, as presiding over one of the convents in Zaitún, whilst Andrew of Perugia ruled the other.

And this appears to be the latest notice bearing upon the history of this venerable man's life, excepting the anecdote related by Odoric[2], and what can be gathered out of the letter of Bishop Andrew given below.

John died, aged upwards of eighty years, sometime about the year 1328[3], as we gather from a letter addressed to the Pope by certain Christians of Cathay, which will be quoted in another section of this book[4]. Pagans as well as Christians followed him to the grave with demonstrations of the deepest grief and veneration[5]. No character so worthy of respect, except Benedict Goës in later days, appears among the ecclesiastical travellers with whom our subject brings us into contact.

He appears to have been not only the first, but the last effective Archbishop of Cambalec[6]. In 1333, after the news of John's death had reached Avignon, one [French] Friar

should unite to destroy the abominable sect of the Mahomedans; the Khan himself belonging to the said sect. (*Rymer*, quoted by *D'Ohsson*, iv, 592–4.) [Cf. *Marco Polo*, i, p. 36 *n.*]

1 *Wadding*, vi, p. 184.

["Quare alios tres ejusdem Suffraganeos creavit hoc anno ex eodem Ordine Pontifex; videlicet fratrem Thomam, fratrem Hieronymum, & fratrem Petrum de Florentia; datis XI. Kal. Martii, & XIII. Kal. Januarii litteris incipientibus; *Rex Regum & Dominus Dominantium.*"]

2 *Ante*, p. 270. 3 [Gams, 1330; others, 1333.]

4 See Introductory Notices of Marignolli.

5 See the *Livre du Grant Caan*, infra.

6 [Angelo de Gubernatis in his *Storia dei Viaggiatori italiani nelle Indie orientali*, Livorno, 1875, has devoted a chapter to the *Viaggiatori italiani nella Cina che visitarono l' India*, pp. 95–98; it is an abstract of *Cathay*.

In his *Saggio di Bibliografia Sanfrancescana*, pp. 409–410, Marcellina da Civezza has only devoted to Monte-Corvino a few extracts from the works of Amat di San Filippo and of Angelo de Gubernatis

Nicholas[1] [professor of Divinity at the Faculty of Paris], was appointed to the See [18th Sept. 1333], and was sent

but he has given a full account of the beginnings of the mission of this celebrated Franciscan brother in his *Storia universale delle Missioni Francescane*, III, cap. vi, p. 252, without adding any new information, however.]

[1] ["At the close of the Yüan Dynasty [A.D. 1278–1368] a native of this country [Fu lin], named Nieh-ku-lun, came to China for trading purposes. When, after the fall of the Yüan, he was not able to return, the Emperor T'ai Tsu, who had heard of this, commanded him to his presence in the eighth month of the 4th year of Hung Wu (=September 1371) and gave orders that an official letter be placed into his hands for transmission to his king, which read as follows: 'Since the Sung dynasty had lost the throne and Heaven had cut off their sacrifice, the Yüan [Mongol] dynasty had risen from the desert to enter and rule over China for more than a hundred years, when Heaven, wearied of their misgovernment and debauchery, thought also fit to turn their fate to ruin, and the affairs of China were in a state of disorder for eighteen years. But when the nation began to arouse itself, We, as a simple peasant of Huai-yu, conceived the patriotic idea to save the people, and it pleased the Creator to grant that Our civil and military officers effected their passage across eastward to the left side of the River. We have then been engaged in war for fourteen years; We have, in the west, subdued the king of Han, Ch'ên Yu-liang; We have, in the east, bound the king of Wu, Chang Shih-ch'êng; We have, in the south, subdued Min and Yuĕh [=Fu kien and Kwang tung], and conquered Pa and Shu [=Sze ch'wan]; We have in the north, established order in Yu and Yen [=Chi li]; We have established peace in the Empire, and restored the old boundaries of Our Middle Land. We were selected by Our people to occupy the Imperial throne of China under the dynastic title of "the Great Ming," commencing with Our reign styled Hung Wu, of which we now are in the fourth year. We have sent officers with this Manifesto except to you, Fu lin, who, being separated from us by the western sea, have not as yet received the announcement. We now send a native of your own country, Nieh-ku-lun, to hand you this Manifesto. Although We are not equal in wisdom to our ancient rulers whose virtue was recognised all over the universe, We cannot but let the world know Our intention to maintain peace within the four Seas. It is on this ground alone that We have issued this Manifesto.' And he again ordered the ambassador Pu-la and others to be provided with credentials and presents of silk for transmission to that country, who thereafter sent an embassy with tribute. But this embassy was, in the sequel, not repeated until during the Wan-li period [A.D. 1573–1620] a native from the great Western Ocean came to the capital who said that the Lord of Heaven, Ye-su, was born in Ju-tê-a [Judaea] which is identical with the old country of Ta Ts'in; that this country is known in the historical books to have existed since the creation of the world for the last 6000 years; that it is beyond dispute the sacred ground of history and the origin of all worldly affairs; that it should be considered as the country where the Lord of Heaven created the human race. This account looks somewhat exaggerated and should not be trusted. As regards the abundance of produce and other

forth accompanied by twenty friars and six laymen. But it is not known what became of the party[1]. Their arrival at Almaliq and civil treatment there were heard of[2], but nothing beyond; there is no indication of their having ever reached the Court of Cathay.

The mission of John de' Marignolli and his companions succeeded (1338), but there was no [residing] bishop at Cambalec in their time. Some time before 1369 a certain Cosmas had been appointed, for we find that in that year he was transferred from the see of Cambalec to that of Saray, and Friar William of Prato (Du Prè?) named in his place[3]. Probably the Pope was not aware of the revolution which had recently ejected the Mongol family, and he could not be aware of its full effect on European intercourse. Guilielmus Pratensis and the friars who followed him are heard of no more.

A list embracing several other Archbishops or Bishops of Cambalec is indeed to be found in Le Quien's *Oriens Christianus*. Some of these it is probable were in fact prelates titularly named to the see, though not approaching it within thousands of miles, but others were certainly

precious articles found in this country, accounts will be found in former annals." *Ming Shih*, translated by Hirth, *China and the Roman Orient*, pp. 64–67.

Bretschneider, *Arabs*, p. 25, makes the following remarks about Friar Nicholas: "Nicholas, in the year 1338, had not yet arrived in Peking, for the Christians there complained in a letter, written at the above date, that they were eight years without a curate. It is therefore possible that the Nie ku lun of the Chinese Annals is identical with the monk Nicholas. The statement of the Chinese that Nicholas carried on commerce does not contradict this view. Perhaps he trafficked in fact, or he considered it necessary to introduce himself under the name of a merchant."

This Nicholas, archbishop of Khan Baliq, must not be taken—Hirth made this mistake, *Roman Orient*, p. 65—for Nicholas of Bantra, who died on the way, see p. 10.]

[1] [Gams gives 1338 as the date of the death of Nicholas.]

[2] See a letter from Pope Benedict XII to the Khan of Chagatai, thanking him for his good reception of Nicholas. (*Mosheim*, p. 111, and *App.* No. lxxix.)

[3] *Mosheim*, p. 120: "Guillelmum Pratensem Franciscanum, qui divinae institutionis praecepta Parisiis docebat, praefecit."

bishops of a different diocese, which has been confounded with that of Cambalec[1].

There is a curious notice of the proceedings and success of John of Montecorvino to be found in the chronicle of John of Winterthur, a Suabian Minorite[2], who finished his annals about the middle of the century. After mentioning the death of the friars at Tana in India, he goes on to say that a few years before that event, a certain Franciscan of Lower Germany had set out on a pilgrimage of evangelization, and had written a letter to the chief of the Northern Vicariate, which the chronicler had seen, and in which a detailed account was given of the traveller's proceedings. The substance of this letter is then recited, and we find it to be in fact the same as that of the first letter of John Montecorvino from Cambalec, though his name is never mentioned, but all is supposed to relate to the acts and sufferings of the Low German friar. Professor Kunstmann[3] identifies this person with that Friar Arnold of Cologne whom Montecorvino mentions as having joined him about the year 1303–4. It is possible that this Arnold is in some way connected with the mistake, but it seems pretty certain that what the chronicler had seen was merely

[1] *Le Quien*, iii, coll. 1346–1356. This see, as Prof. Kunstmann points out, is that of *Cembalo* in the Crimea (I presume the Symbolōn Limēn of Strabo), and now famous under the name of Balaklava.

[The list given by Gams (*Series Episcoporum*, 1873, p. 126) includes: Beatus JOANNES de MONTECORVINO, O.S. Fr., el. 1307: 1308 consecr., † in China, 1330.—NICOLAUS, O.S. Fr., elect. 18. IX, 1333; † 1338.—COSMAS, O.S. Fr., tr. ad Sarai 1369 Christiani expulsi; † 1370.—Hic, et qui sequuntur, non residebant.—GUILIELMUS de PRATO, O.S. Fr., el. 11. III, 1370.—JOSEFUS,—DOMINICUS, O.S. Fr., el. 9. VIII, 1403.—CONRADUS (*Scopper*), O.S. D., el. c. 1408.—JACOBUS, O.S. D., el. 8. I, 1427.—LEONARDUS.—BARTHOLOMAEUS, O.S. Fr., el. 15. IV, 1448.—BERNARDUS.—JOANN. de PELLETZ, O.S. Fr., el. c. 1456.—BARTHOLOMAEUS II.—ALEXANDER de CAFFA, O.S. Fr., captus a Turcis c. 1475, in quorum captivitate 7 annos erat, † in Italia, 1483.—Titulus episcopatus deficit.]

[2] *Jo. Vitodvrani Chronicon*, in *Eccard*, *Corpus Historicum*, etc., Lipsiae, 1723, i, coll. 1895–7. Winterthur is in the modern Swiss canton Zurich.

[3] *Phillips* and *Görres*, xliii, 677.

a copy of Montecorvino's letter. There are one or two slight circumstances in the chronicle which are not mentioned in that letter, but they look very like such amplifications as would be natural in such a case.

John in the first of these letters makes interesting mention of a certain King George of the family of Prester John. This George is mentioned by Marco Polo as exercising a secondary sovereignty in Tenduc, the position of which has been explained in a note on Odoric (p. 244). Marco also names the same George as one of the generals of Kúblái's army in a great battle with Kaidu, the Khan's inveterate rival[1]. This seems the most suitable place to introduce some account of the personage whose name of Prester John is so constantly recurring in the narratives of that age.

The first notice of a potentate so styled appears to have been brought to Europe by the Syrian Bishop of Gabala

[1] *Marco Polo*, i, 183, 186 *n.*, 187, 214 *n.*; ii, 148 *n.*, 333, 334 *n.*, 348, 457–459, 463–467.

["M. Polo and Johannes de Monte Corvino transfer the title of Prester John from Wang-khan, already perished at that time, to the distinguished family of Wang-ku. Their Georgius is undoubtedly K'o-li-ki-sze, Alahush's great-grandson. That this name is a Christian one is confirmed by other testimonies; thus in the Asu (Azes) regiment of the Khan's guards was K'o-li-ki-sze, alias Kow-r-ki († 1311), and his son Ti-mi-ti-r. There is no doubt that one of them was Georgius, and the other Demetrius. Further, in the description of *Chin-kiang* in the time of the Yuen, mention is made of K'o-li-ki-sze Ye-li-ko-wen, i.e. K'o-li-ki-sze the Christian, and of his son Lu-ho (Luke). K'o-li-ki-sze of Wang-ku is much praised in history for his valour and his love for Confucian doctrine; he had in consequence of a special favour of the Khan two Mongol princesses for wives at the same time (which is rather difficult to conciliate with his being a Christian). The time of his death is correctly indicated in a letter of Johannes de M. Corvino of the year 1305: *ante sex annos migravit ad Dominum.* He left a young son *Chu-ngan*, who probably is the Joannes of the letter of Ioannes (Giovani) of M. C., so called *propter nomen meum*, says the missionary. In another Wang-ku branch, Si-ki-li-sze reminds one also of the Christian name *Sergius.*" (Palladius, *Elucidations of Marco Polo's Travels*, p. 23.) Prof. Pelliot has found new proofs of the identification of K'o-li-ki-sze with George, and he has the funerary inscription of this prince, written by Yen fu, which he intends to translate and publish in a book on the Christians in China in the Middle Ages, written jointly with Mr. A. C. Moule.]

[*Jibal*, south of Laodicea in Northern Syria] who came in 1145 as envoy from the King of Armenia to Pope Eugene III. For he reported that not long before a certain John, inhabiting the extreme east, king and Nestorian priest, and claiming descent from the Three Wise Kings, had made war on the [Samiard] Kings of the Medes and Persians, and had taken Ecbatana their capital. He was then proceeding with his army to Jerusalem, but was stopped by the Tigris which he could not cross, etc.[1]. We shall see hereafter what facts appear to lie at the bottom of these rumours of a conquering Christian prince in Central Asia in the first half of the twelfth century. But the Nestorians probably were glad to catch at a story which raised the importance of their sect, whilst the Catholics also greeted with joy this intelligence of a counterpoise to the Mahomedan power rising in a quarter so unexpected. The reports of Prester John's power, opulence, and sanctity expanded without limit, and letters were circulated through-

[1] "Vidimus etiam ibi tunc prætaxatum de Syria Gabulensem episcopum.... Narrabat etiam, quod ante non multos annos, Joannes quidam, qui ultra Persidem et Armeniam, in extremo Oriente habitans, rex et sacerdos, cum gente suâ Christianus est, sed Nestorianus, Persarum et Medorum reges fratres, Samiardos dictos, bello petierit, atque Ecbatani...sedem regni eorum expugnaverit. Cui dum præfati reges cum Persarum, Medorum et Assyriorum copiis occurrerent, triduo utrisque mori magis quam fugere volentibus, dimicatum est PRESBYTER JOANNES (*sic enim eum nominare solent*) tandem versis in fugam Persis, cruentissimâ cæde victor extitit. Post hanc victoriam dicebat prædictum Joannem ad auxilium Hierosolymitanæ Ecclesiæ procinctum movisse, sed dum ad Tygrim venisset, ibique nullo vehiculo traducere exercitum potuisset, ac septentrionalem plagam, ubi eundem amnem hyemali glacie congelari didicerat, iter flexisse. Ibi dum per aliquot annos moratus, gelu expectaret, sed minime hoc impediente aeris temperie, obtineret, multos ex insueto cœlo de exercitu amittens, ad propria redire compulsus est. Fertur enim iste de antiquâ progenie illorum, quorum in Evangelio mentio fit, esse Magorum, eisdemque quibus et isti gentibus imperans, tantâ gloriâ et abundantiâ frui, ut non nisi sceptro smaragdino uti dicatur. Patrum itaque suorum, qui in cunabulis Christum adorare venerunt, accensus exemplo, Hierosolymam iter proposuerat, sed praetaxata causa impeditum fuisse asserunt. Sed hæc hactenus."—*Ottonis Frisingensis Chronicon*, lib. vii, cap. 33, in *Germanic. Historic. Illust.* etc., *Christiani Urstisii Basiliensis*, Francofurdi 1585. [Cf. *Marco Polo*, i, p. 231 *n*.]

out Europe, and survive in many continental libraries, which he was alleged to have addressed to the Emperor of the East and other Christian princes. In these his great power and glory were vaunted with the most extravagant details; India and the tomb of St. Thomas being always claimed as a prominent part of his dominions. Large extracts from such a letter may be seen in Assemani, and a translation has been given by Mr. Layard[1]. By the circulation of these letters, glaring forgeries and fictions as they are, the idea of this great Christian conqueror was planted in the mind of the European nations, and twined itself round every rumour of revolution in further Asia that penetrated to Europe. Even when the noise of the real conquests of Chinghiz began to make itself audible in the west, he was invested with the character of a Christian king, and more or less confounded with the mysterious Prester John[2]. After this delusion was dispelled and the diffusion of the Mongol power had opened up the east, travellers naturally sought traces of the vast monarchy of which Europe for a century past had heard so much, but with invariable disappointment. Eventually the Chief of the Keraite tribe of Tartars became identified as the representative of Prester John, but a portion of the facts which combined with so much fable to form the legend have another source[3].

[1] *Assemani*, pp. 488–493; *Layard's Nineveh*, i, 250.

[2] See *Eccard*, *Corpus Historic.*, ii, 1451, "Relatio de Davide Rege Tartarorum Christiano." The name Prester John does not, I think, occur in this, but the idea seems to be there.

[3] There is a letter in the Ecclesiastical Annals of Baronius, quoted from the Chronicle of Roger Hoveden, addressed, in 1177, from Venice by Pope Alexander III to "*Carissimo in Christo filio illustri et magnifico Indorum regi, sacerdotum sanctissimo.*" The Pope recites how he had heard from his beloved son, Master Philip the physician, about the king's pious desire to have instruction in Catholic doctrine, etc., and to possess a church in Rome and an altar in Jerusalem. He found it too difficult, on account of the length and obstructions of the way, to send any one *a latere*, but he would despatch the said Philip to communicate instruction to him. It is not stated that Philip had

Plano Carpini, the first traveller to Mongolia whose narrative we have, says nothing of Prester John. Rubruquis, a few years later, goes into considerable detail on the subject[1].

"At the time," he says, "when the Franks took Antioch[2] the sovereignty in these regions of Northern Asia was held by a certain Coir-Kham[3]. *Coir* was his proper name, *Cham* his title, the word having the meaning of soothsayer, which is applied to their princes, because they govern the people by means of divination[4]. And we read in the history of Antioch that the Turks sent for succour against the Franks to King Coir-Cham; for all

actually been to the king's court, but only that he had heard of his majesty's pious desires from conversation with honourable persons of his kingdom, whom the physician had met with in those parts (*in partibus illis*). Baronius refers this to "the King of the Indians, vulgarly called *Pretejanni*, reigning far and wide over Ethiopia," and supposes it possible that the church possessed in his own time by the Abyssinians, at the back of the apse of St. Peter's, might have been granted on this occasion. The commentator, Pagius, rejects this, and considers the king to have been Prester John of Asia.

But I suspect that Baronius is right, and that the King of Abyssinia is in question. The *illis partibus* is vague, and may refer to Egypt or to Palestine, where Doctor Philip might well have met with Abyssinian pilgrims. There is no mention of the term *Prester John* in the document itself; and the application of that title to the Abyssinian king was probably a good deal later than this, though earlier than has generally been supposed, as will appear hereafter. (*Annal. Eccles.*, Lucæ, 1746, vol. xix, p. 450.)

A letter given by Matthew Paris, which was written from the Holy Land, in 1237, by Philip, Prior of the Dominicans there, speaks of the heads of the various sects of oriental Christians; and among others, of one who was over all the Nestorians in the east, and whose prelacy extended over India the Greater, and the kingdom *Sacerdotis Johannis*, and other realms still nearer the sun rising. Here it is, doubtless, the Asiatic potentate who is spoken of (*Rerum Angliæ Scriptores*, etc., Francofurti, 1601, p. 301). [On Prester John, we shall refer to the long note in our *Marco Polo*, i, pp. 231–237.]

[1] Page 259 *et seq.* [2] [In 1098.]

[3] ["Belonged to a certain Con cham." Rockhill's edition of *Rubruck*, p. 108.]

[4] The old "medicine men" of the Tartars, before the introduction of Buddhism, were really called *Kams* (*Qāmān* of the Persian writers, see *D'Ohsson*, i, 17, and also between 429 and 435). But I do not suppose there is any connexion between *Khān* or *Qān* and this *Kam*. [There is no confusion possible between *Qām* قام, Persian plural *Qām ān* قامان, "medicine men," and *khān* خان or *Qaān* قآن.]

the Turks came originally from those parts of the world. Now this Coir was of Cara Catay: *Cara* meaning *Black*, and *Catay* being the name of a nation, so that *Cara Catay* is as much as to say the Black Cathayans. And they were so called to distinguish them from the proper Cathayans, who dwell upon the ocean in the far east, of whom I shall tell you something hereafter. But these (Black) Cathayans inhabited certain mountain pastures (*Alpes*) which I passed through; and in a certain plain among those mountains dwelt a certain Nestorian who was a mighty shepherd, and lord over the people called Naiman, who were Nestorian Christians. And when Coir Cham died, that Nestorian raised himself to be King (in his place), and the Nestorians used to call him King John, and to tell things of him ten times in excess of the truth. For this is the way of the Nestorians who come from those parts of the world; out of a mere nothing they will spin the most wonderful stories, just as they have spread all about that Sartach is a Christian, and have told the same of Mangu Cham, and of Ken Cham[1]; the fact being merely that they treat Christians with more respect than other folk, but all the while are not Christians a bit. However in this way great tales went forth about this King John; though even when I passed over the lands that had been his pasture grounds nobody knew anything about him except a few Nestorians. Those pastures are now occupied by Ken Cham, whose court was visited by Friar Andrew, and I passed that way myself on my journey back. Now this John had a brother, who was also a great pastoral chief, whose name was Unc, and he dwelt on the other side of those Alps of Caracatay, some three weeks' journey distant from his brother, being the lord of a certain little town called CARACORUM, and ruling over a people called Crit and Merkit[2]. These people were also Nestorian

[1] [Keu Cham = Kuyuk Khan.]

[2] The Kerit or Kerait [who lived on the Orkhon and the Tula], and

Christians, but their lord had abandoned Christianity and had taken to idolatry, keeping about him those priests of the idols who are all addicted to sorcery and invocation of demons. Beyond his pastures again, some ten or fifteen days, were the pastures of the Moal[1], a very poor tribe without any captain, and without any religion except soothsaying and sorceries, such as are followed by all the people in those parts. Next to the Moal again was another poor tribe called Tartar[2]. Now King John being dead without leaving an heir, his brother Unc was brought in and caused himself to be called Cham, and his flocks and herds were spread about even to the borders of the Moal[3]. And at this time there was a certain Chingḥiz a blacksmith among the tribe of Moal, and he took to lifting the cattle of Unc Cham whenever he had a chance, so that great complaints were made by the herdsmen of Unc Cham to their lord. So Unc got together an army and made a raid into the land of the Moal denouncing Chingḥiz, and the latter fled into the land of the Tartars and hid himself there," etc.

the Merkit, two of the great tribes of Mongolia. [The Merkits were a nomadic people of Turkish stock, with a possible infusion of Mongol blood. They are called by Mohamedan writers Uduyut, and were divided into four tribes. They lived on the lower Selenga and its feeders. *Marco Polo*, i, p. 236 *n.*]

[1] The Mongols.

[2] The tribe of Tartars proper dwelt to the eastward, near Lake Buyar.

[3] ["Friar William's transcription of the word Mongol seems to be taken from the Turki form of that word *Mogal.*" Rockhill's *Rubruck*, p. 112 *n.*]

[Rubruck says that the Naimans were "Nestorian Christians" (Rockhill's ed., p. 110), while Piano Carpini says that they were "pagans." (Rockhill's ed., p. 17.) Rockhill, *l.c.*, p. 17 *n.*, writes: "Supposing they professed the Uigur creed, which Rubruck states to have been a jumble of Manichaeism and Buddhism, with perhaps a slight tinge of Nestorianism, they might be classed among his idolaters (as he, in fact, sometimes does the Uigurs), or among Christians." Conf. Ney Elias (*Tarikhi-rashidi*, 290), where, translating from Jiwani, he speaks of the Naiman as *Tarsa*, which he renders by "Christians."]

In this passage we have the two sources of the story of Prester John, to which we have alluded, mixed up together, as will be seen by a short statement of the histories referred to.

The empire of Kará Khitai was founded by a prince of the Khitan dynasty of Liao [or *Si Liao*, Western Liao], who escaped with a body of followers from Northern China, on the overthrow of that dynasty by the Kin in the beginning of the twelfth century. This chief, called by the Chinese Ye-liu Ta-shi, and by Rashíduddín, Fushi Taifu, was well received by the Uighúrs, and some others of the tribes west of the desert who had been subject to the Khitan empire. Gathering an army, he commenced a course of conquests which eventually extended over the whole of Eastern and Western Turkestan, including Khwarizm. In 1125 he took the title of Gur-Khan, or Universal Khan, fixing his residence at Bela-Sagun [Tokmak, on the Chu River], and establishing the Buddhist faith, to which he adhered, as dominant in this new empire, which was known as Kará [black] Khitai[1]. [Ta Pu-yen (as princess regent) 1136; Ye-liu I-lie (1142); Ye-liu Shi (as princess regent) 1154; Ye-liu Che-lu-ku (1168), second son of Ye-liu I-lie] successively occupied the throne after him; and the latter was still reigning in 1211 or 1212, when the son of the last Khan of the Christian [Turkish] tribe of Naimans [Kuchluk] sought and found shelter at the court of Kará Khitai, and received the daughter of the Gur-Khan in marriage. But he formed a plot to displace his benefactor, and was eventually successful in capturing him, and in mastering a large part of his dominions: he abandoned Christianity for Buddhism at the persuasion of his wife, and eventually was attacked by the Mongols under Chinghiz in 1218, and slain in the mountains of Badakhshan[2].

[1] [*Marco Polo*, i, p. 232. On Prester John, see *ibid.*, pp. 231–237.]

[2] *D'Ohsson*, i, 163, *seq.*; 441, *seq.*

Here we see not only the source of a part of the story of Rubruquis, the domination of Coir Cham (the Gur-Khan) over Kará Khitai, and the usurpation of the chief of the Naiman tribe of Nestorians in his place, but also the probable original of the stories of the conquering lord, brought to Europe by the Bishop of Gabala not many years after the first Gur-Khan had overrun Turkestan to the borders of Persia. This Gur-Khan was indeed a Buddhist, and not a Christian; but we shall have occasion to note hereafter the constant confusions of rumour between the two religions as they existed in Eastern Asia. The source of the other part of Rubruquis's story, and that which in the latter part of the thirteenth century had superseded the memory of the Gur-Khan in connexion with the legends of Prester John, requires the recapitulation of a different history.

The Nestorians, in the centuries succeeding the condemnation of their doctrine in the Roman empire, had sought to penetrate eastward. Their success may be gathered from their old establishment in India and in China, and from the long list of their metropolitan sees in the middle of the thirteenth century, embracing the regions from Armenia and the Persian Gulf in the west to Tangut and Cambalec in the east[1].

[1] These Metropolitan sees were as follow. 1. Of Elamitis or of Jandisbápúr (*Khuzistan*). 2. Nisibis. 3. Perath Mesenæ (*Basrah*). 4. Assyria and Adiabene (*Mosul* and *Arbela*). 5. Beth Garma or Beth Seleucia and Carcha in Assyria. 6. Halavan or Halala (*Zohab* on confines of Assyria and Media). 7. Persia or of Urumiah, Salmasa and Van. 8. Merv, or Khorasan. 9. Hara or Heriunitis, i.e. *Herat.* 10. Razichitis, or Arabia and Cotroba (said to be an island in the Sea of Oman). 11. Of the Sinæ (China). 12. Of India. 13. Of Armenia. 14. Of Syria or Damascus. 15. Azerbijan. 16. Of Rai and Tabaristan (*Rai*, an ancient city, of which vast traces exist near Tehrán). 17. Dailam, south of the Caspian. 18. Samarkand. 19. Cashgar. 20. Balkh. 21. Segestan (*Seistán*). 22. Hamadan. 23. Khanbaleg (*Peking*). 24. Tanchet (*Tangut* or N.W. China). 25. Chasemgarah and Nuachet. (These seem to be Indian names, Hassan- or Kasimghar and Nyakot? but I do not know where.) See *Assemani*, p. 630; and the list as given by *Layard* in his *Nineveh*, i, 257.

To face page 23.

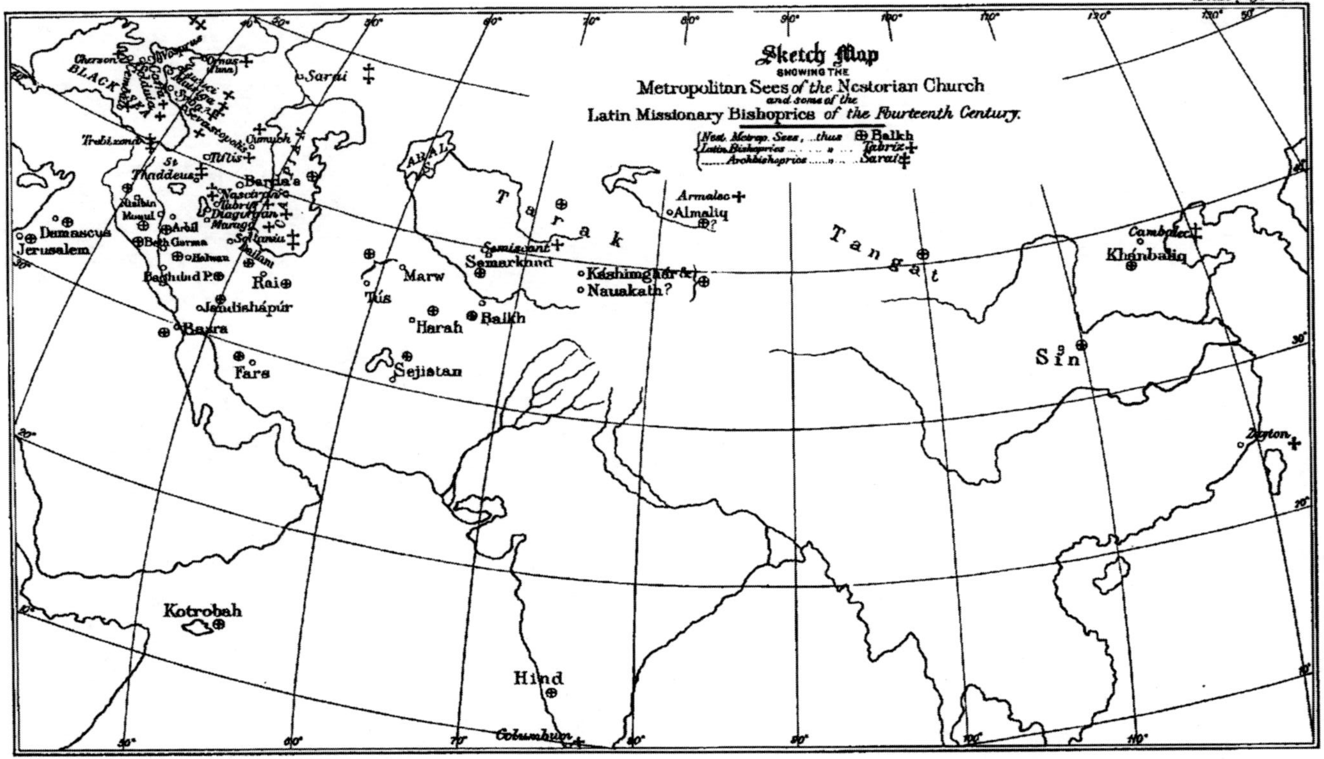

It is related by the Christian historian, Gregory Abulfaragius, that between 1001 and 1012 the patriarch of

The lists of *Metropolitan Sees of the Nestorian Church*, as given by the original authors in Assemani's second volume (pp. 458–9), differ somewhat from these. I take the opportunity of presenting them here, with some more precise geographical explanations.

The earlier list as given by Elias, Metropolitan of Damascus (A.D. 893), is as follows:

1. Province of the Patriarch (resident at Baghdad); 2. Jandisapúr; 3. Nisibis; 4. Mosul; 5. Bethgarma; 6. Damascus; 7. Rai; 8. Herat; 9. Armenia; 10. Kand (supposed *Samarkand*); 11. Fars; 12. Barda'a; 13. Halwán.

The later list as given by Amru, who wrote about 1349, runs thus:

1. JANDISABUR [or Jandishápúr, a city of Khuzistan built by Sapor I; identified by Rawlinson with the traces of a great city at Sháhábád between Dizfúl and Shuster (*J.R.G.S.* ix, 72)].

2. NISIBIN [Nisibis].

3. BASRAH.

4. MOSUL and ATHUR [or Nineveh].

5. ARBIL and HAZAH [*Chazene* and part of *Adiabene*; see p. 53].

6. BAJARMA, i.e. Beth-Garma [in the region of Ptolemy's *Garamæi*, north of Baghdad. The see is also called *Karkha* and *Beth-Seleucia*; and Assemani identifies it with "the ancient Scleucia Elymaidis adjoining the river Hedyphon or Hedypnus"; but here he goes strangely astray, some four hundred miles indeed. Rawlinson points out the true site as that called now Eski Baghdad, a little east of the Tigris, and below Dúr (*J.R.G.S.* x, 93–94). It was apparently the *Charcha* mentioned by Ammianus Marcellinus in the retreat of Jovian after Julian's death (*Ritter*, x, 157; *Am. Marc.*, xxv, 6)].

7. HALWÁN [called also, according to Assem., *Halacha*, and believed to be the *Calah* of Gen. x, 11, and the *Halah* of the Captivity; eight miles south of the modern Zoháb in the Province of Kirmanshah (see Rawlinson, as above, ix, 35). It was a hot-weather residence of the Khalifs].

8. FARS.

9. MERV.

10. HARAH [Herat].

11. KOTROBAH. [According to Edrisi this was an island inhabited by Christians, which by his description must have been near Socotra. As there is no island suiting the description but Socotra itself, and as Polo specifies that the latter island had an archbishop, there can be little doubt that Kotrobah is another name for Socotra.]

12. SÍN [i.e. China. The see was probably at Si-ngan fu].

13. HIND [i.e. India].

14. BARDA'A. [This city was the metropolis of the Province of Ar-Rán on the Kur. It is often mentioned in the History of Timur. Arrowsmith's Map to Burnes marks it on the R. Terter, a considerable distance to the south-east of the modern Elisabetpol. See also *J.R.GS.*, vol. iii, p. 31.]

15. DAMASHK [Damascus].

16. RAI and TABARISTAN [country E. of Tehrán].

17. DAILAM [S.W. of the Caspian, the hill country above *Gilán*].

18. SAMARKAND.

Baghdad received a letter from the metropolitan of Merv, in Khorasan, which related the miraculous conversion of the King of KERITH, a sovereign living far to the north-east, in the interior of the land of the Turks, who had sent to Merv to demand a Christian priest, and 200,000 of whose subjects were ready to follow him to baptism[1]. The patriarch gave the needful orders for the despatch of priests and teachers. The Christianity of the Keraits, as a tribe, is also attested by Rashíduddín, the Mahomedan historian of the Mongols[2].

The seat of these Keraits lay originally about the sources of the Amúr; but on being invaded by the Khitan in the ninth century, a large body of them took refuge in the mountains north of the Hwang Ho, called In shan, and there became powerful, spreading across the river into the territory called in our maps the Ordo country; the region so occupied by them on both banks being, as we have seen[3], the Tenduc of Marco Polo. Here they lived on good terms with their neighbours of the adjoining empire. The connexion between these people in Tenduc, and those of their tribe who had remained north of the desert, appears to have been maintained or renewed; but the light

19. TARK [Turkish Tribes beyond Samarkand probably].
20. HALAHA [as we have already had Halwán, considered to be the same with Halaha, Assem. proposes to read *Balkh*].
21. SEJISTAN.
The remaining names are entered in the margin of the MS., viz.:
22. JERUSALEM. [This became a metropol. see in 1200.]
23. KHANBALIQ and AL FALIQ [qu. *Almáliq*?].
24. TANGAT.
25. KASHIMGHAR and NAUAKATH. [The former name is probably intended for *Kashghar*, as Assemani in one place interprets it, though in the list at p. 22 he has given it in addition to Kashghar. *Nauakath* is found as the name of a place in Turkestan in Edrisi (ii, 217). Here it may possibly represent Yanghi-Hisar near Kashghar, or Yanghikand near Talas, the names of which are of like meaning. The provinces 24 and 25 were probably subdivisions of the former province of Tark.]

[1] So says *Assemani*, pp. 484, 485. But I cannot find the story in *Pococke's Abulfaragius*.

[2] Quoted by *St. Martin*, *Mémoires sur l'Arménie*, ii, 280.

[3] See note on Odoric, p. 244.

on this point is not very distinct. Certainly, however, we find that the chief of the Keraits in the time of Chinghiz and his father occupied the country about Kara Korum; whilst it is seen from Marco Polo that Tenduc was a part of the same chief's dominions. Tribes of Keraite lineage are found to this day in the country which Polo called Tenduc.

The chief of the Kerait just alluded to is he who is introduced as Unc Cham in the second part of the story of Rubruquis, and whom Marco Polo, whilst giving him the same name, identifies with Prester John. His proper name is called Tuli by the Chinese, and Togrul by the Persian historians, the name of Unc being a corruption of the Chinese title *Wang*, or King, which had been conferred on him by the Kin sovereign of Northern China, after which he called himself Wang-Khan. The circumstance mentioned by Rubruquis of his having abandoned Christianity, does not appear to be alluded to by the eastern writers; but one would rather hope that it was true, for his career does no credit to Christianity. He at first obtained the sovereignty of the Keraits by the murder of two of his brothers and several nephews. His father's brother, Gur-Khan by name (and here we have probably the origin of a part of the confusions of Rubruquis), who had taken refuge with the Naimans, got the chief of that tribe to take arms in his favour, and succeeded in displacing Tuli-Wang-Khan. The latter fled for help to Yessugai, the father of Chinghiz, who gave it so effectually that Tuli was again restored to his dominions. After a reign of many years, however, he was again ejected, and reduced to a destitute condition. Hearing, by-and-by, of the rising influence of Temujin, afterwards called Chinghiz Khan, the son of his old friend, he visited him, was received in the most cordial manner, and was treated with the greatest consideration and liberality. This was in 1196. For some years the two chiefs conducted their raids in alliance, but differences sprang up between them; the son of Wang-Khan entered into a plot to kill Temujin, and in 1202–3 they were in open war with one another. In the latter year, Temujin completely defeated the old Kerait in a battle fought between the Tuli and Kerulen rivers; and the vanquished chief, as he fled through the Naiman country, was slain by two of that tribe. This *Potente*, as Marco Polo calls him, it is whom that traveller identifies with Prester John, and in this Polo is followed by Montecorvino and Odoric. The idea must have been derived from the oriental Christians; for the title of *Malik Yūḥannā* (King John) is applied expressly by Abulfaragius to the same Tuli-Wang-Khan. But we have seen that the name reached Europe more than a century before that chief's time[1].

There seems to have been discovered no corroboration from oriental sources of the restoration of a measure of power and dignity to the descendants of the Kerait king who had wronged Chinghiz so grievously. But for this Marco's authority might well suffice, even were it not so fully confirmed by Montecorvino.

Much ingenuity has been expended by learned men to little purpose in devising an origin for the name of Prester John. The *John* alone has been derived from the Chinese title Wang, or has been connected with the old legends of the immortality of John the Evangelist. *Prester John* has been interpreted as a corruption of *Firishtaján*, *Paraster Khan*, *Presbyter Cohen*, and what not, down to the Pedro Juan, and Preto Joam, or Black John, which the Portuguese applied to the King of Abyssinia, and the *Pretiosus Joannes*, with which one of the Popes actually addressed that potentate.

[1] *Pococke's Abulfaragius*, p. 280; and for the preceding paragraphs see *D'Ohsson*, i, 48–83; *Klaproth* in *Journ. Asiat.*, sér. i, tom. ix, 299–306, *Pauthier*, *Le Pays de Tanduc et les Descendants du Prêtre Jean*, Paris, 1862; *Ritter*, vol. ii, pp. 253–295; and especially *D'Avezac* in his introduction to Carpini.

The history of the transfer of the name to the King of Abyssinia, as the phantom conqueror of Central Asia faded into thin air, would too much lengthen this digression. It is sufficient to remark that though this transfer is usually referred, as by Ludolf, to the fifteenth century, when the Portuguese began to get acquainted with the quasi-Christian kingdom of Abyssinia, there is proof in this collection that the name was applied to the African monarch already in the first half of the fourteenth century[1].

[1] See Marignolli in this collection. Friar Jordanus had already, according to my understanding of him, placed Prester John in Africa. In the middle of the next century Fra Mauro expressly identifies him with the King of Abyssinia. In connexion with this subject I may notice that a critic in the *Spectator* (April 2nd, 1864, p. 397) blames me for referring in a note on this passage of Jordanus to the remarks of D'Avezac on Prester John "as if they supported my views," whilst, he says, on turning to those remarks he found they did just the contrary.

The implied censure has no ground. I did not refer to D'Avezac's Essay as supporting any views, but as containing a comprehensive "dissertation on Prester John and the confusions which transferred a Christian prince of Central Asia to Central Africa," and this it certainly does contain. Incidentally D'Avezac indicates the view that the India Tertia of Jordanus is somewhere in Asia or in the far East, and not in Africa as I assumed. But this affects nothing in the reference to him. That the India Tertia and Ethiopia of Jordanus were both in Africa as a matter of fact is plain, whatever the friar's own notions as to their whereabouts might be. India Tertia is the country of rhinoceroses, civet-cats, horned adders, true negroes, ambergris, and zebras; that is to say it is in Africa. Between India Tertia and India Major (i.e. India proper) also lay the Male and Female Islands, which we know from Polo were believed to lie between Persia and Africa, and from Conti to adjoin Socotra. The Ethiopia again of Jordanus is no Asiatic region, but simply Abyssinia. It adjoins India Tertia; its emperor rules over more than fifty kings, according to the old fable regarding the King of Abyssinia (see *Ludolf*, bk. ii, c. 18, § 1, and *Suppt.*, p. 15); its people are all Christians but heretics; and its king, according to another old legend, received a large tribute from the Sultan of Egypt (as a bribe not to stop the Nile; see note on *Marignolli, infra*). I may add that Friar Burchard the Dominican, nearly a century before Jordanus, knows Ethiopia as including Nubia (see above, p. 7).

It is very probable that the application of the name of India to a part of Africa connected itself with geographical notions alluded to by the Reviewer, of which there are indications in Ptolemy and Marcianus of Heraclea, and more plainly in Edrisi, and according to which Africa ran far to the East, and so as to meet, or nearly to meet, the coast of S.E. Asia. Even in Fra Mauro's map the African coast trends considerably eastward from the Red Sea (see cut

The fourth letter in the present section, written in 1326, is from the pen of ANDREW OF PERUGIA, Bishop of Zaitún, the last survivor of the six bishops sent out twenty years before by Pope Clement. Like the first two letters it is derived by Wadding from the chronicle which he ascribed to Odoric, now preserved in the National Library at Paris[1]. The impression which the letter gives of Bishop Andrew is not quite a favourable one, and it is plain that he did not pull well with Archbishop John. I have elsewhere suggested the possibility that this bishop might have been that Andrew the Frank who came to Pope Benedict in 1338 as the head of the Great Khan's embassy[2]. Even an aged man might have been tempted to revisit the Latin world before he died, and Andrew need not have been a very aged man in 1338.

We hear of but one successor to Andrew as Bishop of Zaitún, and of him only his death[3]. Under 1362 Wadding records that "Friar James of Florence, Archbishop of Zaitún, and Friar William the Campanian, two Minorites, were slain as Christian confessors in the empire of the Medes[4]."

The next letters are those of FRIAR JORDANUS the Dominican, the author of the *Mirabilia*, of which a translation was published by the HAKLUYT SOCIETY in 1863.

in *Marignolli*, *infra*). But I believe the India Minor, India Major, and India Tertia of Jordanus will be found to answer pretty closely to the SIND, HIND, and ZINJ of the Arabs, and that these names are the origin of the three Indias.

[1] *Wadding*, vii, p. 53. There is an Andrew of Perugia mentioned by Quétif as writing against the Emperor Lewis in 1330. But even if he were not a Dominican (which Quétif is not sure of) it is most improbable that this should have been our Andrew come back from the East. (*Quétif* and *Echard*, i, p. 567.)

[2] See introduction to Marignolli.

[3] [The list given by Gams (*Series Episcoporum*, 1873, p. 126) includes: GERARDUS, O.S. Fr., el. c. 1313, † in Zaytoun.—ANDREAS de PERUGIA, recus.—PEREGRIN, O.S. Fr., † 6. VII, 1322.—ANDREAS de PERUGIA (iterum scd. el. 1323), † 1326.—JACOBUS de FLORENTIA, martyr, † 1362.—Episcopatus cessat.]

[4] See this expression (*empire of the Medes*) explained in a note on the seventh letter below.

There are a few remarks to make in addition to what was said of Jordanus in the preface to that translation.

We have nothing to guide us as to the age of Jordanus at the time of his appointment to be Bishop in India. But it is just possible that we trace the journey of his party to the East as early as 1302, when Thomas of Tolentino took out with him to Asia twelve friars, of whom it is reported incidentally that they proceeded first to Negropont, and afterwards to Thebes. Now, it is obvious from the second and third pages of the *Mirabilia* that this was precisely the route followed by Jordanus, and as it seems a somewhat peculiar one the coincidence is worthy of note. The company doubtless was chiefly composed of Franciscans, but so was that party with which he went to India[1].

One of the letters translated here appears perhaps to imply that Jordanus had been to Columbum before his landing at Tana with the Franciscans[2]. And it seems to me certain that he wrote the *Mirabilia* before he went out again as bishop. His appointment to that office appears to have taken place in 1328[3], though he did not leave Europe till 1330, and as the heading of the book sets forth his episcopal designation, it is probable that he noted down the *Mirabilia* in the interval between those two dates.

That he had been at Columbum before he was made bishop is confirmed by the following circumstance. Among the Ecclesiastical Records, besides the Pope's letter to the Christians of that place there is another in like terms

[1] *Wadding*, vii, p. 11.

[2] *Loca sunt tria ubi Fratres multum fructificare poterunt et communiter vivere*, quas ego scio: *et unus est Supera...et alter est in contracta de Parocco...et alter Columbus*." This is the only place I know in which the latter name appears in the nominative case, so that it would seemingly have been more correct to call it Columbus than Columbum as I have done, following the French editor of the *Mirabilia*.

[3] *Bzovii Annal. Ecclesiast.*, Coloniæ, 1618, tom. xiv, col. 531.

commending the new bishop "to the whole body of Christian people dwelling in *Molephatam*[1]." Now, this kingdom is mentioned by no one else that we know of except Jordanus himself in his *Mirabilia*, where he spells the name precisely as in the Pope's letter, a very unusual agreement when Asiatic names are in question. Hence, to me it seems certain that the information which led the Pope to write to Molephatam was given by Jordanus himself, and derived from his personal knowledge.

Indications of date, though slight, may also be gathered from the book. In it (p. 54) he speaks of Elchigaday as the reigning sovereign of the second Tartar (or Chagatai) empire. Ilchigadaï became Khan in 1321 [1322?], and the date of his death is not given. Some of the histories, indeed, put the death of his successor in 1327, but this is certainly inaccurate as will be shown below. Still, as that successor (Tarmashirin Khan)[2] had a reign of some length [1322–1334] and certainly was dethroned about 1334 at latest, it seems pretty clear that Ilchigadaï must have been dead long before Jordanus could have *returned* from exercising his episcopate in India. Hence he must have written his work before he went on that mission.

Before the printing of the *Mirabilia* the name of Jordanus was known, from his connexion with the friars put to death at Tana, but it was not known of what country he was. Hence the Portuguese claimed him as a countryman, and the Portuguese Hagiologist Cardoso declares that Jordanus himself was eventually a martyr to the faith, but with no particulars or evidence[3]. It is

[1] *Odoric. Raynaldi Annales Ecclesiast.*, 1330, lv. ["Universis Christianis commorantibus in Molephatam gratiam in præsenti, quæ perducat ad gloriam in futuro."] Molephatam (*Malifatan*) is mentioned by the historian Rashíduddín as one of the cities of Ma'abar, in a passage quoted at the end of the third letter in this collection.

[2] [There is a Khan, Dua Timur (1321–1322), between these two, of very brief reign. This, however, rather strengthens the argument.]

[3] *Kunstmann* in *Phillips* and *Görres*, xxxvii, p. 152.

not known that he ever reached Columbum as bishop; we only know that there is no mention of him or any other bishop on Marignolli's visit twenty years later.

I have taken the opportunity of inserting at the end of these remarks a few additional notes to the *Mirabilia* of Jordanus, in correction of my own mistakes or in further illustration of the author's text.

The last letter is one from PASCAL, a young Spanish Franciscan on a mission to Tartary, written in August 1338 from Almaliq, the capital of the Khans of Turkestan or Chagatai. It describes his proceedings from his quitting his convent at Vittoria in Spain to his arrival at Almaliq, and shows a burning zeal for his work, which had the consummation which he seems almost to have anticipated, in the martyrdom which befel him, together with several of his brethren, probably within less than a year from the date of this letter[1].

The letter is derived from Wadding, who also relates the story of the martyrdom. Its circumstances are likewise briefly told by John de' Marignolli, who was at Almaliq the year after they occurred. And another reference to the story, of earlier date perhaps than the composition of Marignolli's book, is found in John of Winterthur's chronicle[2]. The narrative is given most fully by one of the Franciscan hagiologists, Bartholomew of Pisa, who wrote later in the same century, and his account, with which Wadding's is nearly identical, runs as follows[3]:

"In the Vicariat of Cathay or Tartary, in the city of Armalec in the Middle Empire of Tartary, in the year 1340, the following Minorites suffered for the faith—viz.,

[1] Compare note on Marignolli, with the remarks on that traveller's chronology in the introductory notice. The data appear to fix the death of the friars to 1339, whilst the time of year assigned by the ecclesiastical writers (midsummer) would be probably correct.

[2] *Eccard, Corpus Histor.*, i, col. 1877–8.

[3] *Barthol. Pisan., De Conformitate*, etc. (as above, p. 5) f. lxxx *ver.*

Friar Richard the Bishop of Armalec, Friar Francis of Alessandria, Friar Pascal of Spain, Friar Raymond of Provence; these four were priests; also Friar Lawrence of Alessandria, and Friar Peter of Provence, both lay brethren, and Master John of India, a black man, belonging to the third order of St. Francis, who had been converted by our friars. All these had been very well treated in that empire by the emperor then on the throne. Indeed, he had been cured of a cancer by Friar Francis of Alessandria (more by prayer than by physic), and on this account the emperor used to call Friar Francis his father and physician. And so it came to pass that he bestowed upon the brethren lands and privileges and full authority to preach, and even made over to them his own son, then seven years of age, to be baptised; and so he was, accordingly, by the name of John. But by the permission of God, the emperor himself, on his way to a hunting match, was taken off by poison, and his four sons also were put to death. Then the empire was seized by a certain villain of a falconer[1], a Saracen of the blood-royal, whose name was Alisolda. And as the brethren by their preaching had made many converts to the faith, this new emperor ordered that all the Christians should be made Saracens, and that whosoever should disobey the third order to this effect should be put to death. And so when the brethren aforesaid would not obey this order they were bound and all tied to one rope, which was dragged along by the infuriated mob, who smote and spat upon them, stabbed and slashed them, cutting off their noses and ears, and otherwise mutilating them, till at length they fell by the sword and made a blessed migration to the Lord.

"But the aforesaid emperor before long was himself slain, and his house destroyed by fire. Now, these brethren suffered in the year before-mentioned, about the Feast of

[1] *Falcherius*.

St. John Baptist, and whilst Gerard Odo was General of the Order[1]."

It is impossible to reconcile the revolutions of government, as stated in this ecclesiastical story, with the chronology of the Chagatai empire as given by Deguignes[2]. But the latter admits the dates of succession to be very uncertain, and there seems some ground for believing that the Franciscan statements are substantially correct.

According to the lists of Deguignes Tarmeshirin Khan, the first Mussulman Khan of Chagatai, was dethroned in 1327 by his brother Butan Khan; Butan again was dethroned by Zenkshi or Jinkshi; he by his brother Yesun Timur; and he again by ALI-SULTAN of the descendants of Okkodai, who in 1332 was succeeded by Kazán, who reigned till 1346[3].

[1] There is a little discrepancy in the list of friars. Wadding omits Raymond, and adds that William of Modena, a Genoese merchant, moved by their example, also suffered with constancy. Marignolli omits Raymond, calls Lawrence *of Ancona*, and gives Gilott as the name of the merchant.

The appointment of a bishop to Armalech seems to have escaped the notice of the annalists, nor is any other besides this Richard named by Le Quien in *Oriens Christianus*. [iii, col. 1360: "Is probabiliter est episcopus ille Armalech, nomine Richardus de Burgundia, Ordinis Minorum, quem idem Waddingus refert ad annum 1342. num. 7. pag. 480. hoc anno, circa festum S. Joannis Baptistae, gloriosum, cum pluribus aliis Minoritis, martyrium subiisse in civitate Armalech vicaria Tartariae."] He may have been sent in 1328, when John XXII is stated to have despatched bishops of the two orders with priests to various Asiatic states, including Khorasan and Turkestan. (*Wadding*, vii, 88.) But it is pretty clear that Pope Benedict himself did not know anything of the bishop, for in a letter to two ministers of the Khan of Chagatai, who were Christians, he praises their beneficence "*cuidam Episcopo* de Ord. Frat. Min. in civitate Armalech deputato." (*Mosheim*, *App*., p. 177.)

[According to Gams, p. 454, Richard of Burgundy, O.S. Fr., was appointed bishop of Armalech in 1338, and was martyred in 1342; the pope Benedict XII being elected in 1334, it was during his reign and not under John XXII that the appointment of a bishop, the only bishop of Armalech, was made.]

[2] *Deguignes*, i, p. 286; and iv, p. 311.

[3] [According to Stanley Lane Poole's *Muhammedan Dynasties*, p. 242, the list of these chiefs of the western branch of the line of Chagatai Khans (those of Mávará-un-Nahr or Transoxiana) is: 17. Tarmashirin, began to reign A.H. 722 = 1322; Sanjar? A.H. 730–4?

Again, in the narrative which is given in Astley's collection from Abulghazi and others, the succession of the princes is the same, but Tarmeshirin Khan dies in 1336, and no other date is given except the death of Kazán in 1348.

If the dates in Deguignes be correct, the Ali-Sultan of the history certainly cannot be the Alisolda of the Franciscans. The other statement has nothing inconsistent with this identification which so obviously suggests itself. Now, the first dates are *certainly* incorrect; for Ibn Batuta visited Tarmeshirin Khan not many months before he entered India, and that was in the end of 1333. About two years later, he tells us, he heard of the dethronement of Tarmeshirin by his cousin Buzan Oglu (Butan Khan?)[1]. This would place the event about 1334-5. Ibn Batuta also tells us that this Buzan was an unjust sovereign who persecuted Islam, and allowed the Jews and Christians to rebuild their temples, etc. This looks very like a counterpart, from the Mussulman point of view, of the favourable character given by the missionaries of the sovereign who patronised them.

There is, however, a letter written in 1338, from Pope Benedict XII to the Khan of Chagatai, thanking him for his kindness to the Christians in his territory, and especially to Archbishop Nicholas when on his way to Chambalec[2]. And another letter to the ministers of the Khan, already quoted, speaks of their having granted a piece of land to the mission to build a church on, etc. Now, this Khan is

=1330-4?; 18. Jinkishai, A.H. 734=1334; 19. Buzun, A.H. *c.* 735 =*c.* 1335; 20. Isun Timur, A.H. *c.* 739=*c.* 1339; Ali (of Oktai stock), A.H. *c.* 741=*c.* 1340; 21. Muhammad, A.H. *c.* 743=*c.* 1342; 22. Kazán, A.H. 744=1343; Danishmanja (of Oktai stock), A.H. 747=1346; 23. Buyan Kuli, A.H. 749=1348; anarchy and rival chiefs until the supremacy of Timur, A.H. 760-771=1358-1370 A.D.]

[1] There are some curious difficulties attending the chronology of Ibn Batuta's journey, but though their solution might throw the dates in question later, I believe it could not throw them earlier.

[2] *Mosheim, App.*, p. 175.

called in the Pope's letter *Chansi*, which seems to identify him with the Jinkshi of the historical lists; whilst the circumstances mentioned seem to identify him with the Khan whose kindness to the mission is commemorated in the martyrology, and who would thus appear to be Jinkshi rather than Butan. As Nicholas was named Archbishop late in 1333, the date of his being at Almaliq was probably 1335 or 1336. There is, under these circumstances, nothing inconsistent with the revolt and success of Ali Sultan taking place in 1338 or 1339, or with his being slain soon afterwards, as the ecclesiastical story tells; though there remain some minor discrepancies.

It may be added that we have the positive statement of Friar Pascal in the letter here translated, that when he arrived on the frontiers of Chagatai, the emperor thereof had lately been slain by his natural brother. The letter is dated August 10th, 1338, and the event in question, which might have occurred from half a year to a year earlier, must have been, it seems to me, the dethronement of Jinkshi by YesunTimur. We shall then have the data afforded by Ibn Batuta, the Pope's letter, the ecclesiastical story of the martyrdom, and Pascal's own letter, all quite consistent with one another, though all inconsistent with the accepted historians. The succession of sovereigns will then run:—

Ilchigadai dies probably about		... ...	1321.
Dua-Timur		...	1321–22.
Tarmeshirin Khan dethroned by Butan		...	1334.
Butan	"	by Jinkshi ...	1335.
Jinkshi	"	by YesunTimur,	1337.
YesunTimur	"	by Ali Sultan,	1338–9.
Ali Sultan	"	by Kazán ...	1339–40.

And this Kazán was no doubt reigning when Marignolli was so well treated at Almaliq[1].

[1] See Marignolli, *infra*.

Another piece inserted in this part of our collection is a short account of "The Estate and Governance of the Grand Caan" (*i.e.*, of the Empire of Cathay under the Mongols), which was written in Latin by a certain Archbishop of Soltania under instructions from Pope John XXII. I have not been able to hear of a copy of this Latin original, but at an early date the work was done into French by that diligent John le Long of Ypres who wrought so largely in that way, and seems to be the true prototype of all the Ramusios, Hakluyts, and Purchases. Of this translation two copies exist in the Bibliothèque Nationale[1], and one did exist formerly in the Cottonian collection. This French version was printed at Paris in 1529, and subsequently, as mentioned in the bibliography relating to Odoric[2]. It was again printed from the MS. by M. Jacquet in the second series of the *Journal Asiatique* (vi, pp. 57–72) (and from that impression I have translated) [and pp. 335–346 of the miserable book of Louis de Backer, *L'Extrême Orient au Moyen Âge*, Paris, 1877].

The names of several Archbishops of Sultaniah have been preserved, and as this work fixes its own date approximately as between the death of John Montecorvino, which it alludes to as recent, and that of Pope John, it must have been written about 1330, and therefore almost certainly by JOHN DE CORA, nominated to the see of Sultaniah by that

[1] In MSS. Nos. 1380 (late 7500 c) and 2810 Fr. (late 8392). See the list of MSS. of Odoric, *supra*, p. 68 and 71.

[2] *Supra*, p. 76. LHystore merueilleuse // Plaisante et Recreatiue du grād Empereur de Tar // tarie seigneur des Tartres nōme le grād Can. Côte=// nāt six liures ou parties: Dont....On les vēd a paris en la rue neufue n̄re dame a leseigne. S. Nicolas // et au pallays en la gallerie cōe on va a la chācellerie pour Jehā. S. denys. Small fol. [1529].

Begins f. 142 recto: De la gouūnance du grant caan de cathay.

— Louis de Backer. L'Extrême Orient au Moyen Age d'après les manuscrits d'un Flamand de Belgique Moine de Saint Bertin à Saint-Omer et d'un Prince d'Arménie Moine de Prémontré à Poitiers. Paris, 1877, 8vo.

Cf. H. Cordier, *Bibliotheca Sinica*, col. 1930–1938.

Pope in the beginning of the year just mentioned (or somewhat earlier). It does not seem possible to determine from the text whether the author had himself been in Cathay, or only compiled from the reports and letters of others[1].

This Archbishop John, a Dominican[2], was perhaps also, as Le Quien has suggested, the author of a curious work described in Quétif's *Scriptores Ordinis Prædicatorum*, as existing in the Colbertian library[3], which was presented to the French king, Philip of Valois in 1330, and in which are discussed the various ways by which an army might be conducted to the Holy Land, how the Byzantine Empire might be reconquered by the Latins, and its church subjected to Rome, how the Turks might be subdued, &c. Various passages quoted by Quétif from this work show that the author was in Persia already in 1308, and had more than twenty-four years' experience of residence among the

[1] Cora, this John's name-place, is a town of the Roman Campagna six miles from Velletri. [The see of Sultaniah was created on the 1st May, 1318, for Francus of Perugia, replaced (1st June, 1323) by William Adam, who being transferred to Antivari had for his successor John of Cora, a Dominican, appointed by John XXII on the 9th August, 1329.—I find *Cori*, Province of Rome, Circondario de Velletri.] M. d'Avezac says that the reference to Montecorvino's funeral implies the author's presence at it, but there appears to be a difference in the readings. The passage as given in Jacquet's publication in the *J. A.*, p. 69, runs thus:

"Cilz Arceuesques comme il plot a Dieu est nouuellement trespassez de ce siècle. A son obseque et a son sepulture *vinrent* tres grant multitude de gens crestiens et de paiens, et desciroient ces paiens leurs robes de dueil," etc. M. d'Avezac's quotation, which appears to be taken from the work as printed in 1529, has *vis* instead of *vinrent*.

[2] [There was later at Sultaniah an Archbishop John, promoted in 1398 from the bishopric of Nakhschiwan; he was also a Dominican and was sent in 1403 by Timur as an ambassador to the Court of Charles VI, King of France. Cf. H. Moranvillé, *Mémoire sur Tamerlan et sa Cour, par un Dominicain, en* 1403. (*Bibliothèque de l'École des Chartes*, lv, 1894, pp. 432–464.)]

[3] *Quétif and Echard*, i, pp. 571–4. It is entitled, "*Directorium ad faciendum passagium transmarinum editum per quemdam Fratrem ordinis Prædicatorum scribentem experta et visa potius quam audita, quod dirigitur serenissimo principi & Domino D. Philippo Regi Francorum, compilatum anno Dni* [MCCCXXX] *millesimo ccc° trigesimo.*" There is a MS. of the same work in Magdalen College Library at Oxford.

infidels; that he had been a great labourer in the reconciliation of the Armenians to Rome; that he had seen armies of almost all the nations of the east go forth to war; that he had visited an island of the Indian sea, which appears to have been Socotra[1]; and that he had been present with Don Martin Zacharia, the Genoese Captain of Chios, in some of his victories over the Turks[2]. The rank of the author as Archbishop in the East is gathered by Quétif from the records of the French council, in which the proposals made in this work were discussed, vii Kal. August, 1330.

D'Avezac indeed says that the work in question was written by Fr. Burchard, the author of a celebrated description of the Holy Land, and informs us that this is stated in a French translation of the work, executed for the Duke of Burgundy in 1457, as well as in the catalogue of the Colbert MSS. drawn up by Baluze in the end of the seventeenth century. But there is certainly some mistake here, as Burchard or Brocard the Dominican, who wrote the *Descriptio Terræ Sanctæ*, went to the Holy Land in 1283[3], a century before the date to which the *Directorium* described by Quétif most assuredly belongs. It is curious that so accurate and accomplished a writer as M. d'Avezac should have overlooked this.

[1] See *supra*, p. 7.

[2] See *Jordanus*, p. 56, and additional notes to *Jordanus*, *infra*.

[3] The date 1232 for Burchard's visit to Palestine in the first edition of *Cathay* was taken from the *Biographie Universelle*. But the editor of *Peregrinatores Quatuor*, etc., shows that the journey occurred in 1283. (Yule.)

ADDITIONAL NOTES AND CORRECTIONS TO THE TRANSLATION OF THE *MIRABILIA* OF FRIAR JORDANUS.

(HAK. SOC. 1863.)

Preface, p. iv. The MS. of Jordanus is stated by a reviewer in the *Spectator* to be now in the British Museum.

Page vii. *Bishop of Semiscat.* Prof. Kunstmann takes this place for Meshed, but we are both wrong. M. Coquebert-Montbret, the French editor, was right in identifying it with Samarkand, though the identification did not seem probable in absence of reasons alleged. But it is clear, from reading the records in reference to this appointment in Wadding or Mosheim, that Samarkand is meant. The bishop in question, Thomas of Mancasola[1], is commended by the Pope to Elchigaday, Emperor of *Turquestan*, in whose territories he had been previously labouring, and was now promoted to a bishopric *in civitate Semiscantensi*, as it is written in one place, no doubt, correctly. For we learn from Clavijo that Samarkand was also called *Cimesquinte*. It is called *Sie-mi-se-kan* also in old Chinese annals, which is, perhaps, an indication of the same form (*Deguignes*, iv, 49).

Page ix. *Chronicle in the Vatican.* The doubts as to this chronicle being written by our Jordanus are confirmed by a reference to Muratori (*Antiq. Ital. Medii Ævi*, vol. iv, pp. 949 *et seq.*), who gives a number of extracts, and states the author's apparent interests to be Venetian and Franciscan.

[1] [We read in Gams, *Series Episcoporum*, p. 454: "Eccl. Semiscatensis. 1329. sed. Thomas Mancasola, O.S.D."]

Page xiv. *Note referring to Conti.* Being compelled to finish this preface in great haste, I made a mistake here, for which apology is due to Mr. Major. In the travels, as published in his *India in the Fifteenth Century*, the first name is *Peudefitania*, which Mr. Major explains as "Durmapatnam, near Tellicherry"; the second is *Buffetania*, which he explains as "Burdwan"; I believe, however, that the two names represent the same place, and I do not admit that either could mean *Burdwan*.

In the same note, for *Barandsi* read *Baránasí*.

Page xvii. My surmise as to the reading of the first words of Jordanus is "emphatically wrong," a critic says, in the *Spectator*; and I believe he is "emphatically" right.

Text. Pages 4, 5. *The Catholic Archbishop, Zachary by name.* This personage, Zachary Archbishop of St. Thaddeus, is congratulated by Pope John XXII on his reconciliation and zeal for the Catholic faith, in a letter dated in November, 1321. St. Thaddeus was a celebrated convent immediately south of Ararat (*Od. Raynaldi Annales Eccl.*, sub an. 1321 vi; *Jour. Asiat.*, sér. v, tom. xi, 446).

Page 6. *The tomb of Húlakú.* Húlakú not only did build a castle, called Tala, on an island in the lake, in which were deposited his treasures; but he was himself buried there, and much gold, etc., cast into the tomb with him. His successor, Abaka, was also buried there (*D'Ohsson*, iv, 257, 406–7, 538).

Page 7. *Lake where Ten Thousand Martyrs were crucified*, etc. This lake is not Sevan, north of Ararat, but the great lake of Van, south of the mountain. The great city called Semur must be ancient Van, called by the Armenians *Shamirama Kerta* (the city of Semiramis). There are vast remains. And six miles from Van is a monastery on a hill called Varac, where they relate that ten thousand martyrs were crucified, as Jordanus says. Another authority, however, speaks of their being crucified on Mount Ararat, "under Adrian and Antoninus Pius," and being valorous soldiers who refused to sacrifice. They are said to be celebrated in one of the sermons of Ephraim Syrus (*St. Martin*, in *Journ. As.*, sér. ii, tom. v, 161; *Viaggi Orient. del P. Filippo*, Venice, 1667, p. 1089; *Breve Desc. dello Stato della Christianità, etc., nell' Armenia, per il R. P. Domenico Gravina*, Roma, 1615, p. 38).

Page 10. *Pix, dico seu Pegua.* There is rather a wild question in the note on this last word. I suppose now that it is a form of *pegola*, old Italian for *pitch*.

> "Tal non per fuoco ma per divina arte
> Bollia laggiuso una *pegola* spessa."
>
> Dante, *Inf.*, xxi, 16.

The word *pegola* is applied to the same thing, *viz.* the mineral pitch of Persia, by Cesar Frederic in *Ramusio* (iii, 386 v., ed. of 1606).

Page 12. *Risis autem comeditur atque* Sagina *in aquâ tantummodo cocta.* This is mistranslated; it should be "Rice, however, and *millet* are eaten merely boiled in water." *Saggina* in Italy is the tall Asiatic millet, or *sorghum*, which in India we call *jowar.* The common dictionaries, with their usual imbecility, explain it, some as *Turkey-wheat*, some as *buck-wheat*, some as both!

Page 13. *Pliny's Pala and Ariena, the Jack.* Ritter strangely assumes these to be the *banana.* "Humboldt," he says, "writes, that many Indians (of S. America) make their meal with a very little manioc and three bananas of a larger kind. Still less satisfied the Indian Brahmans, for one fruit of that kind was enough for four." And he refers to the above-cited passage in Pliny. Here the great geographer is all abroad. Four Brahmans would be as ill-pleased to dine off one plantain of the largest kind known in India, as four Germans off one potato. The only feature suggesting the plantain in Pliny's description is the greatness of the leaves; but the form (three cubits by two) is quite different, and the great leaves were probably suggested by the great fruit; also the production of dysentery by the fruit, which Pliny mentions, is entirely foreign to the plantain.

Page 18. *The Rhinoceros in Western India.* The following references will show that the rhinoceros was in Sindh and the Punjab, at least as late as Jordanus's time, and in Peshāwar province two hundred years later (*Ibn Batuta*, iii, 100; *Baber*, pp. 292, 316; *Journ. Asiat.*, sér. i, tom. ix, 201; *Pétis de la Croix*, *Timur*, p. 158).

Page 24. *Alleged Hindu Theism.* On this subject Gasparo Balbi says, that we must not assume that *idol* stands for *God* with those heathen, "*perchè questa gente credono anch' essi che vi sia un Dio che regge e governa la machina di questo mondo;* ma adorano l' idolo come noi adoriamo nelle imagini quello che si rappresentano" (p. 68).

Page 30. *Island of naked folk.* The Carta Catalana exhibits this east of Java (which is there called *Jana*), with the title "Insula nudorum in quâ homines et mulieres portant unum folium ante et retro alium."

Page 34. *A star of great size*, etc., *called Canopus.* Baber, on describing his first invasion of Cabul, and his passage of the Indian Caucasus, says: "Till this time, I had never seen the star *Soheil* (*Canopus*); but on reaching the top of a hill, Soheil appeared below, bright to the south. I said, 'This cannot be Soheil!' They answered, 'It is, indeed, Soheil!' Baki Cheghaniani recited the following verses:

> 'O Soheil! how far dost thou shine, and where dost thou rise?
> Thine eye is an omen of good fortune to him on whom it falls!'"
>
> *Baber*, p. 133.

Page 37. *Even the Devil, too, speaketh to men*, etc. "This, for certain, I can affirm, that oftentimes the Devil doth cry with an audible voice in the night: 'tis very shrill, almost like the barking of a dog. This I have often heard myself, but never heard that he did anybody any harm" (*Robert Knox's Hist. Rel. of the Island of Ceylon*, p. 78; see also *Campbell's Excursions*, etc., i, 311).

Page 40. *Note.* On Fandaraina and Singuyli, see *note* to Odoric (p. 133).

Page 45. *Fifty-two kings under the Lord of Ethiopia.* On the numerous tributaries ascribed to the "Emperor of Ethiopia," *i.e.*, the King of Abyssinia, sometimes one hundred and twenty (as in Fra Mauro), sometimes sixty, sometimes fifty, sometimes forty, see *Ludolf*, book ii, c. xviii, § 1, and suppt., p. 15.

Page 53. *Moorish Sea.* Read Black Sea (*Mare Maurum*), and see note near beginning of Odoric.

Page 54. *Dua, Cayda, Capac, and Elchigaday.* Both Kaidu and Dua reigned in the Turkestan or Chagatai division of the Mongol dominions in the latter part of the thirteenth and the beginning of the fourteenth centuries. Kaidu long disputed with Kúblái the supreme *Khanate*, whilst Dua was the inheritor of the special Khanate of Chagatai. Capac, the *Guébek* of D'Ohsson or Kapak of others, was the fourth Khan from Dua, dying in 1321, and succeeded by *Ilchikdai*, the Elchigaday of our author.

Page 56. *A very noble Genoese, by name Martin Zachary, etc.* The story of this worthy, and how the Emperor (Andronicus Senior) got Chios from him, and took him prisoner, may be read in *Nicephorus Gregoras*, ix, 9, vi, and in *Joannes Cantacuzenus*, ii, c. 10 and 11. In 1338 Pope Benedict XII and King Philip of France wrote to the Emperor of the East to obtain Martin's liberation, and probably with success, for a Genoese Martin Jaqueria is found in command of the Pope's galleys two years later (*Ducange, Hist. de Constant.* Pt. ii, p. 103).

Page 57. *Andreolo Cathani.* For *camp* read *castle.* This castle was that of Phocæa Nova or Foglia Nuova as the Latins called it, three hours from ancient *Phocæa* on the coast of Ionia. Here certain Genoese obtained a grant of the alum-mines in an adjoining hill during the time of Michael Palæologus, and worked them to great profit. When the Turkish power became predominant they made terms with their Mussulman neighbours, and the position was maintained by the Genoese at least till late in the fifteenth century. Andrew Catanea or Cathani, the chief of the settlement in the reigns of the Andronici, is mentioned by several of the Byzantine Historians. The process of extracting the alum at Phocæa is described much as by Jordanus, in the Byz. History of Michael Ducas. (*Ducange, Hist. de Constant.* ed. 1729, Pt. ii, p. 136; *Georg. Pachymeres*, v, 30; *Ducæ Michaelis Nepotis Hist. Byz.*, cap. xx.)

Page 58. *St. John supposed to be asleep at Ephesus.* I find this belief is spoken of not only by Sir John Mandeville (p. 136), but by Saint Augustine himself as reported to him by respectable Christian folks of Ephesus. (*Romance of Travel*, ii, 88.)

LETTERS AND REPORTS OF MISSIONARY FRIARS.

No. I. FIRST LETTER OF JOHN OF MONTECORVINO[1].

. . . . . .

I, FRIAR John of Monte Corvino, of the order of Minor Friars, departed from Tauris, a city of the Persians, in the year of the Lord 1291, and proceeded to India. And I remained in the country of India, wherein stands the church of St. Thomas the Apostle, for thirteen months, and in that region baptized in different places about one hundred persons. The companion of my journey was Friar Nicholas of Pistoia, of the order of Preachers, who died there, and was buried in the church aforesaid.

I proceeded on my further journey and made my way to Cathay, the realm of the Emperor of the Tartars who is called the Grand Cham. To him I presented the letter of our lord the Pope, and invited him to adopt the Catholic Faith of our Lord Jesus Christ, but he had grown too old in idolatry[2]. However he bestows many kindnesses upon the Christians, and these two years past I am abiding with him.

[1] [No. XXXXIIII. Ex L. Waddingi *Annal. Minor.*, T. vi, p. 69, *s.*: "Ego frater Ioannes de Monte Corvino de Ordine Fratrum Minorum, recessi de Thaurisio ciuitate Persarum anno Domini MCCXCI. et intraui in Indiam....Data in Ciuitate Cambaliech regni Catan, anno Domini MCCCV. die VIII. mensis Ianuarii." (Mosheim, App., pp. 114–117.)]

Cf. Wadding, vi, anno 1321, 359–361.—Raynaldus, iv, 401.—Marcellino da Civezza, *Storia*, Vol. iii.

[2] The expression "*nimis inveteratus est idololatria*" might seem to point to old Kúblái. But the expressions that follow seem to imply that the same emperor continued to reign up to the date of the letter. This was Timur, grandson of Kúblái (1294–1307), who had a strong propensity to the Lamas and their doctrines (*Quatremère's Rashideddin*, p. 191).

The Nestorians, a certain body who profess to bear the Christian name, but who deviate sadly from the Christian religion, have grown so powerful in those parts that they will not allow a Christian of another ritual to have ever so small a chapel, or to publish any doctrine different from their own.

To these regions there never came anyone of the Apostles, nor yet of the Disciples. And so the Nestorians aforesaid, either directly or through others whom they bribed, have brought on me persecutions of the sharpest. For they got up stories that I was not sent by our lord the Pope, but was a great spy and impostor; and after a while they produced false witnesses who declared that there was indeed an envoy sent with presents of immense value for the emperor, but that I had murdered him in India, and stolen what he had in charge. And these intrigues and calumnies went on for some five years. And thus it came to pass that many a time I was dragged before the judgment seat with ignominy and threats of death. At last, by God's providence, the emperor, through the confessions of a certain individual, came to know my innocence and the malice of my adversaries; and he banished them with their wives and children.

In this mission I abode alone and without any associate for eleven years; but it is now going on for two years since I was joined by Friar Arnold, a German of the province of Cologne.

I have built a church in the city of Cambaliech, in which the king has his chief residence. This I completed six years ago; and I have built a bell-tower to it, and put three bells in it. I have baptised there, as well as I can estimate, up to this time some 6000 persons; and if those charges against me of which I have spoken had not been made, I should have baptized more than 30,000. And I am often still engaged in baptizing.

Also I have gradually bought one hundred and fifty boys,

the children of pagan parents, and of ages varying from seven to eleven, who had never learned any religion. These boys I have baptized, and I have taught them Greek and Latin after our manner. Also I have written out Psalters for them, with thirty Hymnaries and two Breviaries. By help of these, eleven of the boys already know our service, and form a choir and take their weekly turn of duty[1] as they do in convents, whether I am there or not. Many of the boys are also employed in writing out Psalters and other things suitable. His Majesty the Emperor moreover delights much to hear them chaunting. I have the bells rung at all the canonical hours, and with my congregation of babes and sucklings I perform divine service, and the chaunting we do by ear because I have no service book with the notes.

A certain king of this part of the world, by name George, belonging to the sect of Nestorian Christians, and of the illustrious family of that great king who was called Prester John of India, in the first year of my arrival here attached himself to me, and being converted by me to the truth of the Catholic faith, took the lesser orders, and when I celebrated mass he used to attend me wearing his royal robes. Certain others of the Nestorians on this account accused him of apostacy, but he brought over a great part of his people with him to the true Catholic faith, and built a church on a scale of royal magnificence in honour of our God, of the Holy Trinity, and of our lord the Pope, giving it the name of the *Roman Church*[2].

This King George six years ago departed to the Lord a true Christian, leaving as his heir a son scarcely out of the cradle, and who is now nine years old. And after King George's death his brothers, perfidious followers of the errors

[1] "*Tenent chorum et hebdomadas.*" The passage is quoted under *Hebdomadæ* by Ducange, with the explanation of that word which the text gives.

[2] Probably in Tathung, towards the Hwang Ho; see note to Odoric, pp. 244–245.

of Nestorius, perverted again all those whom he had brought over to the church, and carried them back to their original schismatical creed. And being all alone, and not able to leave his Majesty the Cham, I could not go to visit the church above-mentioned, which is twenty days' journey distant[1].

Yet, if I could but get some good fellow-workers to help me, I trust in God that all this might be retrieved, for I still possess the grant which was made in our favour by the late King George before mentioned. So I say again that if it had not been for the slanderous charges which I have spoken of, the harvest reaped by this time would have been great!

Indeed if I had had but two or three comrades to aid me 'tis possible that the Emperor Cham would have been baptized by this time! I ask then for such brethren to come, if any are willing to come, such I mean as will make it their great business to lead exemplary lives, and not to make broad their own phylacteries.

As for the road hither I may tell you that the way through the land of the Goths, subject to the Emperor of the Northern Tartars, is the shortest and safest; and by it the friars might come, along with the letter-carriers, in five or six months[2]. The other route again is very long and very

[1] "This is precisely the distance which the Imperial Geography assigns as the distance from the capital of the country occupied by the tribe of *Urat* [a branch of the old Kerait still occupying the country adjoining Tathung], that is to say, 1520 *li*, or 152 leagues, of which about 7½ go to a day's journey." *Pauthier*, *Le Pays de Tanduc*, etc., p. 38.

[2] This first route is the way by Tana and Sarai as described by Pegolotti. He, however, makes upwards of eight months actual travelling from Tana to Cambalec.

Respecting the Goths of Gazaria see Rubruquis (p. 219), in Rockhill's ed., p. 42, and Barbaro in Ramusio (ii, 97 vers.). Both of these travellers attest the Germanic dialect, and the latter had a German servant who spoke with them. "They understood each other reasonably well, much as a man of Forli might understand a Florentine." Busbeck, who was the emperor's ambassador at Constantinople between 1554 and 1560, saw two of these Crimean Goths,

dangerous, involving two sea-voyages; the first of which is about as long as that from Acre to the province of Provence, whilst the second is as long as from Acre to England. And it is possible that it might take more than two years to accomplish the journey that way[1]. But, on the other hand, the first-mentioned route has not been open for a considerable time, on account of wars that have been going on[2].

It is twelve years since I have had any news of the Papal court, or of our Order, or of the state of affairs generally in the west. Two years ago indeed there came hither a certain Lombard leech and chirurgeon, who spread abroad in these parts the most incredible blasphemies about the court of Rome and our Order and the state of things in the west, and on this account I exceedingly desire to obtain true intelligence. I pray the brethren whom this letter may reach to do their possible to bring its contents to the knowledge of our lord the Pope, and the Cardinals, and the agents of the Order at the court of Rome.

I beg the Minister General of our Order to supply me with an Antiphonarium[3], with the Legends of the Saints,

and gives a list of some forty of their vocables, which are pure Teutonic, some of them pure English (one at least pure Scotch, *criten*, to weep or *greet*); other words which he gives are apparently not Teutonic at all. Their numerals are Germanic up to 100, but 100 itself and 1000 are Persian (*Sada* and *Hazar*). (*Busbequii Opera Omnia*, Amst., 1660, pp. 321–326.) The Goths of the Crimea are also mentioned by the comrade of Plano Carpini, Benedict the Pole (776), who calls them *Saxons*; by Nicephorus Gregorias (*Hist. Byzant.*, i, 5); by Laonicus Chalcondylas (iii, p. 68), and probably by many others.

[1] This alternative route is that which John himself had followed to Cathay. The first sea voyage alluded to is that from Hormuz to Malabar, and the second that from Malabar, or from St. Thomas's (Madras) to China. The distances do fairly correspond with the voyages from Acre which he adduces in illustration.

[2] The wars carried on, since thirty years, against the Grand Khan by Kaidu; or perhaps rather the wars of succession in Turkestan after his death in 1301 at a very great age (see *D'Ohsson*, ii, 451, 512, etc. and *Marco Polo*, ii, pp. 458–9 *n.*).

[3] The *Antiphonæ* now are short anthems from the Psalms and similar parts of Scripture, which are chanted in whole or in part before the appointed Psalms, and in whole after these. The Antiphonæ, or part of one, before the Psalms, determines the pitch for the intona-

a Gradual[1], and a Psalter with the musical notes, as a copy; for I have nothing but a pocket Breviary with the short Lessons[2], and a little missal: if I had one for a copy, the boys of whom I have spoken could transcribe others from it. Just now I am engaged in building a second church, with the view of distributing the boys in more places than one.

I have myself grown old and grey, more with toil and trouble than with years; for I am not more than fifty-eight. I have got a competent knowledge of the language and character which is most generally used by the Tartars[3]. And I have already translated into that language and character the New Testament and the Psalter, and have caused them to be written out in the fairest penmanship they have; and so by writing, reading, and preaching, I bear open and public testimony to the Law of Christ. And I had been in treaty with the late King George, if he had lived, to translate the whole Latin ritual, that it might be sung throughout the whole extent of his territory; and whilst he was alive I used to celebrate mass in his church, according to the Latin ritual, reading in the before-mentioned language and character the words of both the preface and the Canon[4].

tion of these. It would seem that the etymological meaning of the term has been abandoned. But an *Antiphonarium* is or was also a name applied to a book containing all that is sung by the choir during vespers.

[1] *Graduale* is a psalm or part of a psalm sung at mass between the Epistle and Gospel, some say because read on the steps of the altar. But *Graduale* is also a name applied to a book containing all that is sung by the choir in the service of the mass.

[2] The *Lectio Brevis* is a short passage of Scripture read at the end of *Prime* and the beginning of *Complines*.

[3] The original seems to be corrupt here, and does not bear closer rendering: "*Didici competenter linguam et litteram Tartaricam, quæ lingua usualis Tartarorum est.*" *Tartaricam* can scarcely be the true reading. Perhaps it should be *Tarsicam*; see passage in the following letter.

[4] *Præfatio* is that part of the service of the mass commencing with the words *Sursum Corda* which immediately precedes the *canon*, by

And the son of the king before-mentioned is called after my name, John; and I hope in God that he will walk in his father's steps.

As far as I ever saw or heard tell, I do not believe that any king or prince in the world can be compared to his majesty the Cham in respect of the extent of his dominions, the vastness of their population, or the amount of his wealth. Here I stop.

Dated at the city of Cambalec in the kingdom of Cathay, in the year of the Lord 1305, and on the 8th day of January[1].

No. II. SECOND LETTER OF JOHN OF MONTECORVINO[2].

To the Reverend Father in Christ the Vicar General of the Order of Minor Friars, and to the Vicar of the said Order, and to the Master of the Order of Preachers, and to

which name is implied the series of prayers and ceremonies followed in the consecration of the Eucharist. In explaining these terms of the Roman service I have consulted Ducange; a modern Italian encyclopædia (*N. Encic. Popol. Italiano*); and an Italian priest of my acquaintance.

[1] I think that here January 1305 must mean *our* January 1305, and not 1306. The next letter we shall find to be written about a year after this one. And that next letter had been read by the Pope when he created John Archbishop, for the fragments of his bull on that occasion (see *Wadding*, vi, 93; or *Mosheim*, App., p. 124) contain allusions to its contents. Now, though the date of this bull is not preserved, it is fixed by other circumstances to the spring of 1307. Hence, letter No. II could not have been written later than 1306, nor this letter, No. I, later than 1305.

[2] No. XXXXV. Ex L. Waddingi *Annal. Min.*, T. vi, p. 69 *s.*: "Reuerendo in CHRISTO Patri Fratri NN. Vicario Generali Ministro Ordinis Fratrum Minorum, et Vicario Fratrum, et Magistro Ordinis Praedicatorum, et Fratribus Ordinis vtriusque in provincia Persarum manentibus: frater IOANNES DE MONTE CORVINO de Ordine Fratrum Minorum, inutilis CHRISTI seruus, praedicator fidei sacrae Christianae, Legatus et Nuncius Sedis Apostolicae Romanae, salutem et caritatem in eo qui est vera caritas et salus omnium.

Ordo eximiae caritatis inuitat, ut longe lateque distantes, et maxime, qui peregrinantur pro lege CHRISTI, cum revelata facie se inuicem videre non possunt, saltem verbis et litteris se inuicem consolentur... Baptizaui ibi circa centum personas cet: *Deest finis.*" (Mosheim, App., pp. 117–120.)

the Friars of either Order abiding in the province of the Persians;

From Friar John of Montecorvino of the Order of Minor Friars, an unprofitable servant of Christ, Preacher of the Holy Christian Faith, Legate and Nuncio of the Apostolic See of Rome;

Health and Love in Him who is the True Love and Health of all.

The requirements of blessed brotherly love demand that those who are separated far and widely, and especially those who are Missionaries of Christ's Law in distant lands, when they cannot see each other face to face, should at least send one another comforting communications by letter.

I have been thinking that you had some reason to be surprised that during my long residence in so distant a region you had never yet received a letter from me[1]. And I also was surprised that until this year I never received a letter from any friend or any Brother of the Order, nor even so much as a message of remembrance, so that it seemed as if I was utterly forgotten by everybody. And most of all I was grieved at this when I heard that rumours of my death had reached you.

But now I wish to tell you that last year, in the beginning of January, by a certain friend of mine who was attached to the court of the Lord Kathan Khan[2], and who had come to his majesty the Cham, I sent a letter to the father vicar and the friars of the Province of Gazaria, giving a short account of the whole state of affairs with me. And

[1] This is clearly what he means. But he *says*: "*Vos non sine causâ mirari, quod tot annis in Provinciâ tam longinquâ consistentes, nunquam meas litteras recipistis.*"

[2] "*Qui fuit ex sociis Domini Kathan Chamis.*" This seems to refer to Ghazan Khan, sovereign of Persia; but, according to Deguignes and D'Ohsson, he died in 1304. It is, therefore, perplexing that in 1306 the writer should still speak of the "Messengers of the said Lord Kathan" as just arrived, which he does a little further on.

in that letter I begged the said vicar to send you a copy; and now I have learned from some persons who have just arrived with the messengers of the aforesaid Lord Kathan to his majesty the Cham, that my letter did reach you, the bearer of it from this having after a while gone on from the city of Sarai to Tauris. I do not therefore think it necessary to detail the contents of my former letter nor to write them over again. I will only mention that the first matter spoken of was about the persecutions which the Nestorians raised against me, and the second was about the church and houses which I had completed.

I have now had six pictures made, illustrating the Old and New Testaments for the instruction of the ignorant[1]; and the explanations engraved in Latin, Tarsic[2], and Persian

[1] This is the passage alluded to in the Pope's bull appointing John to the archbishopric (see note above, p. 51).

[2] "Tarsic letters," says Rémusat, quoting this passage, are "those of the Uighúrs, to whose country the relations of that age gave the name of *Tarsia* from a Tartar word signifying *infidel*, and which appears to have been applied in Tartary successively to the followers of Zoroaster, and to the Nestorian Christians." (*Nouv. Mélanges Asiat.*, ii, 198.)

[According to Palladius, *Tie sie* is the Chinese transcription of the word *tersa*, used by the Persians since the time of the Sassanides to designate the Christians, and sometimes also the Fire-worshippers and Magi. Cf. Bretschneider, *Med. Res.*, i, p. 67 *n.* We read in Ney Elias' translation of the *Tarikh-i-Rashidi*, p. 290: "Now the tribe of Náimán were mostly Christians [*Tarsa*]." In a long note Elias makes the following remark regarding Rémusat's passage: "Thus the name was applied also to the Uighúrs as a nation, but probably only on account of their Christianity or Buddhism—for both religions were prevalent among them."]

[Devéria thinks that by *Tarsicis* Monte Corvino means the writing of the Unfaithful, *i.e.* of the Mongols. Bonin, *Jour. As.*, May–June 1900, p. 587, says the word refers to "Syrian letters."]

The name of Tarse is applied expressly to the kingdom of the *Yogurs* by Hayton the Armenian; and Marino Sanudo the Elder also speaks of the kingdom of Tarse where the Tartars first learned letters and also idol worship; he is probably drawing from Hayton. (*Secreta Fidel. Crucis*, p. 235.) Carpini likewise (p. 709) has *Tarci* in his list of nations conquered by the Mongols, but the reading is doubtful. *Tharze* appears in Fra Mauro and *Tarssia* in the earlier Catalan map, somewhere about Turkestan. The author was apparently also following Hayton, as he states that the Three Kings came from that country. Trigautius tells us that in his time (the beginning of the seventeenth century) the Mahomedans in China spoke of the old professors of

characters, that all may be able to read them in one tongue or another.

Christianity in that country as *Terzai*, the origin of which appellation he was ignorant of; but he heard from an Armenian that the Armenian Christians in Persia were called by the same name. (*De Christiana Exped. apud Sinas*, 1617, p. 137.) The word is apparently that given by Meninski as "*Tarsá*, a Christian, an infidel, a fire-worshipper." Its application to the Uighúrs and their character perhaps indicates the extensive prevalence of Nestorian Christianity among them.

Quatremère quotes the author of a book called *Tabakati Naseri*, as saying that the inhabitants of a certain city of Tibet professed the *Dín Tarsáyi*, which he renders *religion Chrétienne*, though considering that the writer had mistaken Buddhism for Christianity. (*Rashid-eddin*, p. 198.)

The Uighúr [or rather the *Soghdian*] character was the original source of those still used by the Mongols and Manchus, and was itself almost certainly derived from the old Syriac character through the Nestorians.

The modern Tartar characters are written (and, I presume, read) in vertical lines from top to bottom of the page, the lines succeeding each other from left to right. It seems doubtful whether the Uighúr itself was thus written; at least, Rémusat says that the only document in that character which was known to him was written in horizontal lines, though the language of Rubruquis as to the Uighúr writing most precisely describes the vertical direction of the modern Tartar alphabets. Rémusat thinks that the vertical direction may have been acquired by the frequent necessity of interlining Chinese documents, a suggestion which seems ingenious rather than convincing. It has, indeed, been maintained by some authorities that the ancient Syriac itself was vertical, and an old line is cited,

"E cœlo ad stomachum relegit Chaldæa lituras,"

but Rémusat denies this. [The Syriac part of the inscription of Si-ngan fu is in vertical lines.]

I may venture to remark that the direction in which a character is *read*, and not that in which it is written, is the essential distinction. Everyone has acquaintances whose characters run, if not vertically, at least in a resultant direction between vertical and horizontal; and the Indian Munshi in *writing* the Persian character on a paper in his hand, according to the usual practice, does really by some natural necessity write *e cœlo ad stomachum*, a practice which, by becoming systematised or copied by a people to whom writing was a new acquirement, might give rise to a modified character, *read* as well as written vertically.

The language of the Uighúrs appears to have been Turkish. So Rubruquis, who shows unusual discernment for his time in all linguistic matters, expressly testifies. Rashíduddín says that Mangú Khan had secretaries to write his orders in Chinese, Tibetan, Tangutan, and Uighúr. Unless the latter represent Turkish, that language, which was spoken over so great a part of his empire, was omitted altogether.

Mr. Schmidt, the translator of Ssanang Setzen, maintains against the general opinion that Uighúr was Tangutan or Tibetan; his arguments are not convincing, and his temper does not beget confidence. Whatever Uighúr may have meant in Mongol authors, the people and language so called by the Western Asiatics were Turkish.

As regards a third subject (I may add that) some of the boys whom I purchased and baptized have departed to the Lord. A fourth matter mentioned was that since my first coming to Tartary I have baptized more than five thousand souls.

In that same year of the Lord 1305, I began another new place before the gate of the Lord Cham, so that there is but the width of the street between his palace and our place, and we are but a stone's throw from his majesty's gate. Master Peter of Lucolongo, a faithful Christian man and great merchant, who was the companion of my travels from Tauris, himself bought the ground for the establishment of which I have been speaking, and gave it to me for

The "Ugaresca" of the Genoese in the Crimea, and the Uighúr character which Friar Pascal learned at Saray (see below) could have nothing to do with Tibetan.

Captain Valikhanoff speaks of the language now in use at Kashgar as being *Uighúr*, but it is not clear whether he means that this term is known to the natives. (*Russians in Cent. Asia*, p. 67.)

On the original seat and migrations of the Uighúrs, see D'Ohsson (i, 107 *seq.*, and 429 *seq.*) [and Introductory Essay].

(*Rubruquis*, pp. 288, 289; *Plano Carpini*, 651; *Klaproth* in *J. As.*, sér. i, tom. v, 203; *Rémusat, Rech. sur les langues Tart.*, 38, 39, 60–63; *St. Martin, Mém. sur l'Arménie*, ii, 275; *Schmidt, Ssanang Setzen*, etc., pp. 211, 386, 396–8, 406, 412.)

[According to Dr. Von le Coq (*Exploration archéol. à Tourfan*, *J. As.*, Sept.–Oct. 1909, p. 325) the Uighúr, who go back to the Hiung nu, were a mixed race, of Scythic, Iranian, and Turkish elements; their language was a Turkish dialect somewhat similar to that of the Tu kiue. Their tribe was the first Turkish tribe reaching a high degree of civilisation; most of them were Buddhist, but many were Manichaeans and Nestorian Christians. These Uighúr, called *Hwei-ho* by the Chinese, at the time of the Wei (Toba) dynasty were known as the *T'ie-le* (Tölös) tribes and were then subject to the Tu-kiue; these Hwei-ho became gradually powerful from the beginning of the VIIth century, after they had defeated Ch'u-lo kagan; Hami, Kashgar, Turfan fell into their hands; subsequently they were known to the Chinese as *Wei-wu-rh*; at the height of their power, it extended from Pei-t'ing (Gu-chen) to Aqsu. They had several capitals; among others Kao ch'ang, Kho cho or Idiqut-shahri (Turfan), and Kara balgasun near the Orkhon river. The Uighúr character is of Syriac origin, introduced into Eastern Turkestan by the early Nestorian missionaries; it is the basis of the modern Mongol and Manchu characters. According to Palladius, the Uighúr writing was introduced by Chinghiz among his people a few years after Ch'ang ch'un visited Mongolia. (*Marco Polo*, i, p. 28 *n.* Bretschneider, *Med. Res.*, i, pp. 53, 236, 263. Chavannes, *Tou-kiue.*)]

the love of God. And by the divine favour I think that a more suitable position for a Catholic church could not be found in the whole empire of his majesty the Cham. In the beginning of August[1] I got the ground, and by the aid of sundry benefactors and well-wishers it was completed by the Feast of St. Francis with an enclosure wall, houses, offices, courts, and chapel, the latter capable of holding two hundred persons. On account of winter coming on I have not been able to finish the church, but I have the timber collected at the house, and please God I hope to finish it in summer. And I tell you it is thought a perfect marvel by all the people who come from the city and elsewhere, and who had previously never heard a word about it. And when they see our new building, and the red cross planted aloft, and us in our chapel with all decorum chaunting the service, they wonder more than ever. When we are singing, his majesty the Cham can hear our voices in his chamber; and this wonderful fact is spread far and wide among the heathen, and will have the greatest effect, if the divine mercy so disposes matters and fulfils our hopes.

From the first church and house to the second church which I built afterwards, is a distance of two miles and a half within the city, which is passing great. And I have divided the boys into two parties, putting one of them in the first church and the other in the second, and so each party performs the service by itself. But I act as chaplain and celebrate mass in each church on alternate weeks, for none of those boys are priests.

As regards the regions of the East, and especially the

[1] This may perhaps mean August 1304, though, if we look at the beginning of this paragraph only, we should suppose it to be August 1305. But in his preceding letter written in January 1305, he says he was already in *actu edificandi ecclesiam.* And from August to St. Francis's day (4th October) in the same year seems too short a time for the amount of work reported.

empire of the Lord Cham, I give you to know that there is none greater in the world. And I have a place in the Cham's court, and a regular entrance and seat assigned me as legate of our Lord the Pope, and the Cham honours me above all other prelates, whatever be their titles. And although his majesty the Cham has heard much about the court of Rome, and the state of the Latin world, he desires greatly to see envoys arriving from those regions.

Here are many sects of idolaters holding various beliefs; and here also are many persons attached to religious orders of different sects, and wearing different habits; and these practise greater abstinence and austerity than our Latin monks.

I have seen the greater part of India and made inquiries about the rest, and can say that it would be most profitable to preach to them the faith of Christ, if the brethren would but come. But none should be sent except men of the most solid character; for those regions are very attractive, abounding in aromatic spices and precious stones. But they possess few of our fruits, and, on account of the great mildness and warmth of the climate, the people there go naked, only covering the loins. And thus the arts and crafts of our tailors and cordwainers are not needed, for they have perpetual summer and no winter. I baptized there about a hundred persons....

Here the letter, as given by the chronicler from whom Wadding copies, breaks off. But the same authority gives, as the substance of part of another letter that had been presented, what in fact appears to have been the end of this letter, perhaps accidentally separated from what goes before[1]:

"Besides what he wrote in the preceding year (*i.e.* 1305) Friar John of Monte Corvino this year relates in another letter of his that a solemn deputation had come to him from a certain part of Ethiopia, begging him either to go

[1] See introductory notice, *supra*, p. 6.

thither to preach, or to send other good preachers; for since the time of St. Matthew the Apostle and his immediate disciples they had had no preachers to instruct them in the faith of Christ, and they had an ardent desire to attain to the true Christian faith.

"Friar John also said that after the Feast of All Saints he had baptized four hundred persons. And as he had heard that a number of friars, both Minors and of the other Order, had arrived in Persia and Gazaria, he exhorted them to preach fervently the faith of our Lord Jesus Christ and so to win a harvest of souls. The letter was dated at Cambalec, a city of Cathay, in the year of the Lord 1306, on Quinquagesima Sunday and in the month of February."

No. III. LETTER FROM FRIAR MENENTILLUS, A DOMINICAN, FORWARDING COPY OF A LETTER FROM JOHN OF MONTE CORVINO.

To you Friar Bartholomew of Santo Concordio[1], your brother in all things, Menentillus of Spoleto, wisheth health and wisdom in Christ[2]!

[1] This Bartolomeo a Santo Concordio, a Dominican monk, a Pisan by birth, and eminent for his learning in canon and civil law as well as his accomplishments in Latin and Tuscan literature, flourished in the early part of the fourteenth century and died in 1347. He was best known afterwards as the author of a *Summa de Casibus Conscientiæ*, arranged alphabetically, which he completed in 1338. This was printed at a very early date and often again, being apparently much used as a handbook by confessors, and known familiarly as the *Magistruccia* or *Pisanella*. (*Quétif*, *Scriptores Ord. Praed.*, i, 623–625.) There is a work of the same author "*De origine civitatis Pisanæ*" in *Muratori*, *Ital. Rer. Scriptores*, tom. vi.

[2] The opening of this letter may be given as a sample of the style of the original :—

"A vo' in Cristo frate Bartolomeo de Santo Concordio suo per tutte le cose frate Menentillo di Spuleto salute e sapienzia! Perciò che conosco che voi grande cura avete in iscienzia, e molto sapete e vorreste tutte le cose sapere, spezialmente quelle che non sapete, e vorrest' avere sapimento e cognoscienzia di tutte le cose; imperciò scrivo a voi certe cose le quali aguale sono scritte delle parte d' India Superiore per uno frate Minore, lo quale fue compagno di frate Nicolaio da Pistoia, lo quale moritte in India Superiore, andando

And because I wot of the great curiosity that you have in regard to all science, and that, much as you do know, you would fain know everything and especially things that are new to you; and in truth that you are one whose desire is to have knowledge and information of all kinds; therefore transcribe I for you certain matters just as they have been written from India by a certain Minorite Friar (the travelling companion of Brother Nicolas of Pistoia, who died in Upper India), when on his way to the court of the Lord of all India. The bringer of the letter I have seen and spoken with, and it was in his arms that the said Brother Nicholas did die. The letter was to the effect following[1]:

"The state of things [with regard to climate] in the Indies is such as shall now be related.

"In India it is always warm, and there never is any winter; yet the heat is not extravagant. And the reason is, that there be at all times winds which temper the heat of the air. And the reason why there can be no winter is the position of the country with respect to the zodiac, as I shall now tell. That is to say, the sun when entering *Virgo*, i.e. on the 24th day of August, sends down his rays, as I have seen and in particular noted with my own eyes, quite perpendicularly, so as to cast no shadow on either side. And in like manner when he is entering *Aries*, i.e. at the end of March. And when he has gone through *Aries* he passes towards the north, and casts shadows towards the south until...[the summer solstice] and then turns to *Virgo*, and after he has past through the sign of *Virgo* he then casts his shadow towards the north. And thus there

al Signore di tutta l' India. Lo messo viddi e parlai con lui, in delle cui braccia lo ditto frate Nicolaio moritte. E cosi testificava."

[1] Professor Kunstmann speaks of Menentillus having met John of Montecorvino at the court of the Khan and got the information that follows from him. But this must surely rest on some misunderstanding. Menentillus is merely a monk in Italy, who chances on a letter of John's and sends it to a learned friend to gratify his curiosity.

is never so great an elongation[1] of the sun as to admit of cold, and there are not two seasons. Or, as I have said before, there is no winter or cold season.

"As regards the length of the day and the night I have tried to determine them by such measures and indications as I could. I have observed that at the two epochs before mentioned, when the sun's rays strike perpendicularly without casting any shadow, the day is fifteen hours long, and the night nine. And when the sun is at the solstice of *Cancer*, the day is a little less than fourteen hours long, and the night is a little more than ten, perhaps by a quarter of an hour. But when the sun is in the solstice of *Capricorn*, that is to say in the month of December, the day has a length of eleven hours and the night of thirteen. For the sun's elongation is somewhat greater when it is in *Capricorn* than when it is in *Cancer*[2].

"Moreover, the star which we call the Pole-star is there so depressed, i.e. so low, that it can scarcely be seen. And methought that if I had been on a lofty point I could have seen the other Pole-star which is in the opposite quarter[3]. I looked many a time for a sight of it, and I saw several constellations which moved round about it, from observing which I gathered that they were exceedingly near to it[4].

[1] The transcript made for me gives *congiungimento*, but Professor Kunstmann's has *elongamento*.

[2] I am afraid we cannot throw the blame of these extraordinary statements on anybody but Friar John himself. He considers that at a given north latitude within the tropic the day is at its longest when the sun passes towards the north, and *diminishes* up to midsummer day, increases again till it repasses the given latitude, and then diminishes till midwinter.

[3] "*L' altra tramontana la quale è posta in contrario.*"

[4] This runs: "Molto guardai di vederla e vidi più segni che gl' andavano intorno per li quai li *conovi* et parvemi ch' elli fusseno vicini veramente, perchè la fumosità vi sono continue chontra quella parte *si tene* per li calori e per li venti ella è molto al disotto non me ne potei certificare." The words in italics are read by Prof. Kunstmann *Conobbi* and *Sottane*. The last I have adopted, but not the former, which he understands to be the name (*Canopi*) given to the stars, certainly a misapprehension.

But because of the continual haze on the horizon in that quarter, caused by the heat and the winds, and because of the stars being so low, I never could satisfy myself. However India is a very extensive region, and perhaps in some places it would be seen at a greater elevation, in others at a less. I have examined the matter to the best of my ability. So much as to [the climate of] Upper India, which is called MAEBAR, in the territory of St. Thomas.

"*Concerning the state of things as to the country itself in Upper India.* The condition of the country of India aforesaid is this. The land is well enough peopled; and there be great cities therein, but the houses are wretched, being built of sandy mud, and usually thatched with leaves of trees. Hills there are few; rivers in some places are many, in others few. Springs there are few or none; wells in plenty; and the reason is this, that water is generally to be found at the depth of two or three paces, or even less. This well water is indeed not very good to drink, for it is somewhat soft and loosens the bowels; so they generally have tanks or excavations like ponds, in which they collect the rain water, and this they drink. They keep few beasts. Horses there are none, except it be in possession of the king and great barons. Flies there be few, and fleas none at all[1]. And they have trees which produce fruit continually, so that on them you find fruit in every stage up to perfect ripeness at one time[2]. In like manner they sow and reap at almost all seasons, and this because it is always warm and never cold. Aromatic spices are to be had good cheap, some more so and some less so, according to what spices they be. They have trees that produce sugar, and others that produce honey, and others that produce a liquor that has a smack of wine. And this the natives of thos

[1] They must have come with the Portuguese then!

[2] The sentence is apparently corrupt, but this seems to be the meaning.

countries use for drink. And those three things are to be had at very small cost. And the pepper plant is here also. It is slender and knotty like a vine; and indeed 'tis altogether very like a vine, excepting that it is more slender, and bears transplanting.

"Ginger is a reed-like plant, and, like a cane-root, it can be dug and transplanted. But their canes here are more like trees, being sometimes a cubit in girth and more, with slender prickly branches round about, and small leaves.

"The Brazil tree[1] is a slender lofty and thorny tree, all red as it were, with leaves like fern. The Indian nuts are as big as melons, and in colour green like gourds[2]. Their leaves and branches are like those of the date tree.

"The cinnamon tree is of a medium bulk, not very high, and in trunk, bark, and foliage, is like the laurel; indeed, altogether it resembleth the laurel greatly in appearance. Great store of it is carried forth of the island which is hard-by Maabar[3].

"As regards men of a marvellous kind, to wit, men of a different make from the rest of us, and as regards animals of like description, and as regards the Terrestrial Paradise, much have I asked and sought, but nothing have I been able to discover.

"Oxen are with these people sacred animals, and they eat not their flesh for the worship they bear them. But they make use of cows' milk, and put their cattle to labour like other folk.

"The rain falleth at fixed seasons.

[1] *Bersi.*

[2] The word is *chocosse*. I can find nothing nearer than *cocuzza*, which is given as a South Italian word for a gourd (*cucurbita*). The comparison seems probable.

[3] Ceylon. I believe this is one of the earliest notices of the Ceylon cinnamon trade. Sir Emerson Tennent, I think, quotes Ibn Batuta as the earliest.

"The state of things as regards the inhabitants of India is as follows:—The men of this region are idolaters, without moral law, or letters, or books. They have indeed an alphabet which they use to keep their accounts, and to write prayers or charms for their idols; albeit they have no paper, but write upon leaves of trees like unto palm leaves. They have no conscience of sin whatever. They have idol-houses in which they worship at almost all hours of the day; for they never join together in worship at any fixed hour, but each goes to worship when it pleases himself. And so they worship their idols in any part of these temples, either by day or by night. They frequently set forth their fasts and feasts, but they have no fixed recurring day to keep, either weekly or monthly. Their marriages take place only at one time of the year; and when the husband dies the wife cannot marry again. The sin of the flesh they count not to be sin, nor are they ashamed to say so.

"In the regions by the sea are many Saracens, and they have great influence[1] but there are few of them in the interior. There are a very few Christians, and Jews, and they are of little weight. The people persecute much the Christians, and all who bear the Christian name.

"They bury not their dead but burn them, carrying them to the pile with music and singing; whilst apart from this occasion the relatives of the deceased manifest great grief and affliction[2] like other folk.

"But India is a region of great extent, and it hath many realms and many languages. And the men thereof are civil and friendly enough, but of few words, and remind

[1] As to the great influence of the Saracens on the coast of Maabar see the extract from Rashid *infra*, which shows that at this very time a "Saracen" was the king's chief minister and governor of the seaports of Pattan, Malipattan, and Káíl (in the original *Wazír wa Mushír wa Sahib-i-tadbír*).

[2] *Rancori*. Kunstmann has *ramori*.

me somewhat of our peasants[1]. They are not, strictly speaking, black, but of an olive colour, and exceedingly well formed both women and men. They go barefoot and naked, except that they wear a cloth round the loins, and boys and girls up to eight years of age wear nothing whatever, but go naked as they came from their mother's womb. They shave not the beard; many times a day they wash; bread and wine they have none. Of the fruits that we make use of they have few or none; but for their daily food they use rice and a little milk; and they eat grossly like pigs, to wit, with the whole hand or fist, and without a spoon. In fact, when at their food they do look more like pigs than men!

"There is great security in the country. Bandits and robbers are seldom met with; but they have many exactions to pay[2]. There are few craftsmen, for craft and craftsmen have little remuneration, and there is little room for them. They commonly use swords and daggers like ourselves; and if actually they have a battle they make short work of it, however great the forces be, for they go to battle naked, with nothing but sword and dagger. They have among them a few Saracen mercenaries, who carry bows.

"The state of things in regard to the Sea of India is this. The sea aboundeth greatly with fish; and in some parts of it they fish for pearls and precious stones. The havens are few and bad; and you must know that the sea here is the Middle Sea or Ocean. Traversing it towards the south there is no continent found but islands alone, but in that sea the islands are many, more than 12,000 in number. And many of these are inhabited, and many are not.

"You can sail (upon that sea) between these islands

[1] "*Sono li omini assai dimestichi e familiari e di poche parole, e quasi come omini di villa.*"

[2] "*Pedaggi molti vi si pagano.*" This I take from Kunstmann. My transcript has "*Per arti molti vi si pagano.*"

and ORMES and (from Ormes) to those parts which are called [MINIBAR] is a distance of 2,000 miles in a direction between south and south-east; then 300 miles between east and south-east from Minibar to Maabar, which (latter however) you enter steering to the north; and from Menabar [Maabar?] you sail another 300 miles between north-east and north to SIU SIMMONCOTA[1]. The rest I have not seen, and therefore I say nothing of it.

[1] I have endeavoured to reduce to shape and congruity this passage, which is a good deal bungled in the MS. It runs thus: "*Navicavisi da isse* (or *da Issa*) *infine ad Ormesse et a quelle parti le quali si dice che siano due miglia migliaia di miglia e intra scilocco e levante da Minabar a Maabar ch' entra a tramontana ccc miglia intra levante e scirocco da Menabar a Siu Simmoncota altre ccc migliaia navicavisi intra greco e tramontana.*"

In the text I have taken *da isse*, as read by Kunstmann (for *esse*), to refer to the islands, and this requires rather a forced translation to be intelligible. But if it be a proper name, ISSA, as in my transcript, then we should read—"You can sail from Issa to Ormes and so to those parts," etc. In that case Issa must be a port of the Persian Gulf, perhaps Al-Ahsa, which is a port on the west shore below Al-Katif, and is mentioned by our author's contemporary, Rashíd, in connexion with Indian trade, in a passage which will be given presently.

The first section of the voyage, then, I understand to be from the Persian Gulf to one of the ports of Malabar (called Minabar, see p. 132, *supra*); the second from the said port to some city on the Gulf of Manaar; and the third from the Gulf of Manaar to some place on the Coromandel coast, at least as far north as the church of St. Thomas, *i.e.*, Madras. I say "some city on the Gulf of Manaar," because we shall see presently that Mabar is, with the present writer, a city, and is probably to be identified with that where Marco Polo locates his chief king of Mabar. As Polo seems to specify this as sixty miles west of Ceylon, I judge that it must have been somewhere near Ramnad. It is not Cail, because he says distinctly that Cail was subject to another of the chiefs, and Cail is a good deal more than sixty miles from any part of Ceylon.

The extreme point which our author visited, whether Siu Simmoncota or Giu Gimmoncota (for it is so read by Kunstmann), I cannot determine. It must have been *at least* as far up the coast as Madras, because he tells us in the first letter that his companion Nicholas of Pistoia was buried in the church of St. Thomas. Samulcotta (*S'yâmala Kotta*—Black Fort, or Fort of Durga?), the nearest approach to the name that I can trace among existing towns, seems to be too far north. The Buddhists were called *Samanas* and Samanals in South India, and *Saman-Kotta*, "The Fort of the Buddhist," might be a probable enough name.

The name, however, taking it abstractedly as it stands, would most nearly represent *Siva-Samundra-Kotta*. *Siva* appears constantly in

"The shores of the said sea in some places run out in shoals for 100 miles or more[1], so that ships are in danger of grounding. And they cannot make the voyage but once a year, for from the beginning of April till the end of October the winds are westerly, so that no one can sail towards the west; and again 'tis just the contrary from the month of October till March. From the middle of May till the end of October the wind blows so hard that ships which by that time have not reached the ports whither they are bound, run a desperate risk, and if they escape it is great luck. And thus in the past year there perished more than sixty ships; and this year seven ships in places in our own immediate neighbourhood, whilst of what has happened elsewhere we have no intelligence. Their ships in these parts are mighty frail and uncouth, with no iron in them, and no caulking. They are sewn like clothes with twine. And so if the twine breaks anywhere there is a breach indeed! Once every year therefore there is a mending of this, more or less, if they propose to go to sea. And they have a frail and flimsy rudder like the top of

popular pronunciation as *Siu* or *Seo*, as in *Seodasheogarh*, *Seopoor*, *Seoganga*, etc., and we find the analogous name of Dwara-Samudra to be written by the Persian and Arabian historians *Dur-sammund* and *Dur-Saman* (see *Dow's Ferishta*, i, 256, 281; *Masálak al-ábsár* in *Not. et Extr.*, xiii, 170; and *Wassaf* in *Von Hammer*, op. inf. cit., ii, 202). The only place I can trace bearing at present the name of Siva-Samundra (the Sea or Lake of Siva) is a very holy and ancient site on an island in the Caveri south-east of Seringapatam, whilst the site we seek must have been on the coast. Perhaps, however, there is some indication of the existence of a place of importance on the coast in the name of which Samudra was an element, in passages of Firishta and Wassaf. The latter, in speaking of the civil wars of Maabar about this very time, says that the Raja had laid up 1200 *krors* of gold besides jewels in the treasures of *Shahrmandi*; whilst the former, after describing the prodigious spoils carried from the Peninsula by Malik Kafur in 1310, observes that he understood Dwara Samudra to have been since *destroyed by the encroachment of the sea*, and to lie in ruins. But Dwara Samudra the capital of the Belal Rajas was an inland city, which has been identified with Halabidu in Mysore (*Wassaf* in *Hammer Purgstall's Ilchane*, ii, 204; *Brigg's Firishta*, iv, 374).

[1] Here he refers apparently to the reefs and shoals between Ceylon and the mainland.

a table, of a cubit in width, in the middle of the stern; and when they have to tack, it is done with a vast deal of trouble; and if it is blowing in any way hard, they cannot tack at all. They have but one sail and one mast, and the sails are either of matting or of some miserable cloth. The ropes are of husk[1].

"Moreover their mariners are few and far from good. Hence they run a multitude of risks, insomuch that they are wont to say, when any ship achieves her voyage safely and soundly, that 'tis by God's guidance, and man's skill hath little availed.

"This letter was written in MAABAR, a city of the province of SITIA in Upper India, on the 22nd day of December in the year of our Lord MCCX (CII or CIII)[2]."

[1] *Resti.* I am doubtful of the meaning of the word.

[2] The date in the MS. at Florence is obscure, but M.CC.X...at least is legible. Quétif, in his mention of it in *Script. Ord. Prædicatorum*, gives the date as M.CCC.XX. But this is not correctly transcribed. John left Tauris in 1291, and on his way passed thirteen months in Southern India. Hence the date is doubtless M.CC.XCII or M.CC.XCIII. It is worth noting that as Marco Polo, if Rashíd's statements quoted below be exact, could not have been later than 1292 in visiting Maabar on his way westward, the two Italian travellers may have met in that region.

The "Province of Sitia" is named by no other traveller that I know of. The island or peninsula of Ramisseram was, however, called *Sethu*, "The Bridge" or Causeway, from which the chiefs of the adjoining territory of Ramnad or Marawa derived their title of *Sethupati* or "Lord of the Bridge," and perhaps this name is disguised under the form Sitia. It is possible that the same name is intended in a passage quoted by Von Hammer Purgstall from the Persian historian Wassaf, where the chiefs of Maabar are mentioned, and where they are unaccountably spoken of (without attempt at comment or explanation on the part of the editor) as "sharing the lordship of the land of *Sind.*" This may have been سيت or سيتو (*Set*, or *Setú*) misread as سنت or سنتو (*Sint* or *Sintu*); if it were not *Pandi*, misread as *Sindi*, which is equally possible.

It seems impossible to derive any distinct notion of the political state of this part of the peninsula at the end of the fourteenth century from the confused and mystified genealogies of the Tamul chronicles as exhibited by Professor Wilson and Mr. W. Taylor. Something however is to be learned from Marco Polo and his Persian contemporaries, whose statements are in remarkable agreement as to the leading facts.

Marco [ii, p. 331] tells us that going sixty miles westward from

Ceylon you come to the noble province of Maabar, which in his time was divided among five kings who were brothers (*the Ramusian Polo says* four *kings*). The chief of these, who reigned at Maabar proper, was called SONDER BANDI DAVAR; another, who reigned at Cail, was called ASCIAR (Ishwar?); the names of the others he does not state. It seems also to be implied that the territory of these chiefs extended at least as far north as St. Thomas's. The brothers were constantly at strife, and Marco expresses his opinion that as soon as their mother, who tried hard to keep peace among them, should die, they would infallibly quarrel and destroy each other. He tells us also that the treasure accumulated by the sovereigns of this kingdom was immense: and that as no horses (or at least only ponies with crooked legs) were reared in the country, large revenues were expended in procuring them.

["You must know that the merchants of Kis and Hormes, Dofar and Soer and Aden collect great numbers of destriers and other horses, and these they bring to the territories of this King and of his four brothers, who are kings likewise as I told you. For a horse will fetch among them 500 *saggi* of gold, worth more than 100 marks of silver, and vast numbers are sold there every year. Indeed this King wants to buy more than 2000 horses every year, and so do his four brothers who are kings likewise" (*Marco Polo*, ii, p. 340).]

Now read what Rashíduddín says on the same subject: "Maabar extends from Kulam to Silâwar (this should be *Nilâwar*, i.e. Nellore, as we shall see presently) 300 *farsangs* along the shore,... The king is called DEWAR, which means in the Maabar tongue 'lord of Wealth.' Large ships called *junks* bring merchandize thither from Chin and Machin...Maabar is as it were the key of India. Within the last few years SINDAR LEDI" (ليدي *Ledi*, misread for بندي BANDI), "who with his three brothers obtained power in different directions, and Malik Taki-ullah bin Abdarrahman bin Muhammed Et-Tibi, brother of Sheikh Jamaluddín, was his minister and adviser, to whom he assigned the government of FATAN MALIFATAN" (the Molephatam of Jordanus, see p. 184), "and BAWAL" (probably a misreading for *Kâvil* or *Kail*). "And because there are no horses in Maabar, or rather those which are there are weak, it was agreed that every year Jamaluddín Ibrahim should send to the Dewar 1400 Arab horses obtained from the islands of Kais, and 10,000 (1000?) from all the islands of Fars, such as Katif, L'Ahsa, Bahrein, Hormuz, Malkat (Maskat?), etc. Each horse is reckoned worth 220 *dinars* of red current gold. In the year 692 H. (A.D. 1292) the Dewar died, and Sheikh Jamaluddín who succeeded him obtained, it is said, an accession of 7000 bullock loads of jewels and gold, and Takiuddín, according to previous agreement, became his lieutenant. Notwithstanding his immense wealth he established a rule that he should have the first option of purchasing all imports," etc. (In *Sir H. M. Elliott, Historians of Muham. India*, p. 44.)

The statements of Wassaf are more diffuse, and have been confused either by the scribe or by Von Hammer in quoting them. The latter seems content, as we have seen, to accept the confusion of Sind with the peninsula, and proceeds on his own authority to confound Maabar with Malabar. An abstract of Wassaf's statements, as well as I can understand Von Hammer's extracts, may be given as follows: "Maabar is the coast which stretches from the Persian Sea through a length of 300 *farsangs* to NILAWAR. Its princes are called DIWAR or lord. Three princes at this time shared the dominion of the country, of whom the most powerful was Taki-uddín Abdarrahman bin Muhammed Et-Thaibi, who had a contract for the supply of horses with Jamal-uddín, the Malik-ul-Islam and Farmer-General of the Customs of the Persian Gulf, who resided at Kish. The contract price of the horses was fixed at 220 ducats a head, whilst the cost of those lost at sea was borne by the contractor in Persia. In the time of Abubekr, the Salghur Atabeg of Hormuz, when that kingdom was in its glory, 10,000 horses yearly used to be shipped to India, bringing to the sellers a revenue of 3,500,000 pieces of gold!

"Two of the native chiefs of Maabar who contended for the throne were SINDARBANDI and PIREBANDI, the former the legitimate, the latter the illegitimate son of Gilishdiur Raja of Maabar" (probably *Kulesa-Dewar*; Von Hammer does not seem to see that this *diur* is the title Dewar which has just been specified), "a prince who had reigned prosperously for forty years without ever having been laid up by illness or attacked by a foe. He had named Pirebandi his successor, which so enraged Sindarbandi that he slew his father, and took forcible possession of Shahrmandi, where his enormous treasures were laid up. Pirebandi gathered an army to avenge his father's murder, and a battle took place beside a lake which the people of India called Taláji" (*Talà*, a Tank? and perhaps the same as the *Celai* (for *Telai*) of Odoric, p. 123). "Eventually Pirebandi, aided by his cousin Bermal (Perumal?) was successful; whereon Sindarbandi fled to the court of Delhi, and sought help from Alauddín against his brother." This led to the invasion of Kafur.

This historian also speaks of Jamaluddín Abdarrahman Et-Thaibi as the Farmer-General and Keeper of the Marches of Maabar, apparently the same whom Rashíd states to have succeeded to the Dewar in 1292. His son Surajjuddín, it is also stated, was plundered of all his wealth by the army of Kafur, upon which his son Nizamuddín betook himself to Delhi to make complaint, and obtained, with some partial restoration of property, the administration of the finances in Maabar, which had been held by his father and grandfather. (See *Hammer Purgstall, Gesch. der Ilchane*, ii, 51 *seq*., and 197 *seq*.) There are evident discrepancies between the accounts of Rashíd and Wassaf, which it would be vain to attempt to reconcile without further knowledge. Nor do either their notices nor anything that I can gather from the works of Wilson and Taylor suffice to show to what dynasty belonged these princes of Maabar of whom Polo and the Persian historians speak. The names of the chiefs, Sindarbandi (Sundara-Pandi), Parebandi (Vira-Pandi), Gilish (Kalesa), are all indeed such as occur repeatedly among the half-mythical lists of the Pandyan dynasty of Madura, but there seems some reason to believe that the chiefs in question may have been rather princes of Marawa, or of some family of adventurers. The title *Dewar*, though not peculiar to the Setupatis has been specially *affected* by all the Marawas down to our own time, and Professor Wilson finds reason to believe that these were for a long time paramount over Madura, and for three reigns held the whole of that kingdom in their hands. (*Catal. of Mackenzie Coll.*, i, 195; *J.R.A.S.*, vol. iii, 165 and 223; *Madras Journ.*, 1836, p. 35, *seq.*) The time indeed of this is left undetermined, except that it was before the rise of Vijayanagar in the fourteenth century.

The nearest approach in the Tamul Annals to an indication of the period with which we are dealing appears to be the following. After a great deal of stuff about reigns of many thousand years, it is said:—

"After that the Pandyan race became extinct; the children of concubines and of younger brothers in former ages, fought against one another; and dividing the country into factions they caused themselves to be crowned in various parts of the Pandyan kingdom, and ruled each over his own town, and the surrounding neighbourhood. No one being permitted to rule in Madura, each party strove in battle against the other; and their several children continued for some generations to rule in those various places." (*Taylor*, *Orient. Hist. MSS.*, i, 25.) The Mahomedans are stated then to have come in during this state of anarchy, in the twelve hundred and forty-sixth year of Salivahana (A.D. 1324). But it is obvious that they had great power in the Peninsula thirty years before that date, and the invasion by the armies of Ala-uddín took place some years before.

M. Pauthier, in his new Marco Polo, has adduced curious references to Maabar, and to the five brother princes, from the Chinese Annals, and has also anticipated me in bringing forward the passage from Rashíd at p. 68 in illustration of the traveller. It is curious that its remarkable concurrence with the latter's statements should have escaped Sir Henry Elliott from whom we both derive the extract. Whilst referring to this part of Marco's narrative it seems worth while to point out that when M. Pauthier concurs with Marsden and others in identifying the kingdom of MUTFILI, which the traveller describes, with *Masulipatam* he does the same injustice to his author's accuracy which he so severely blames in others. Masulipatam, he says, is *Machli*-patam and *Machli*-bander, "*d'où est venu sans doute le nom de* Mustfili." But Marco's name is *Mutfili*, and requires no torture. The name and place still exist. Mutapali or Mootapilly, which the Arab sailors would call Mutafilly, as they call Pattan Fattan, is a port in the Gantur district south of the Krishna, which still has, or had at the beginning of this century, a considerable amount of coasting trade. The kingdom of Mutafili was no doubt, as Marsden perceived, that of Warangal or Tiling. "It is subject to a queen of great wisdom, whose husband died forty years ago, and her love to him was such that she has never married another. During this whole term she has ruled the nation with great equity, and been beloved beyond measure by her people" (*Polo,* iii, 21). The just and good queen of whom Marco here speaks can also be identified as Rudrama Devi, the daughter of the ruler of Dewagiri, and widow of Sri Kumara Kakatiya Pratapa Ganapati Rudra Deva King of Warangal, who made extensive conquests on the coast. This lady ruled after her husband's death for twenty-eight, or thirty-eight years, and then in 1292 or 1295 transferred the crown to her daughter's son Pratapa-Vira-Rudra-Deva, the Luddur Deo of Firishta. (See *Taylor*, *Oriental Hist. MSS.*, ii, 81; *Ditto, Catalogue Raisonné*, etc., iii, 483; *C. P. Brown*, *Carnatic Chronology*, pp. 54–55. The latter does not mention the queen.)

P.S. After this went to press a brief examination of the passage quoted from Rashíd (at page 68) as it is in the MS. in the India Office Library, shows its readings as *Nildwar*, *Sindar Bandi*, and *Káil*, for *Silawar*, *Sindar Ledi*, and *Bawul.* That is, the letters will *bear* the readings stated, and not those of Sir H. Elliott's copy, but there are no diacritical points.

[See the long notes to *Marco Polo's* Chapters xvi. and xvii. of Book III, ii, pp. 331–352.]

No. IV. LETTER FROM ANDREW BISHOP OF ZAYTON IN MANZI OR SOUTHERN CHINA, 1326[1].

Friar Andrew of Perugia, of the Order of Minor Friars, by Divine permission called to be Bishop, to the reverend father the Friar Warden of the Convent of Perugia, health and peace in the Lord for ever!

...On account of the immense distance by land and sea interposed between us, I can scarcely hope that a letter from me to you can come to hand....You have heard then how along with Friar Peregrine, my brother bishop of blessed memory, and the sole companion of my pilgrimage, through much fatigue and sickness and want, through sundry grievous sufferings and perils by land and sea, plundered even of our habits and tunics, we got at last by God's grace to the city of Cambaliech, which is the seat of the Emperor the Great Chan, in the year of our Lord's incarnation 1308, as well as I can reckon.

There, after the Archbishop was consecrated, according to the orders given us by the Apostolic See, we continued to abide for nearly five years; during which time we

1 [No. XXXXVI. L. Waddingi *Annal. Minor.*, T. vii, p. 53 *s.*: Frater ANDREAS de PERUSIO de Ordine Minorum Fratrum diuina permissione vocatus Episcopus, R. P. Fratri Guardiano Perusini Conuentus salutem et pacem in Domino sempiternam.

Nam propter immensam terrarum mariumque distantiam, inter me et vos interjectam, vix sperare possum, quod litterae ad vos per me transmissae ad manus vestras valeant peruenire. *Et infra sequitur.* Nouistis me itaque cum bonae memoriae fratre PEREGRINO Coepiscopo, et meae peregrinationis indiuiduo comite, praeter multos labores et languores, inedias, variaque tormenta atque pericula in terra pariter et in mari, ubi fuimus rebus omnibus, etiam tunicis et habitibus spoliati, demum, Deo juuante, ad Sambaliensem ciuitatem, quae Sedes est Imperii Magni Chanis, anno Dominicae Incarnationis MCCCVIII. vt credo peruenisse, vbi secundum mandatum a Sede Apostolica nobis datum, Archiepiscopo consecrato, moram ibi per quinquennium ferme contraximus; infra quod temporis spatium procurauimus Alafa ab Imperatore magnifico pro victu et vestitu octo personarum...Data in Cayton anno Domini MCCCXXVI. in mense Januarii. (*Mosheim*, pp. 120–3.)]

obtained an *Alafa*[1] from the emperor for our food and clothing. An *alafa* is an allowance for expenses which the emperor grants to the envoys of princes, to orators, warriors, different kinds of artists, jongleurs[2], paupers, and all sorts of people of all sorts of conditions. And the sum total of these allowances surpasses the revenue and expenditure of several of the kings of the Latin countries.

As to the wealth, splendour, and glory of this great emperor, the vastness of his dominion, the multitudes of people subject to him, the number and greatness of his cities, and the constitution of the empire, within which no man dares to draw a sword against his neighbour, I will say nothing, because it would be a long matter to write, and would seem incredible to those who heard it. Even I who am here in the country do hear things averred of it that I can scarcely believe....

There is a great city on the shores of the Ocean Sea, which is called in the Persian tongue Zayton[3]; and in this city a rich Armenian lady did build a large and fine enough church, which was erected into a cathedral by the Archbishop himself of his own free-will. The lady assigned it, with a competent endowment which she provided during her life and secured by will at her death, to Friar Gerard the Bishop, and the friars who were with him, and he became accordingly the first occupant of the cathedral.

After he was dead however and buried therein, the

[1] *Arab.* 'alaf, *pabulum*, and 'ulúfa, *a soldier's wages, a stipend or provision.* (*Freytag.*) But Quatremère points out that the exact word used here, *'alafah* is employed by Rashídeddin to signify (1) the allowance made by the prince for the keep of animals such as elephants, and (2) *an allowance for the entertainment of ambassadors and other like personages.* He refers to the passage in the text. (*Quat.*, *Rashideddin*, p. 371.)

[2] "*Jaculatoribus*," but I suppose a misprint for *Joculatoribus.*

[3] Wadding has *Cayton.* No doubt it was Çayton, for we constantly find the ç for z. But printing it Cayton has led Ritter into the mistake of putting Bishop Andrew at Canton. (*Ritter's Lectures*, Berlin, 1861, p. 224.)

Archbishop wished to make me his successor in the church. But as I did not consent to accept the position he bestowed it upon Friar and Bishop Peregrine before mentioned. The latter, as soon as he found an opportunity, proceeded thither, and after he had governed the church for a few years, in the year of the Lord 1322, the day after the octave of St. Peter and St. Paul[1], he breathed his last.

Nearly four years before his decease, finding myself for certain reasons uncomfortable at Cambaliech, I obtained permission that the before mentioned *alafa* or imperial charity should be allowed me at the said city of Zayton, which is about three weeks' journey distant from Cambaliech[2]. This concession I obtained as I have said, at my earnest request, and setting out with eight horsemen allowed me by the emperor, I proceeded on my journey, being everywhere received with great honour. On my arrival (the aforesaid Friar Peregrine being still alive) I caused a convenient and handsome church to be built in a certain grove, quarter of a mile outside the city, with all the offices sufficient for twenty-two friars, and with four apartments such that any one of them is good enough for a church dignitary of any rank. In this place I continue to dwell, living upon the imperial dole before-mentioned, the value of which, according to the estimate of the Genoese merchants, amounts in the year to 100 golden florins or thereabouts[3]. Of this allowance I have spent the greatest part in the construction of the church; and I know none among all the convents of our province to be compared to it in elegance and all other amenities.

And so not long after the death of Friar Peregrine

[1] July 7th.

[2] This is very short allowance, and an error in the number may be suspected.

[3] In intrinsic value something less than £50; but with respect to both time and place equivalent to a vastly greater sum of money doubtless than £50 is to us.

I received a decree from the archbishop appointing me to the aforesaid cathedral church, and to this appointment I now assented for good reasons. So I abide now sometimes in the house or church in the city, and sometimes in my convent outside, as it suits me. And my health is good, and as far as one can look forward at my time of life, I may yet labour in this field for some years to come: but my hair is grey, which is owing to constitutional infirmities as well as to age.

'Tis a fact that in this vast empire there are people of every nation under heaven, and of every sect, and all and sundry are allowed to live freely according to their creed. For they hold this opinion, or rather this erroneous view, that everyone can find salvation in his own religion[1]. Howbeit we are at liberty to preach without let or hindrance. Of the Jews and Saracens there are indeed no converts, but many of the idolaters are baptized; though in sooth many of the baptized walk not rightly in the path of Christianity.

Four of our brethren have suffered martyrdom in India, at the hands of the Saracens; and one of them was twice cast into a great blazing fire, but came out unhurt. And yet in spite of so stupendous a miracle not one of the Saracens was converted from his misbelief[2]!

All these things I have briefly jotted down for your information, reverend father, and that through you they may be communicated to others. I do not write to my spiritual brethren or private friends, because I know not which of them are alive, and which departed, so I beg them to have me excused. But I send my salutation to

[1] The Chinese "hold that all the sects may agree without dispensing with their own observances, and have a text which says *San chiao ye tao*, i.e., The doctrines are three, but the reason of them is one." (*Alvaro Semedo, Rel. Della Cina*, 116.)

[2] No doubt Odoric had brought this history to Zaytún with the bones of the martyrs a year or two before.

all, and desire to be remembered to all as cordially as possible, and I pray you, father Warden, to commend me to the Minister and Custos of Perugia, and to all the other brethren. All the suffragan bishops appointed to Cambaliech and elsewhere by our lord Pope Clement have departed in peace to the Lord, and I alone remain. Friar Nicholas of Banthera, Friar Andrutius of Assisi, and another bishop[1], died on their first arrival in Lower India, in a most cruelly fatal country, where many others also have died and been buried[2].

Farewell in the Lord, father, now and ever. Dated at Zayton, A.D. 1326, in the month of January[3].

No. V. LETTER OF FRIAR JORDANUS OF THE ORDER OF PREACHERS.

To the reverend fathers in Christ, the Preaching and Minorite Friars dwelling in TAURIS, DIAGORGAN, and MAROGA, Friar Jordanus of the Order of Preachers, the least of all, after saluting them and kissing their feet humbly, commends himself with tears[4].

[1] Probably Ulrich Sayfustordt (see p. 10 *supra*).

[2] Probably at Hormuz.

[3] ["Omnes Episcopi suffraganei facti per Dominum Papam Clementem Cambaliensis Sedis migrarunt in pace ad Dominum, ego solus remansi. Frater Nicolaus de Banthera, frater Andrutius de Assisio, & unus alius Episcopus mortui fuerunt in ingressu Indiae inferioris, in terra quadam crudelissima, ubi & plures alii mortui sunt & sepulti. Valeat in Domino vestra Paternitas nunc & semper. Data in Cayton anno Domini MCCCXXVI. in mense Januarii."]

[4] It is needful to remark on this and the following letter, the former of which is taken from Quétif and the latter from Wadding, though both are understood to be derived from the same MS., that both begin in the same manner, an identity which continues down to "*all our books.*" My impression is, however, that these paragraphs belong properly to this first letter, and have been transferred to the other by some mistake. There is an intense despondency about the second letter, of which there is no trace in these paragraphs. Nor is it easy to see how he could talk of leaving his things (*robbam*) and those of the deceased friars, and all the books, after he had been stripped to the shirt, as he represents himself in the second letter.

I have taken the names of the places partly from the version in

All your venerable company of fathers is aware that I am left alone a poor pilgrim in India, where for my sins I have been allowed to survive after the passion of those blessed martyrs, Thomas the holy, James the glorious, Peter, and Demetrius. Nevertheless blessed over all be God who disposeth all things according to his will!

After their blessed martyrdom, which occurred on the Thursday before Palm Sunday in Thana of India[1], I baptized about ninety persons in a certain city called PAROCCO[2], ten days' journey distant therefrom, and I have since baptized more than twenty, besides thirty-five who were baptized between Thana and Supera[3]. Praise be to Christ the Creator of all things; if I had but a comrade I would abide for some time longer. But now I will get ready

Quétif, and partly from that in Wadding. In Wadding they run "Tauris, Diagorgan, and Merga." In Quétif, "Tauris, Tongan, and Maroga." When publishing the *Mirabilia* of Jordanus I supposed Tongan to stand for Daumghan in Northern Persia, not knowing the grounds on which the French editor suggested "Djagorgan." There is no doubt, however, that Diagorgan is the proper reading. This is *Dekergán* (properly Dehi-Kherkán or Dehi-Kherján), a city of some antiquity, and still the capital of a district, between Tabriz and Maragha. The name of Diacoregan appears several times in Wadding's Annals in connexion with the Pope's correspondence with the Armenian clergy. A Catholic bishop, Bernard of Gardiola, was appointed to the see of Diagorgan in 1329. There were also Latin bishops of Maraga. At least one, Bartholomew [Parvus, O.S.D.], is named in 1320. [*Le Quien*, iii, 1394–1402, mentions one in 1375, without giving his name.] (See *F. Jordanus*, HAK. SOC., *pref.*; *Journ. R. G. S.*, x, 3, 4; *Le Quien*, iii, pp. 1378–1394.)

[1] See note to Odoric on the date of the event, p. 125.

[2] Bharūch or Broach, originally *Bharukachha*, Gujarāt.

[3] Respecting Supera, see note to *Jordanus*, p. vi, to which the following notices may be added. It is perhaps the Sibór of Cosmas, which he mentions as one of the chief ports of (the west of) India. It has been plausibly supposed to be the Ophir of Solomon, and to be connected with the name which the Coptic language gives to India. It is called Subára by Ibn Haukal and Edrisi, the former placing it four days, the latter five days from Kambaia, and specifying it as one of the chief Indian entrepôts. It is the Sufálah of Abulfeda. Gildemeister says of it, "*de cujus situ omnis interiit memoria.*" The following references, however, may assist, with those in the note already quoted, to ascertain it. Supera or Sufála, according to Reinaud quoting Langlois, answers to the place called by the Sanskrit writers *Subahlika*, which, if true, shows that *Sufala* rather than Supera

a church for the friars who may be coming, and I will leave my things and those of the martyrs, and all our books.

I must come away myself, both on account of the canonization of the holy brethren above-mentioned, and on account of religious and other business of a sufficiently perplexed and difficult kind. The bearer hereof will be able to explain to you what I cannot write myself for lack of time. I will only say a word as to the harvest to be expected, that it promises to be great and encouraging. Let friars be getting ready to come, for there are three places that I know where they might reap a great harvest and where they could live in common. One of these is Supera, where two friars might be stationed; and a second is in the district of Parocco, where two or three might abide; and the third is Columbus; besides many others that I am not acquainted with. But I have been told by our Latin merchants that the way to Ethiopia is open for any one who wishes to go and preach there, where once St. Matthew the Evangelist did preach. I pray the Lord that I may not die until I have been a pilgrim for the faith into those regions, for this is my whole heart's desire. I bid you farewell; and pray ye for me and commend me

was the genuine form of the name. Now, Padre Vincenzo Maria, in the middle of the seventeenth century, when proceeding to Surat, tells us that he landed at *Suali*. Tavernier also says that ships for Surat moor at *Suali*, which is only four leagues from Surat, and two to the north of the Tapti; and Suali is shown in the same position by Rennell, agreeing with that assigned by Ptolemy to Suppara *north* of the Tapti. Is it rash to say that Suali, which is thus precisely identified, may mark for us the true site of Sufala or Supera? (*Montfaucon, Coll. Nova Patrum*, ii, pp. 336–339; *Jaubert's Edrisi*, i, 171; *Gildemeister*, pp. 45, 179, 189; *Reinaud, Mém. sur l'Inde*, 221; *P. Vincenzo Maria, Viag.*, p. 109.) Lassen, however, gives *Súrpáraka* as the Sanskrit name of Suppara, without noticing the alleged *Subahlika* or the recently existing Suali, and identifies the ancient city in site with the modern Surat. (*Ind. Alterthumsk.*, i, 107; iv, 957, and Map in the third volume.) [See French edition of Odoric, p. 91.] [There is still a *Sofāle* (Safāle), a village in the Thāna District. Cf. *Gaz. of India.*]

to all the faithful. Dated from CAGA[1] the 12th day of October, in the year of the Lord 1321.

No. VI. A SECOND LETTER FROM FRIAR JORDANUS[2].

. . . .

After the martyrs obtained their glorious crowns I came to Thana, as I have before related, and buried the bodies of those saints. Since then I have continued alone in the said city and the adjoining territory, for two years and a half, going out and in, but unworthy to partake of the crown of my happy comrades. Alas me, my fathers! alas me, thus left an orphan and a wayfarer in this pathless and weary wilderness! Alas for the evil and hateful day which, for the salvation of other souls, so haplessly separated me from my sainted comrades, unwitting of their coming crowns! Would that it had pleased the Lord most High that then the earth had swallowed me quick, and that I had not been left behind them, unhappy that I am, amid such miseries! Who is able to tell all the hardships that I have since endured? For I have been taken by pirates, cast into prison by the Saracens, been accused, cursed, reviled, and left this long time past like some good-for-nothing vagabond, to go about in my shirt, without the habit of my holy order. O, what hunger and thirst, what cold and heat, yea burning rather, what curses, what diseases, what

[1] Not having seen these letters when I translated the *Mirabilia* of Jordanus, I was led by the French editor's remarks on them to suppose that Caga was to be looked for in the Persian Gulf. With the letters before us we see that it is obviously to be looked for in the west of India, and there can be little doubt that it is, as has been explained by Professor Kunstmann, the port of Gujarāt, which we call *Gogo*, opposite to the Paroço and Supera of Jordanus. Gogo appears in the Catalan Map of 1375, and is mentioned by Ibn Batuta as Kúkah. [Gogha, in the Ahmadàbàd District, Bombay, in the peninsula of Kāthiāwār, on the gulf of Cambay.]

[2] The address and first part of this letter, as given by Wadding, are borrowed from the preceding letter. But the *address* probably *was* the same.

poverty and persecutions, what detraction from false Christians, what severities of climate, and what an infinite number of other hardships have I not endured since those holy martyrs won their crowns! Where shall I find tears sufficient to bewail my desolate position! But these things and more, even unto death, I am ready to bear gladly for the sake of the beloved Jesus; and may He in the end reunite me in blessedness to my blessed comrades.

In addition to all that I have mentioned, and to the extremity of poverty, I suffer continually from bodily ailments. Tortured by pains, sometimes in the head, sometimes in the chest, in the stomach, or in all my limbs in turn, here am I left in my solitude with no human aid. For there is a horrid schism among the people in reference to me. One day they are well disposed; another day quite the reverse, because of those who mislead them. I have, however, been happy enough to baptize more than a hundred and thirty of either sex, and there would be a glorious harvest if the holy friars would come; but they must be ready to bear all things with patience, and martyrdom with gladness. To you then I turn, dear brethren, beseeching you with tears to grant this consolation to a hapless pilgrim bereft of his holy comrades. Let the holy friars come then, let them come with souls established in patience, that the harvest of baptized souls may be kept from the evil one, and after it has been threshed, in the Lord's own time may be treasured in His garner!

But I must say a word as to the voyage to Ethiopia, which it would be very fitting that some friar willing to go thither to preach should undertake. He might go thither at small cost from the place where I now am, and, from what I have heard, it would be a glorious journey for the diffusion of the faith.

Let me tell you that the fame of us Latins is more

highly thought of among the people of India than among us Latins ourselves. Nay, they are in continual expectation of the arrival of the Latins here, which they say is clearly predicted in their books[1]. And, moreover, they are continually praying the Lord, after their manner, to hasten this wished-for arrival of the Latins. If our lord the Pope would but establish a couple of galleys on this sea, what a gain it would be! And what damage and destruction to the Soldan of Alexandria! O, who will tell this to his holiness the Pope[2]? For me, wayfarer that I am, 'tis out of the question. But I commit all to you, holy fathers. Fare ye well, then, holy fathers, and remember the pilgrim in your prayers. Pray for the pilgrim of Christ, all of you, that the Indian converts, black as they are, may all be made white in soul before the good Jesus, through his pitiful grace. I end my words with many a sigh, most heartily recommending myself to the prayers of all.

Dated in THANA of India, the city where my holy comrades were martyred, in the year of the Lord 1323, in the month of January, and on the feast of the holy martyrs Fabian and Sebastian[3].

[1] These prophecies are also mentioned by Jordanus in his *Mirabilia* (p. 23). Nieuhof says the Chinese also had an old prophecy that a nation of white men from afar should one day conquer their country. The like tales of the Mexicans will be remembered; and such also were said to be current among the Karens of Burma.

[2] Marino Sanuto also looked forward to the Pope having a fleet in the Indian Ocean, but he was first to get Egypt under his thumb. (*Secreta Fidel. Crucis*, etc., p. 94.)

[3] 20th January. The date (January 1323) must mean, I think, our January 1324. For he has been *two and a half years* alone since the martyrdom, whereas if 1323 were meant the time would really be considerably under two years. [See French edition of Odoric, pp. 89–91.]

No. VII. LETTER FROM PASCAL OF VITTORIA, A MISSIONARY FRANCISCAN IN TARTARY, TO HIS BRETHREN OF THE CONVENT OF VITTORIA, 1338[1].

Dearly beloved fathers, your sanctities are aware that when I quitted you I proceeded to Avignon in company with the dear father Friar Gonsalvo Transtorna. Thence we went, with the blessing of the reverend the general, to get the benefit of the Indulgence at Assisi; and after that we embarked at Venice on board a certain carrack, and sailed down the Adriatic sea. We next sailed through the sea of Pontus[2], leaving Sclavonia to the left and Turkey to the right, and landed in Greece at Galata near Constantinople, where we found the father Vicar of Cathay in the Vicariat of the East. Then, embarking on another vessel, we sailed across the Black Sea[3], whose depth is unfathomable, to Gazaria[4] in the Vicariat of the North, and in the empire of the Tartars. Then traversing another sea which has no bottom[5], we landed at TANA.

[1] [No. LXXXXII. Ex L. Waddingo T. vii, pp. 256 *s.*: Reuerendis in CHRISTO et dilectis, Guardiano, et Fratribus, Conuentus Victoriensis, cum totius Custodiae Patribus, et dulcissimis Fratribus, frater PASCHALIS Ordinis Minorum salutem cum omni benedictione, non etiam immemor aliis nostris parentibus, ac notis, et amicis reuerentiam filialem.

Nouerit vestra Sanctitas, Patres dilectissimi, quod cum a vobis recessissemus cum caro Patre fratre Gonsalvo Transtorna, profecti sumus, vsque ad Auenionem. Inde Generalis reuerendi benedictione, iuimus ad Indulgentiam Assisii; et post Venetiis ascendentes quamdam carracam, transivimus per mare Adriaticum, et post, per Mare Ponticum ad sinistram admittentes Sclauoniam, et ad dexteram Turquiam, applicuimus Graeciam, scilicet Galatas, iuxta Constantinopolim, et ibi inuenimus Patrem Vicarium de Catay, in Vicaria Orientis...Data in Armalech, in Festo Sancti LAVRENTII, Anno Domini MCCCXXXVIII. in Imperio Medorum. (Mosheim, pp. 193-6.)]

[2] The Propontis or Sea of Marmora, is what he calls Mare Ponticum. It is curious to find the country so near the capital of the empire called *Sclavonia.*

[3] "*Mare nigrum.*"

[4] The Gazaria of Rubruquis is precisely the Crimea, but I believe the term sometimes is extended towards the Don.

[5] A curiously erroneous notion of the Palus Mæotis. *Tana* is Azov.

And having got thither sooner than my comrade, I found my way with some Greeks by waggons as far as SARRAY[1]; whilst my comrade, with some other friars, was carried on further to URGANTH[2]. I was willing enough to go with him, but after taking counsel on the matter, I determined

[1] *Sarai*, the capital of the Khans of Kipchak, founded by Bátú, stood on the left bank of the Akhtuba or northern branch of the Volga. Pallas describes the remains of *two* cities on the river mentioned, one not far below its bifurcation from the main Volga on a salt and sterile plain called Zarefpod, about two hundred and forty miles from the Caspian, the other at Selitrennoi Gorodok, much further down. The latter position seems more consistent with Pegolotti's statement that you could go from Gittarchan to Sarai in one day (even supposing that Gittarchan or old Astrakhan was somewhat higher than the present city), and also with the statements of Arabian geographers that Sarai was only two days from the Caspian. There are modern Russian authorities on the site and ruins of Sarai referred to by Von Hammer and Reinaud, but these are not available to me. The name of the city merely means the *Palace* (Serai, Serail, Seraglio). Ibn Batuta says that starting at early morning to traverse the city he did not reach the opposite side till past noon. Sarai was twice taken by Timur, and was entirely destroyed by him (1395–6). (*Pallas, Voyages*, Paris, An. II, vii, 175, 388; *Hammer-Purgstall, Gesch. der Goldenen Horde*, pp. 9 and 431, etc.; *Reinaud's Abulfeda*, II.) [Cf. *Marco Polo*, i, pp. 5–6.]

[2] Urghanj [Urghandj] or Jorjaniah, formerly the chief city of Khwarezm, the country now known as Khiva. It stood on both banks of the [ancient channel of the] Oxus, with a bridge connecting them. It was the scene of awful devastation and massacre by the Mongols under Chinghiz in 1221, and a hundred thousand of the only class spared, the artisans, are said to have been transported to Mongolia. It must have recovered to some considerable extent in the next hundred years, from the notices in Pegolotti and Ibn Batuta; but the river deserted it and it fell into entire decay. It is the Urgence of Anthony Jenkinson, who describes it in 1558 as an ill-built mud town in a depressed state. New Urghanj, which is the present commercial capital of Khiva, is some sixty miles east of the site of the old city, near the present channel of the Oxus. The lists of Minorite convents in Kipchak, given by Wadding, contain a name which looks as if meant for Urghanj (*Organae, Orgune*), but it seems unlikely, considering the bigoted Islamism of the people, that this should have been the place.

[*Djordjanieh*, according to Ibn Haukal, was the Arabic name of *Urghandj*, the Mongol name according to d'Ohsson (i, 265). It was visited by Marignolli. In 1388 Urghandj was destroyed by Timur, but was subsequently rebuilt (*Zafernameh*, iii, 1). The capture of Urghandj by the Mongols is mentioned in the *Yuen shi*, and the name is spelt there *Yü-lung-ghie-ch'i*. The *Yuen chao pi shi* writes it *Urungechi*. Cf. Bretschneider, *Mediæval Res.*, ii, pp. 92–3.]

Col. James Abbott visited the ruins of Urghanj on his journey from Khiva, but mentions nothing of much interest. (*D'Ohsson*, i, 265–270; *Wadding*, under 1400; *Abbott's Journey*, i, 214.)

first to learn the language of the country. And by God's help I did learn the Chamanian language, and the Uigurian character[1]; which language and character are commonly used throughout all those kingdoms or empires of the Tartars, Persians, Chaldæans, Medes, and of Cathay. My comrade turned back from Urganth and went to you again. But I could not bear to return, like a dog to his vomit, and I was desirous to obtain the grace conceded by his holiness the Pope, so I would not turn back. For you must know that all of us friars who come into these parts have the same privileges as those who go with licence to Jerusalem; that is to say, the fullest indulgence both *a pœnâ* and *a culpâ*, and those who persevere unto the end, a crown of life.

Therefore, my fathers, from the time when I had acquired the language, by the grace of God I often preached without an interpreter both to the Saracens and to the schismatic and heretical Christians. I then received a mandate from my vicar to the effect that on receipt of his letter I should in salutary obedience to him, as in duty bound, proceed to finish the journey which I had commenced.

I had now been staying more than a year in the aforesaid Sarray, a city of the Saracens of the Tartar empire, in the Vicariat of the North, where three years before a certain friar of ours, Stephen by name, suffered honourable martyrdom at the hands of the Saracens[2]. Embarking on a certain vessel with some Armenians, I departed thence

[1] The Comanians were Turkish according to Klaproth, and Rubruquis says, "*Apud Iugures est fons et radix idiomatis Turci et Comanici.*" The name is supposed to be connected with the River Kuban. As to the character, see note above, p. 53.

[2] Pascal no doubt resided in one of the convents of his Order, of which there was one at Sarai, and a second, called St. John's, three miles from the city. The story of Friar Stephen of Peterwaradin, belonging to the latter convent, may be read in Wadding, and is very interesting. This young monk, in 1334, resenting some severe discipline, deserted and publicly professed Islam; but was afterwards seized with remorse, repented and as publicly recanted his apostasy. The

by the river called Tygris[1], and then along the shore of the sea which is called VATUK[2], till I came in twelve days'

enraged Mahomedans hacked him in pieces in sight of the fire that was to have burnt him. (*Wadding*, vii, 159–166.)

It may be noticed here that Wadding gives from old documents, under the year 1400, ix, 233, but apparently referring to a much earlier period in the fourteenth century, lists of convents of the Order in the empire of Uzbek. These amounted, according to his most complete list, to ten convents in the Custodia of Sarai, besides four in that of Gazaria or the Crimea. Those of the Custodia of Sarai are as follows :—

Thana . . .	*i.e.*	*Azov.*
Agitarcan . .	„	*Astrakhan.*
Sarai . . .	„	The capital.
Comuch or Coinuch	„	The province of *Kumuk* or Land of the *Kumuk* Tribe south of R. Terek (*Gumik* of Mas'udi, ii, 40).
Tarchis . . .	„	*Terki* at the mouth of the Terek, previously *Samander*; now represented by Kisliar higher up. Distinct from modern *Tarkhu* (see *Laprimandaie*, p. 269; *Hammer, Gold. Hord.*, p. 8; *Prairies d'Or*, ii, 7; *V. du Chev. Gamba*, ii, 351).
Mamuvi or Manviti	„	Perhaps *Memak*, near Sarai (*Hammer*, p. 10; *Pétis de la Croix*, i, 294; ii, 101).
Mager . . .	„	*Majar* on the Kuma; see Intr. to Ibn Batuta, *infra.*
Ugueth, Uguech .	„	*Ukek*, a city between Sarai and Bolgar on the Volga (*Pétis de la Croix*, ii, 355, 383), the Oukaka of Marco Polo, Utak of Ibn Batuta (ii, 414). Perhaps *Oweke* of Anth. Jenkinson, which he places in 51° 40′.
Ac-Sarai . .	„	"White Building," perhaps *Al Baidha* (same signif.), which Edrisi couples with Samander, and possibly the *Abserai* (for A*k*serai?) of the Catalan Map, on coast below Terki.
Organæ, Orgune .	„	See note, page 82.

From another list given by Wadding under 1314, we may add *Beler*, probably Bolar or Bolgar on the Volga, and S. Joannes, the Monastery of Stephen above-named. The last may be identical with one of those already named. [This note, p. 233 of the first edition of *Cathay*, has been altered and corrected in some of the copies as we give it here; other copies have but an abbreviated note.]

[1] The Volga; but why does he call it Tigris? Polo also calls the Volga by this name, as Pauthier shows (p. 8); whilst Josafat Barbaro gives the same name to the Araxes (*Ram.*, ii, 98). These errors look as if they arose from some *double entendre*, but I cannot suggest what. *Tigris* is said to be derived from a word signifying *arrow*, connected, I suppose, with the Persian *Tír*.

[2] Vatuk, for Bacuk or Bákú; the Caspian, see note, p. 105.

travel to SARACHIK[1]. From that place I got on a cart drawn by camels (for to ride those animals is something terrible), and on the fiftieth day reached Urganth, which is a city at the extremity of the empire of the Tartars and the Persians. The city is otherwise called HUS, and the body of the blessed Job is there[2].

Thence I again mounted a camel-cart, and travelled with a party of accursed Hagarenes and followers of Mahomet, I being the only Christian among them, with a certain servant called Zinguo, until by God's grace we reached the empire of the Medes[3]. What my sufferings have been there, how many and how great, God himself

[1] Saraichik, "The Little Palace," on the river Jaic or Ural, at a day's journey from the Caspian, in a low bad situation, was the head-quarters of the Nogai Horde. Jenkinson mentions it as a place existing in 1558. Pallas found the fortifications still to be seen with a circuit of four or five versts (two and two-thirds to three and one-third miles). Ruins were traceable, with tiles of great size and many tombs.

[The Serachuk of Ibn Batuta, iii, 1.—According to Lerch ("Khiva," 23) quoted by Bretschneider (*Med. Res.*, ii, p. 57) the ruins of this place can still be seen near *Guriev*, at the mouth of the Ural.]

[2] So Ibn Batuta says that between Sarai and Urghanj is a journey of thirty or forty days, in which you do not travel with horses, for lack of forage, but in carts drawn by camels. Water is found at intervals of two or three days (ii, 451, and iii, 2–3). Pegolotti makes the distance twenty days in camel-waggon. Jenkinson's companion, Richard Johnson, allows fifteen days only, but all his times appear too short.

I can find nowhere else any story connecting Urghanj with Job or Hus. It looks like some misapprehension. There is a tomb of Job in Oudh!

[3] This title, given by the writer to the Tartar Khanate of Chagatai or Transoxiana, is a curious misnomer, originating no doubt in a blunder easily explained. This empire, lying as it did intermediate between Cathay and Persia, was called "The Middle Empire," *Imperium Medium*, as we actually find in a letter of Pope Benedict XII addressed to its sovereign (*Wadding*, vii, 212), and in John Marignolli. In Andrea Bianco's Map of the World in St. Mark's library it is called "*Imp. de Medio*, i.e., *seu Côbalek*" (for Armalek). But the Carta Catalana makes the same mistake as Pascal, calling it the empire of "*Medeia*," and the Portulano Mediceo also, in the Laurentian library, makes *Armaloc* capital of the "*Imp. Medorum.*" Media seems always to have bothered mediæval travellers and geographers, who thought it their duty to find Medes extant as well as Persians. Hayton's Media embraces Kurdistan and Fars; Clavijo puts it between Persia proper and Khorasan.

knoweth, and it would be a long story to tell in a letter. However, the Emperor of the Tartars had been slain by his natural brother, and the caravan of Saracens with which I travelled was detained by the way in the cities of the Saracens, for fear of war and plunder.

Hence I was long tarrying among the Saracens, and I preached to them for several days openly and publicly the name of Jesus Christ and his gospel. I opened out and laid bare the cheats, falsehoods, and blunders of their false prophet; with a loud voice, and in public, I did confound their barkings; and trusting in our Lord Jesus Christ I was not much afraid of them, but received from the Holy Spirit comfort and light. They treated me civilly and set me in front of their mosque during their Easter[1]; at which mosque, on account of its being their Easter, there were assembled from divers quarters a number of their *Cadini*[2], *i.e.* of their bishops, and of their *Talisimani*[3], *i.e.* of their

[1] The *Bairam*, one of the great Mahomedan festivals entitled *'Id*, is (Herbelot says) "commonly called the Easter of the Turks." (See *Note* at p. 257.) The Christians applied this name to it, because of its following the fast of Ramazan, which was (more appropriately) termed the Mahomedan Lent. And the Mahomedans also conversely applied the term *Bairam* to the Easter of the Christians.

[2] *Kadhi* or *Kazi* is properly a judge, but from the quasi-identity of Mahomedan law and divinity, he deals with both. He is a Dr. Lushington rather than a bishop.

[3] I cannot make out what this word is. It is used (*Thalassimani*) in the same sense by Barbaro in Ramusio (ii, 107); and, as Mr. Badger tells me, also (*Talismans*) in Rycaut's *History of the Present State of the Ottoman Empire* (p. 204). *Talismani* are also repeatedly mentioned in the Turkish Annals translated by Leunclavius, and in his *Pandectæ* appended thereto he explains *Talismani* to occupy a certain degree among the learned in Mahomedan law. He borrows a passage, which compares the chief mufti to the pope, the chief cadis to archbishops, cadis to bishops, hoggias (khwajas?) to presbyters, talismans to deacons, and dervishes to monks. (*Corpus Byzant. Histor.*, xxiv, pp. 318, 414, etc.)

My friend Mr. Badger thinks that the title has probably been "derived from *Tailasán*, a kind of hood of goat's or camel's hair, '*quale philosophi et religiosi, imprimis apud Persas, usurpare velut pro insigni solent*,' just as *Cappuccino* comes from *Cappuccio*." If this is not the origin, may it be a Frank corruption of *talámiz*, scholars, students? [Cf. Ducange, *s. v.* "*Talismanus.* Ita Sacerdotes suos vocant Turcae." He refers to Wadding, ann. 1342, No. 10.]

priests. And guided by the teaching of the Holy Ghost I disputed with them in that same place before the mosque, on theology, and regarding their false Alchoran and its doctrine, for five-and-twenty days; and in fact I was barely able once a-day to snatch a meal of bread and water.

But by the grace of God the doctrine of the Holy Trinity was disclosed and preached to them, and at last even they, in spite of their reluctance, had to admit its truth; and, thanks be unto the Almighty God, I carried off the victory on all points, to the praise and honour of Jesus Christ and of Holy Mother Church. And then these children of the devil tried to tempt and pervert me with bribes, promising me wives and hand-maidens, gold and silver and lands, horses and cattle, and other delights of this world. But when in every way I rejected all their promises with scorn, then for two days together they pelted me with stones, besides putting fire to my face and my feet, plucking out my beard, and heaping upon me for a length of time all kinds of insult and abuse. The Blessed God, through whom poor I am able to rejoice and exult in the Lord Jesus Christ, knoweth that 'tis by his marvellous compassion alone I have been judged worthy to bear such things for his name.

And now I have been graciously brought to ARMALEC[1], a city in the midst of the land of the Medes, in the Vicariat of Cathay. And thus, beginning at Urganth, which is the

[1] Armalec, the *Almálik* of the Mahomedan writers, which again is the corruption of a Turkish name, and called by the Chinese *Alimali*, was the capital of the Khans of the family of Chagatai. It had been, however, the seat of a Turkish principality before the rise of the Mongols. (*D'Ohsson*, i, 111.) ["It seems the Persian historians first mention Almalik *s.a.* 1211, in which year Ozar, prince of Almalik, is stated to have acknowledged the supremacy of Chinghiz. This prince was subsequently slain by Guchluk, gurkhan of Karak'itai." (Bretschneider, ii, p. 33.)] It stood on or near the Ili River; Klaproth says, "in the vicinity of thè Kurgos of our day on the banks of the Alimatu, a tributary of the Ili from the north." It is, perhaps, however *Old Kulja* (some twenty-six or twenty-eight miles above the modern Chinese frontier city of that name on the Ili), which is mentioned in

last city of the Persians and Tartars, all the way to Armalec, I was constantly alone among the Saracens, but by word and act and dress, publicly bore the name of the Lord Jesus Christ. And by those Saracens I have often been offered poison; I have been cast into the water; I have suffered blows and other injuries more than I can tell in a letter. But I give thanks to God under all that I expect to suffer still greater things for his name, in order to the forgiveness of my sins, and that I may safely reach the kingdom of Heaven through His mercy. *Amen!*

Fare ye well in the Lord Jesus Christ, and pray for me, and for those who are engaged, or intend to be engaged, on missionary pilgrimages; for by God's help such pilgrimages are very profitable, and bring in a harvest of many souls. Care not then to see me again, unless it be in these regions, or in that Paradise wherein is our Rest and Comfort and Refreshment and Heritage, even the Lord Jesus Christ.

And for that He hath said that when the Gospel shall have been preached throughout the whole world, then shall the end come, it is for me to preach among divers nations, to show sinners their guilt, and to declare the way of salvation, but it is for God Almighty to pour into their souls the grace of conversion.

Dated at Armalec, on the feast of St. Laurence, A.D. 1338, in the Empire of the Medes[1].

recent Russian surveys. If this was Almalik it stood in about 80° 58½' east longitude, and 43° 55' north latitude. We shall find it spoken of again by Pegolotti and Marignolli. [" The name of Almalegh appears in the Zafernameh, book iii, 9, in the relation of Timur's expedition against the Jetes in Moghulistan in the year 1390." (Bretschneider, *Med. Res.*, ii, p. 38.)] According to the translators of Baber the name of the city signifies in Túrki "a grove of apple-trees" (p. 1). The Russian Captain Valikhanof says that Almálik is now "a Turkestan village," and that he obtained gold coins and ornaments dug up on its site, but unfortunately he neglects to indicate that essential point. (*The Russians in Central Asia*, etc., London, 1865, pp. 62, 63.)

[1] If souls transmigrate, that of Henry Martyn was in Friar Pascal!

No. VIII. THE BOOK OF THE ESTATE OF THE GREAT CAAN, SET FORTH BY THE ARCHBISHOP OF SOLTANIA, CIRCA 1330.

(*Supposed to be the Dominican John de Cora.*)

Here beginneth the Book of the Estate and Governance of the Great Caan of Cathay, the Emperor Suzerain of the Tartars, and concerning the administration of his empire, and that of the others his princes, as these are set forth by a certain archbishop, called the Archbishop of Soltaniah, by command of Pope John the XXIInd of that name; translated from Latin into French by Friar John the Long, of Ypres, monk of the monastery of St Bertin at St Omer[1].

1. The Great Caan of Cathay is one of the most puissant of all the kings in the world, and all the great lords of that country be his lieges and do him homage; and in chief three great emperors; to wit, the Emperor of Armalech[2], the Emperor Boussay[3], and the Emperor Usbech[4]. These three emperors send year by year live libbards, camels, and gerfalcons, and great store of precious jewels besides, to the said Caan their lord. For they acknowledge him to be their lord and suzerain. And great

[1] [*Begins* fol. 136 verso of French MS. 2810 fr., of the Bibliothèque Nationale in Paris: "Cȳ commence le Liure de lestat du grant Caan. Cȳ commence de lestat et de la gouuernance du grant kaan de cathay souuerain empereur des tartares. et de la disposicion de son empire. et de ses autres princes. Interprété par vn arceuesque que on dist larceuesque Saltensis, au commant du pappe ichan. xxij[e] de ce nom. Translate de latin en francois p frere iehā le lōc dyppre moisne de s'. b'tī en s'. aumer."]

[2] This is *Cambalech* in the text, but it is obviously an error of transcription; Cambalech being correctly mentioned afterwards as the chief city of Cathay itself.

[3] The Ilkhan of Persia, Abu Said Bahádur, 1317–35 [Died 13 Rebi aul akhir 736].

[4] Khan of Kipchak, 1313–41.

power and renown have these three emperors as it appeareth. For when the Emperor Usbech had war with the Emperor Boussaye and went forth to fight him, he brought upon the field 707,000 horsemen, without pressing hard on his empire[1]. What like then and how great must needs be the power of the Great Caan who hath such and so puissant barons for his lieges under him?

His empire is called Cathan or Cathay[2]. It beginneth at the extremity of the east, and runneth down even unto Ynde the Greater; and stretcheth in a right line westward as far as one may travel in six months.

In this empire there be two great cities, Cambalec and Cassay. And all that are of the Caan's realm, great and small, be his serfs and slaves. And the folk of the land have so great obedience and fear for their lord the Great Caan of Cathay that they dare not to oppose him in any matter or transgress his commandment. Insomuch that once when one of his great princes had misbehaved in battle so as to deserve death, the Grand Caan when he knew it sent him a message desiring that he would send him his head. And as soon as he had read the letter, straightway there in the midst of his people without the slightest opposition or resistance he bowed his head and patiently let them cut it off. The Caan maintaineth justice right well, and that as well for great as for small.

Once a year, on the first day of the new moon of March, which is the first day of their year, the said emperor shows himself to his people dressed out in purple and gold and

[1] This was probably in 1318 when there was war between Abu Said and Uzbeg, and the latter threatened the northern frontier of Persia with a great army of horsemen. "He advanced," says the historian Wassaf, "with a vast army; the horses were clad in mail; the swords of countless horsemen flashed in the sun; every rider had three led horses behind him; like a roaring flood and a raging lion this host devastated the country round Darband." (V. Hammer-Purgstall, *Gesch. der Ilchane*, pp. 272, 372.)

[2] *Khitan*, and *Khitai*.

silver and precious stones. Then all the folk drop on their knees before him, and adore him, and say, "Lo this is our God upon earth, who giveth us in lieu of scarcity plenty and great riches, who giveth us peace and maintaineth justice!"

Then the emperor refuseth justice to no man, but thanks be to God Almighty, he delivereth the prisoners, and bestoweth his mercies and acts of compassion on all manner of people, who have need thereof, and require a favour at his hand. Only there be three manner of folk to whom he rendereth never mercy: to wit, such an one as hath laid violent and reprobate hands upon his father or his mother; such as hath forged the king's money, which is of paper; and such as hath done any one to death by giving him poison to drink. To these three rendereth he never mercy.

On this day also he bestoweth many gifts, and great plenty of gold and silver and precious stones. And the smallest of the gifts that he bestoweth is worth at the least a *balisme*[1] of gold, whilst they are often worth...[2] balismes. And one balisme is worth a thousand golden florins.

And the said emperor is pitiful and very compassionate. He provideth always for himself and for his lieges stores of wheat and of rice and of all manner of corn; and for this he hath barns and garners uncountable; and so when there is dearth in the land he openeth his garners, and giveth forth of his wheat and his rice for a half what others are selling it at. And thus he maketh great abundance to arise in the time of greatest dearth[3]. Likewise he maketh great alms to the poor for the love of God,

[1] See note to Odoric, p. 196.
[2] Wanting in the original.
[3] On these magazines for public relief, see *Marco Polo*, i, 29.

and when any one is so infirm of body that he cannot win his bread, or so reduced to poverty that he hath not wherewithal to live, nor hath friends to do him good, then the emperor causeth provision to be made for all his needs[1]. And thus doth he throughout all his kingdom, nor doth he oppress any man throughout all his realm by extraordinary and strange exactions. And know ye for sure that he hath such riches from his revenues, and from the produce of his taxes and customs[2], that his wealth and power are past telling. And he hath treasuries and great houses all full of gold and silver, and gems, and of other kinds of wealth and precious things, and especially in his chief towns.

Also in all his realm from city to city hath he other houses wherein dwell couriers who are sped both on foot and on horseback. And these couriers and messengers have bells hung to their waists or to their whips. And so when one of these couriers cometh bringing the despatches of the emperor, and draweth near unto one of those houses aforesaid, he maketh his bells to jingle; and know that at this sound one of the other couriers in the house girdeth himself and taketh those despatches, and carrieth them off to another house; and so with the rest. And they stop not running, day nor night, until the letters be arrived whither they were to go. And thus the Emperor shall have in XV days news of a country that shall be as far off as three months' journey[3]. He receiveth also right courteously envoys and ambassadors from any foreign country or lordship, and furnisheth them with all that they require in coming and in going, throughout the extent of his realm[4].

[1] See *Jordanus*, p. 46, and *Marco Polo* as above.

[2] "*Gables de truuaiges et de malestoultes.*"

[3] See *Odoric*, p. 233.

[4] See the narrative of Marignolli, and that of Shah Rukh's ambassadors in *Notices et Extraits*, tom. xiv. The rules for the provision

2. *Concerning the Sovereign Bishop, who is the Pope of the Empire of Cathay.*

This realm of Cathay hath a sovereign bishop, such as the Pope is with us. Those of the country and of his religion call him the *Grand Trutius*[1]. He is liegeman of the aforesaid Emperor the Great Caan, and obeyeth him as his sovereign lord. But the Emperor honoureth him above all other men. And when the Emperor rideth in his company he maketh him ride close by his side. And the Emperor withholdeth from him no favour that he seeketh. This *Grand Trucins* hath always the head and the beard shaven, and weareth on his head a red hat, and is always clothed in red[2]. He hath the lordship and supremacy over

of accommodation, etc., to ambassadors, may be seen in Pauthier's *Chine Moderne*, p. 212.

[1] Afterwards written the Grand *Trucins*. I cannot track the word, or say which is right. I suspect it is a mistranscription for *Tyuinus*. *Tuin* was a name used among the Tartars (among the Uighúrs properly, according to Quatremère) for a Buddhist priest. See Rubruquis, pp. 352, 355; Quatremère's *Rashideddin*, p. 198; Hammer, *Gesch. der Goldenen Horde*, p. 217; King Hethum's Narrative in *Jour. As.*, s. ii, tom. xii, p. 289; and *Odoric*, *ante*, p. 144. Yule added in his notes: *Trucins* is perhaps after all a correct reading. For Mendoza says the Generals of the Chinese orders of Monks were called in their language *Tricon*. I cannot find an elucidation of this word unless it be a corruption of *Ta Ho-shang*, which is given as an appellation of the Superiors of the Bonzes. (Mendoza, Hak. Soc., i, 56; *Astley*, iv, 209.)

[I do not find any title resembling *Trutius* or *Trucins* in the ecclesiastical hierarchy of China. Confucius' heir is the *Yen-sheng-kong*; a doctor is a *Po-she*; the Head of the bonzes of Pe-king is the *Seng-lu-sze*; of the Taoists at Pe-king the *Tao-lu-sze*; but Rockhill, *Rubruck*, p. 159 *n.* explains it: "The word *Tuin* would seem to be an Uigur term. Quatremère (p. 198) says, that in a certain Uigur-Chinese Vocabulary of the Paris National Library (title and number not given) this word is explained by the Chinese *shih*, 'scholar'; and that in a Persian-Chinese vocabulary it is rendered by *sêng* 'a Buddhist priest.' The term *Tuin* is used by King Heythum. He says of them that they shaved their heads and beards, wore yellow cloaks, married at twenty, and lived with their wives to the age of fifty. In using the term, our traveller generally applies it to Buddhists, though here at least it would seem to include Uigur priests also." See Odoric, *supra*, p. 144 *n.*]

[2] See *Jordanus*, p. 46 and note.

all the clergy and all the monks of his law throughout all the said realm. And to him it belongeth to correct them in doctrine and in discipline; nor do the Emperors meddle with him or his orders. And among those clerks and monks of theirs be great prelates, bishops, and abbots, but all be subject to the Grand Trucins.

In every city of the said empire there be abbeys of men under vows, and also of women, who dwell in them according to the religion of that country, subject to the obedience and discipline of the Grand Trucins; so that there shall hardly be one city or town in the said empire wherein you shall not find an abbey, whilst in some there be eight or ten or more. And every abbey shall have at the least two hundred inmates. They be passing rich, and with that great wealth of theirs they do much alms before God. They live in great order, and keep their hours of service seven times a-day, and they get up early to matins. They have bells made of metal in the shape of a pent-roof on which they strike their hours. They keep chastity, and none of their clerks and monks do marry. They be idolaters and worship divers idols. And over these idols they say that there be four gods; and these four gods they carve in gold and silver, so as to stand out entire before and behind. And above these four gods they say that there is a greater God who is over all the gods, great and small[1].

[1] The four gods may be the four past terrestrial Buddhas who are found in Burma occupying the four sides of some temples, and the greater God over all may be the Adi Buddha of the Theistic Buddhists, who, according to Huc and Gabet, seems to be recognized in Mongolia and China, though unknown to the Buddhists of Ceylon and the Indo-Chinese countries.

3. *Concerning the state and condition of the realm of Cathay.*

The realm of Cathay is peopled passing well; and it hath no few cities that be greater than Paris or Florence; and a great multitude of places full of inhabitants, and smaller cities past counting. It hath likewise store of fine meadows and pastures, and of sweet-smelling herbs. And there be many great rivers, and great sheets of water throughout the empire; insomuch that a good half of the realm and its territory is water. And on these waters dwell great multitudes of people because of the vast population that there is in the said realm. They build wooden houses upon boats, and so their houses go up and down upon the waters; and the people go trafficking in their houses from one province to another, whilst they dwell in these houses with all their families, with their wives and children, and all their household utensils and necessaries. And so they live upon the waters all the days of their life[1]. And there the women be brought to bed, and do everything else just as people do who dwell upon dry land. And if you ask of those folk where they were born? they can reply nought else than that they were born upon the waters, as I have told you. And seeing that there be these great multitudes dwelling thus both on water and on land, the folk are in such great numbers that the cattle of the country suffice not for them, wherefore they have to bring them from other countries and for that reason flesh-meat is dear there. But in this country there is great store of wheat, rice, barley, and other kinds of corn. And so the Great Caan year by year collecteth of this great plenty, and storeth it in his garners, as hath been

[1] See John Marignolli, *infra*.

told above. And they have a rice harvest twice in the year.

There groweth not any oil olive in that country, nor wine of the vine, and they have none except what is brought from abroad, and for that reason the price thereof is high. But they make oil and wine from rice[1]; and all fruits grow there in very great abundance, excepting filberts[2] which they have not. Sugar, however, they have in very great quantities, and therefore it is very cheap there.

The country is mighty peaceable, nor dare anyone carry arms or stir war therein, except those only who are appointed by the emperor to guard him or any city of his[3].

In the empire of Boussaye aforesaid groweth a certain manner of trees which from their sap are of great help to the folk of the country. For there be some of them which from their bark give forth a white liquor like milk, sweet, savoury, and abundant, and the people of the country make drink and food of it as if it were goat's-milk, and that right gladly. And when they cut those trees anywhere, whether it be in the branches or elsewhere, they give forth where they were cut a manner of juice in great plenty, which juice hath the colour and savour of wine. And other trees there be which bear a manner of fruit as big as filberts, or as nuts of St. Gratian; and when this fruit is ripe the folk of the country gather it, and open it, and find inside grains like wheat, of which they make bread and maccaroni[4] and other food which they are very glad to eat[5].

1 "Wine from rice and oil and from other seeds," he should have said.

2 [auellanes].

3 See Andrew of Perugia's letter, *ante*, p. 72, and Ibn Batuta, *infra*.

4 "*Paste.*"

5 I cannot explain these statements; nor tell what is called a *nut of St. Gratian*; (St. Gratian's day is December 18th.)

["Parmi les variétés de noisettes, on donne le premier rang aux

4. *On the ordering of the two cities of Cambalec and Cassay.*

These two cities are very great, and right famous. Each one of them hath good thirty miles of compass round the walls thereof. And so vast is the number of people that the soldiers alone who are posted to keep ward in the city of Cambalec are forty thousand men, by sure tale. And in the city of Cassay[1] there be yet more, for its people is greater in number, seeing that it is a city of very great trade. And to this city all the traders of the country come to trade; and greatly it aboundeth in all manner of merchandize. And the Saracens[2] aforesaid do very diligently guard the said cities by night and by day.

5. *Concerning the money which is current in the said realm.*

The Grand Caan there maketh money of paper. And this hath a red token right in the middle, and round about there be letters in black. And this money is of greater or of less value according to the token that is thereon;

noisettes de Saint-Gratien ou *avelines*, ainsi appelées parce que les arbres qui les produisent sont originaires d'Avellino, ville du royaume de Naples." (Charles Saint-Laurent, *Dict. encyclop. usuel*, Paris, 1841, p. 959.) This Saint-Gratien is a village of the Department of the Somme, Amiens arrondissement, Villers-Bocage Canton. Vivien de Saint Martin's *Nouveau Dictionnaire de Géographie* has *s.v.*: "Noisettes renommées."

F. Godefroy, *Dict. de l'ancienne langue française*, v, has: "*Nois de Saint Gratien*, subst. composé, coing: Coctanus, arbre de pepin, *nois de saint Gratien*. (*Olla patella*, p. 27, Scheler.)

Coactanus, arbre de pepin, et fructus ejus est *nois* de saint Grascien. (*Gloss. rom. Lat. du XVe s.*, p. 38, Scheler.)

Dans La Haute-Normandie, vallée d'Yères, on appelle *nois de saint Gratien* les grosses nois franches."]

[1] The Cansay of Odoric, etc., *q.v.* Pegolotti also calls it Cassay.

[2] There are no Saracens mentioned before. But the word translated *soldiers* is "*servans*," which perhaps was "*Sarazins*." Or *vice versâ*, the *Sarazins* in the second passage should be *servans*.

one is worth a groat[1] and another is worth a denier; and so some are worth more and some less. And they fix the value of their money of gold and silver with reference to their paper money[2].

You find in this country a greater variety of merchandize than in the territories of Rome or of Paris. They have great store of gold and silver and of precious stones. For when any merchants from foreign parts come thither to trade, they leave there their gold and silver and precious stones, and they carry away the products of the country; spices, silk, cloths of silk and cloths of gold, of which they find great quantities for sale here.

The emperor above mentioned hath very great treasuries; indeed it is a marvel to see them; and these are for this paper money. And when the said paper money is too old and worn, so that it cannot be well handled, it is carried to the king's chamber, where there be moneyers appointed to this duty. And if the token or the king's name is at all to be discerned thereon, then the moneyer giveth new paper for the old, deducting three in every hundred for this renewal. All their royal grants are also made on paper.

6. *Concerning the manner of life of the people of this country.*

The emperor's people are very worthily arrayed, and live in a rich and liberal manner. And though silk and gold and silver are in great plenty, they have very little linen, wherefore all have shirts of silk; and their clothes

[1] "*Maille.*"

[2] The phrase is *avaluent leur monnoie dor et dargent à leur monnoie de pappier*, which Jacquet explains as in the text. The explanation does not seem very satisfactory, and the statement certainly is not true.

are of Tartary cloth[1], and damask silk[2], and other rich stuffs, oft-times adorned with gold and silver and precious stones. They wear long sleeves, coming down over their finger nails. They have sundry kinds of dishes made of canes, which are there very great and thick[3]. They eat meat of all kinds of beasts, and when they will make a great feast they kill camels, and make fine dishes of the flesh after their own fashion. They have fish in great abundance, and other things; and on these they live after their manner, as other people do after theirs.

7. *Of the manner in which they do bury their dead.*

When a child is born they take good heed to register the day of his birth, and when he dies his friends and kinsfolk put the body on a bier of paper adorned with gold and with silver; and on this bier they place myrrh and incense with the body. And then they put the bier upon a car, and this car is drawn by all of the dead man's kin to the place appointed specially; and there they burn the dead, with bier and car and all. And they give a reason for this, for they say that it is thus with fire that gold is purged, and so must the human body also be purged by fire, in order that it may rise again in all purity. When they have thus burned their dead they

[1] *Tartary cloth* is mentioned by Mandeville and other medieval writers. No doubt it was some rich Chinese stuff, for the Tartars proper could scarcely have been entitled to a reputation for fine textures: Dante alludes to it—

> "Con più color sommesse e sopraposti
> Non fer mai in drappo Tartari ne Turchi
> Ne fur tai tele per Aracne imposta";

and his expressions seem to imply that it was of variegated colours; shawl-work or embroidery perhaps. I find that Dozy says *Tatariyát* were robes of satin garnished with borders of gold stuff. (*Dict. des noms des vêtements chez les Arabes*, p. 94.)

[2] *Tamotas* (for *Camocas*, regarding which see a note upon Pegolotti, *infra*).

[3] See Ibn Batuta, *infra*, and note.

return to their houses, and in memory of the dead they cause an image to be made in his likeness. And this image they set in a certain place, and every year on his birthday they burn before this image lignaloes and other manner of fragrant spices; and so they keep the dead man's birthday in remembrance[1].

8. *Concerning the Minor Friars who sojourn in that country.*

In the said city of Cambalec there was an archbishop, whose name was Friar John of Montecorvino, of the Order of Minor Friars, and he was legate sent thither by Pope Clement. The archbishop did establish in the said city three houses of Minor Friars, and these are a good two leagues apart one from another[2]. He made also two others in the city of Zaitún[3], which is distant from Cambalec a three months' journey, and standeth upon the seashore. In those two houses were two Minor Friars as bishops. The one was by name Friar Andrew of Perugia, and the other was by name Friar Peter of Florence[4]. That Friar John the archbishop converted a multitude of people to the faith of Jesus Christ. He was a man of very upright life, pleasing to God and men, and stood in high grace with the emperor. The emperor at all times caused him and all his people to be furnished with all that they required; and much was he beloved by all, pagans as well as Christians. And certes he would

[1] Though burial of the dead appears to be the universal custom in China now, it is seen from many passages of Marco Polo that cremation was a usual practice in his day. [*Marco Polo*, ii, pp. 133–135 *n.*] See also Ibn Batuta, *infra.*

[2] We have seen the history of two of the churches in the archbishop's letters. The third must have been built at a later date.

[3] See Odoric, p. 183, and Ibn Batuta and Marignolli, *infra.* The latter about 1346 found three churches at Zaitún also.

[4] One of the second batch of bishops, sent to the East in 1312.

have converted that whole country to the Christian Catholic faith, if the Nestorians, those false Christians and real miscreants, had not hindered him and done him hurt.

The said archbishop was at great pains with those Nestorians to bring them under the obedience of our mother the holy Church of Rome; for without this obedience, he told them, they could not be saved. And for this cause those Nestorian schismatics held him in great hate.

This archbishop, as it hath pleased God, is lately passed from this world. To his obsequies and burial there came a very great multitude of people, both Christians and pagans. And those pagans rent their mourning garments as their manner is; and both Christians and pagans devoutly laid hold of the clothes of the archbishop, and carried them off as reliques with great reverence.

So there he was buried with great honour, after the manner of faithful Christians. And they still visit the place of his interment with very great devotion.

9. *Concerning the Schismatics or Nestorian Christians who dwell in that country.*

In the said city of Cambalec there is a manner of schismatic Christians whom they call Nestorians. They follow the manner and fashion of the Greeks, and are not obedient to the holy Church of Rome, but follow another sect, and bear great hate to all the Catholic Christians there who do loyally obey the holy Church aforesaid. And when that archbishop of whom we have been speaking was building those abbeys of the Minor Friars aforesaid, these Nestorians by night went to destroy them, and did all the hurt that they were able. But they dared not do any evil to the said archbishop, nor to his friars, nor to other faithful Christians in public or openly, for that the emperor did love these and showed them tokens of his regard.

These Nestorians are more than thirty thousand, dwelling in the said empire of Cathay, and are passing rich people, but stand in great fear and awe of the Christians. They have very handsome and devoutly ordered churches, with crosses and images in honour of God and the saints. They hold sundry offices under the said emperor, and have great privileges from him; so that it is believed that if they would agree and be at one with the Minor Friars, and with the other good Christians who dwell in that country, they would convert the whole country and the emperor likewise to the true faith.

10. *Concerning the great favour which the Grand Caan beareth towards the Christians before mentioned.*

The Grand Caan supporteth the Christians in the said kingdom who are obedient to the holy Church of Rome, and causeth provision to be made for all their necessities; for he hath very great devotion towards them, and sheweth them great affection. And when they require or ask anything from him, in order to furnish their churches their crosses or their sanctuaries to the honour of Jesus Christ, he doth most willingly bestow it. But he desireth that they should pray God for him and for his health, and especially in their sermons. And most willingly doth he suffer and encourage the friars to preach the faith of God in the churches of the pagans which are called *vritranes*[1]. And as willingly doth he permit the pagans to go to hear the preachment of the friars; so that the pagans go very willingly, and often behave with great devoutness, and bestow upon the friars great alms. And so, also, this

[1] I have not been able to trace this term, but it probably contains the Sanscrit *Vihâra*, a Buddhist monastery; perhaps *Vihârasthâna*, if there be such a compound.

emperor most readily sendeth his people to lend aid and succour to the Christians when they have any need, and ask it of the emperor.

Here endeth the discourse concerning the governance of the state of the Grand Caan, sovereign Emperor of the Tartars[1].

[1] [*Ends* fol. 140 verso of French MS. 2810 fr., of the Bibliothèque Nationale in Paris: "Explicit de la gouuernance et de lestat du grant kaan souuerain empereur des Tartars."]

III

CATHAY UNDER THE MONGOLS

III

CATHAY UNDER THE MONGOLS. EXTRACTED FROM RASHÍDUDDÍN

INTRODUCTORY NOTICE

IT has appeared desirable to present these extracts here, both as an appropriate variety, and as in some measure at least a sample of the literature which flourished under one of the Mongol dynasties to which we have so often occasion to refer.

The translation is borrowed from the French, chiefly from that published by Klaproth in the *Journal Asiatique* for 1833 (sér. ii, tom. xi, pp. 335–358, and 447–470). This was put forth in correction of a previous version by Von Hammer Purgstall, with which Klaproth found much fault, especially in the defective decipherment of proper names, of outlandish expressions, and sometimes even of simple Persian words; but in some of these respects he would himself also seem occasionally to have missed the mark. There is another translation, with considerable omissions and some additional matter, by D'Ohsson, in the Appendix to the second volume of his history of the Mongols, and I have followed that wherever it appeared to give better sense than Klaproth's version. An elaborate introduction to a paper of so little pretension as a translation thus prepared would be quite out of place, and a few paragraphs of explanation as to the author and his works are all that need be given.

FAZL-ULLAH RASHÍD, otherwise Rashíd-ud-dín, son of 'Imád-ud-daulah Abu'l Khair, was born at Hamadan about A.D. 1247. His enemies, in the latter part of his life, called him a Jew both by birth and religion[1]. The latter part of the assertion is disproved, both as to himself and his immediate predecessor, but Quatremère is inclined to think that he was possibly of Jewish descent, as he shows an acquaintance with Jewish rites and customs singular for a Mahomedan statesman.

He was a physician by profession, and, in that capacity apparently, passed a considerable part of his life at the court of Abaka Khan and his immediate successors. All treated him with distinction, but he came into no great prominence before the accession of Ghazan Khan in 1295. The Wazir, Sadr-ud-dín, was an old friend of Rashíd's, but mischief-making embittered the minister against the latter, and eventually (1298) the Khan taking Rashíd's part violently, caused Sadr-ud-dín to be executed. Rashíd himself was then named Wazir of the Persian empire in conjunction with Saad-ud-dín. Oljaïtu, the brother and successor of Ghazan, maintained both ministers in office, but they disagreed, and a succession of quarrels between them ended in Rashíd's denouncing his colleague, and causing him to be put to death. This recurring fatality to Rashíd's rivals and colleagues tends to raise serious doubts as to the high character claimed for him, and to abate our pity for his own catastrophe. He did not get on better with Saad's successor, one Ali Shah Jabalán, though selected by himself. Rashíd kept his ground till the death of Oljaïtu, but on the succession of Abu Said (1317) his enemy succeeded in prejudicing the king against him, and

[1] Ibn Batuta (ii, 116), who saw Rashíd's son attending as Wazir on Abu Said Khan at Baghdad, says that "the father Khwaja Rashíd had been an emigrant Jew." Saiduddaulat, the chief minister and favourite of Arghún the father of Oljaïtu, was a Jew. (*Mod. Univ. History* in Fr. trans., iii, 646).

he was displaced. Such confusion ensued that the old statesman had soon to be recalled, but he speedily fell again. He was now accused of having caused the death of Oljaïtu by a potion administered by the hands of his own son Ibrahim, who had been the Khan's chief butler. A doctor's quarrel (*spreti injuria dicti*) aided the conspirators. For one of the chief physicians declared that Oljaïtu's death was attributable to a purgative urged upon him by Rashíd strongly against the legitimate opinion of the physician. He and his son, a noble youth of sixteen, were condemned. Ibrahim was killed before his father's eyes, and then the old man was hewn in two. His head was borne through the streets of Tabriz, and proclaimed as that of a blaspheming Jew, the property of his family was confiscated, and the *Raba' Rashídí*, a quarter which he had built, was given up to pillage. This was in 1318. The colleague who had brought destruction on Rashíd survived in power for six years, and died in his bed. Abu Said then had to confess that affairs had never gone well since the removal of Rashíd, and that he had sorely erred in listening to the calumniators. As some amends to his memory the king raised Ghaiassuddín, the eldest son of Rashíd, to his father's former office. He was a man of noble, liberal and gentle character, but perished in the troubles which followed the death of Abu Said.

What is told of Rashíd's wealth, magnificence, acquirements, and labours, reads like a bit of French romance. In addition to the sciences connected with his original profession, he had studied agriculture, architecture, and metaphysics; he was an adept in Mussulman theology and controversy; and was acquainted with Persian, Arabic, Mongol, Turki, and Hebrew. In the space of eleven months, whilst administering a great kingdom, he declares himself to have composed three important works, besides numerous minor treatises on a variety of intricate subjects.

The *Raba' Rashídí* was a magnificent suburb, the buildings of which were laid out with great regularity and elegance; it was built entirely at his expense, as well as supplied with water by a canal which he caused to be cut through the rock. When Oljaïtu founded Soltania, his minister built there also a quarter consisting of one thousand houses, with a mosque, a college, a hospital, and a monastery, and all these he furnished with considerable endowments. In the transcription and binding of copies of his own works he is said to have laid out 60,000 dinars, equal, according to Quatremère, to about £36,000.

Rashíd stoutly declares the integrity and justice of his own administration, and in this he is corroborated, not merely by contemporaries, but also by the authors of the next generation.

His greatest work was called by the author the *Jamí'-ut-Tawáríkh*, "Collection of Histories" or Historical Cyclopædia, which in fact it is. It contained histories of the Tartar and Turkish tribes, of Chinghiz and his race, and of the Persian khans in particular, including his master Oljaïtu; of various dynasties of Western Asia, of Mahomed and his companions, of the prophets of Israel, the Cæsars and other Christian princes; of China and of India. It concluded, or was intended to conclude, with a universal geography, but it is doubtful if this was ever written, though the existing portions of the work contain many geographical notices.

A general judgment cannot be formed of the worth of these copious writings by the unlearned, for only portions and fragments have been translated. D'Ohsson, who makes much use of Rashíd's *History of the Mongols*, says that though in some parts he copies from those who had gone before him, his history is altogether the most complete, and the most eminent for orderly arrangement and noble simplicity of style. Many of his facts are to be found in no other history; it is the only one which gives information as to the ancient nations of Tartary, and the ancestry of Chinghiz. He was aided with information by Púlad Chingsang, a great Mongol prince, who was the Great Khan's envoy at Tabriz, and who was said to have better knowledge of such subjects than any man living. To him, probably, he owed much of the information in the chapters here translated.

Even from such fragments as this, and those which Sir Henry Elliot has introduced in his *Biographical Index to Historians of India*, it may be gathered that Rashíd had far more correct ideas of geography than any of his contemporaries with whom we have to do in this book. This indeed might have been expected from a man so accomplished, and occupying a position which was not merely that of first minister of Persia, but that of a statesman in one great branch of an empire whose relations embraced nearly all Asia with a closeness and frequency of intercourse to which there has never been an approach in later days.

In 1836 Quatremère commenced the publication of a text and translation of the *Mongol History* of Rashíd, at the expense of the French government, and on a most costly and cumbrous scale. It went no further than the first volume, containing a life of Rashíd and an account of his works, the author's own preface, and the history of Húlakú.

The late Mr. Morley was engaged on an English translation of the whole of the *Jamí'-ut-Tawáríkh*, as may be seen from his letters in vols. vi and vii of the *Journal of the Royal Asiatic Society*. But it never was published, and I am not aware what progress had been made[1].

[1] This sketch has been derived from Quatremère, from D'Ohsson's Preface, from Mr. Morley's letters just mentioned, and from Sir H.

Elliot's Index. But the last seems to draw his material from Quatremère and Morley.

[M. E. Blochet, of the Bibliothèque Nationale, Paris, is editing for "E. J. W. Gibb Memorial" Series the text of the *Jamí'-ut-Tawáríkh*; the work will include: Introduction à l'Histoire des Mongols de Fadl Allah Rashid ed-Din, 1910; I: Histoire des tribus turques et mongoles, des ancêtres de Tchinkkiz-Khan depuis Along Goa, et de Tchinkkiz-Khan; II: Histoire des successeurs de Tchinkkiz-Khan, d'Ougédeï à Temour Kaan, des fils apanagés de Tchinkkiz-Khan, et des gouverneurs mongols de Perse d'Houlagou à Ghazan; III: Histoire de Ghazan, d'Oldjaïtou, et de Abou-Saïd. The Introduction and the first volume were published in 1910 and 1911.]

CONTEMPORARY NOTICES OF CATHAY UNDER THE MONGOLS

EXTRACTED FROM THE HISTORICAL CYCLOPÆDIA OF RASHÍDUDDÍN

CATHAY is a country of vast extent and cultivated in the highest degree. Indeed the most credible authors assert that there is no country in the world to compare with it in culture and population. A gulf of the ocean, of no very great width, washes its south-eastern shores and extends along the coast between MANZI and KOLI[1], running into Cathay so as to reach within (twenty)-four parasangs of Khanbaliq[2], and ships come to that point. The vicinity of the sea causes frequent rain. In one part of the country the climate is a hot one, whilst in others it is cold. In his time Chinghiz Kaan had conquered the greater part of the provinces of Cathay, whilst under the reign of Okkodaï Kaan the conquest of the whole was completed. Chinghiz Kaan and his sons, however, as we have said in relating their history, never took up their residence in Cathay; but after Mangu Khan had transmitted the empire to Kúblái Kaan[3], the latter thought it not well to remain at such

[1] On Manzi, see note *supra*, II, p. 177. Koli is the Chinese Kao li, *i.e.* Corea, and the Gulf is of course the Yellow Sea.

[2] The reading is *four* both with Klaproth and D'Ohsson. But as the real distance is *twenty-four*, the former supposes it originally stood so.

[3] [Mangu died during the seventh month of 1259, while besieging Ho chau, in the Sze chu'an province, north of Ch'ung K'ing, and he was replaced by his brother Kúblái, who was proclaimed as Emperor at K'aip'ing in the third month of 1260.]

a distance from a country so populous, and which was reckoned to surpass all other kingdoms and countries in the world. So he fixed his residence in Cathay, and established his winter quarters in the city of Khanbaliq, which was called in the Cathayan tongue CHUNG-TU[1].

This city had been the residence of the former kings. It was built in ancient times according to the indications of the most learned astrologers, and under the most fortunate constellations, which have always continued propitious to it. But as it had been destroyed by Chinghiz Kaan, Kúblái Kaan desired to spread his own fame by restoring it. The city which he built was close to the former capital and was called DAÏDU[2].

The wall of this city is flanked by seventeen towers, with intervals of a parasang between every two. The population of Daïdu is so great that even outside of the fortifications there are great streets and numerous houses. And there are extensive gardens, planted with various kinds of fruit trees brought together from every quarter. In the middle of this city Kúblái Kaan established his *Ordu*, in a palace of great extent which they call the *Karsi*[3].

The pavements and columns of this palace are all of marble or of the finest cut stone. Four walls enclose and defend it, and there is an interval of a bow-shot from one wall to the next.

The outer court is assigned to the palace-guards; the next to the nobles, who assemble there every morning; the third is occupied by the great officers of the army; and the fourth by the sovereign's most intimate associates. The picture of the palace which follows is reduced from one which was painted for his majesty Ghazan Kaan.

[*Here the original MS. seems to have had an illustration.*]

[1] *Supra*, II, p. 216.   [2] *Supra*, II, pp. 216—217.

[3] *Karsi* is a Mongol word signifying the hall in which the Emperor sits on state occasions. (*Klapr.*)

Two important rivers pass by Khanbaliq and Daïdu. After coming from the direction of the kaan's summer residence in the north, and flowing near Jamjál, they unite to form another river. A very large basin, like a lake in fact, has been dug near the city and furnished with a slip for launching pleasure boats[1]. The river had formerly another channel, and discharged itself into the gulf of the ocean, which penetrated within a short distance of Khanbaliq. But in the course of time this channel had become so shallow as not to admit the entrance of shipping, so that they had to discharge their cargoes and send them up to Khanbaliq on pack-cattle. And the Chinese engineers and men of science having reported that the vessels from the provinces of Cathay, from the capital of MÁCHIN[2], and from the cities of KHINGSAÏ and ZAITÚN no longer could reach the metropolis, the Khan gave them orders to dig a great canal, into which the waters of the said river and of several others should be introduced. This canal extends for a distance of forty days' navigation from Khanbaliq to Khingsaï and Zaitún, the ports frequented by the ships that come from India and from the capital of Máchin[2]. The canal is provided with many sluices intended to distribute the water over the country; and when vessels arrive at these sluices they are hoisted up by means of machinery, whatever be their size, and let down on the other side into the water. The canal has a width of more than 30 ells. Kúblái caused the sides of the embankments to be revetted with stone in order to prevent the earth

[1] The two rivers are the Sha-ho and Pei-ho, which unite below Pe king, afterwards bearing the latter name. The lake is that called *Thaï-i-tchi* or *Si-haï-tsu*, to the east (*west*) of the imperial palace. (*K.*)

[2] Here we find the "capital of Machin" distinct from King sze. It is probably Chinkalan or Canton that is meant. See *supra*, II, p. 179. The author refers here to the extension of the Great Canal towards Pe king by Kúbláí. [Hwang ho to Pe king, 1289–1292. Cf. Gandar, *Canal Impérial*, p. 21.]

giving way[1]. Along the side of the canal runs the high road to Máchin, extending for a space of forty days' journey, and this has been paved throughout, so that travellers and their animals may get along during the rainy season without sticking in the mud. The two sides of the road are planted with willows and other shady trees, and no one is allowed, whether soldier or otherwise, to break branches off those trees or to let cattle feed on the leaves. Shops, taverns, and villages line the road on both sides, so that dwelling succeeds dwelling without intermission throughout the whole space of forty days' journey.

The ramparts of the city of Daïdu are formed of earth. The custom of the country in making such ramparts is first to set up planks, and then to fill in moist earth between them, ramming it hard with great wooden rammers; they then remove the planks, and the earth remains forming a solid wall. The Kaan, in his later years, ordered stone to be brought in order to face the walls, but death intervened, and the execution of his project remains, if God permit, for Timur Kaan.

The Kaan's intention was to build a palace like that of Daïdu at KAIMINFU, which is at a distance of fifty parasangs, and to reside there[2]. There are three roads to that place from the winter-residence. The first, reserved for hunting matches, is allowed to be used only by ambassadors[3]. The

[1] "The earthen embankments in this part of the canal were supported by retaining walls of coarse grey marble cut into large blocks, and cemented together with a kind of mortar. Those walls were about twelve feet in thickness, and the large stones on the top were bound together with clamps of iron." (*Staunton*, ii, 392.)

[2] K'aimingfu, the K'ai-p'ing fu of the Chinese and the Clemenfu (probably miswritten for Chemenfu) of M. Polo, is at the place thirty-six leagues beyond the Great Wall, where Kúbláí, as here related, established his summer residence, changing the name of the town to Shang tu (*supra*, p. 227).

[3] Lord Macartney, on his way from Jehol, found a road reserved only for the emperor. Another, parallel to it, was for the attendants of the emperor, and on this the ambassador was allowed to travel. All other travellers were excluded, and had to find a track where they could. (*Staunton*, ii, 279.)

second road passes by the city of CHÚ-CHÚ[1], following the banks of the Sanghín river, where you see great plenty of grapes and other kinds of fruit[2]. Near the city just named there is another called SEMALI, most of the inhabitants of which are natives of Samarkand, and have planted a number of gardens in the Samarkand style. The third road takes the direction of the Pass of Siking[3], and after traversing this you find only prairies and plains abounding in game until you reach the city of Kaiminfu, where the summer palace is. Formerly the court used to pass the summer in the vicinity of the city of Chúchú, but afterwards the neighbourhood of Kaiminfu was preferred, and on the eastern side of that city a *karsi* or palace was built called LANGTIN, after a plan which the Kaan had seen in a dream and retained in his memory[4].

[1] Cho chau is a town a short distance to the south-west of Peking, on the other side of the river, named the Júju of Polo.

["When you leave the Bridge (*Pul-i-Sangín*), and ride towards the west, finding all the way excellent hostelries for travellers, with fine vineyards, fields and gardens, and springs of water, you come after 30 miles to a fine large city called Júju, where there are many abbeys of idolaters, and the people live by trade and manufactures." *Marco Polo*, ii, p. 10.]

[2] The Sanghín river is that otherwise called Lu-kou and Yung ting, a few miles to the west of Peking, over which stood the bridge which Marco Polo describes (ii, pp. 4–8). The Venetian calls the river Pulisanghin, which is the Persian *Pul-i-sangín* or Stone bridge, as Marsden suggested.

["By *Sanghin*, Polo renders the Chinese *Sang-Kan*, by which name the River Hun-ho is already mentioned, in the 6th century of our era. *Hun-ho* is also an ancient name; and the same river in ancient books is often called *Lu-Kou* River also. All these names are in use up to the present time; but on modern Chinese Maps, only the upper part of the River is termed *Sang Kan-ho*, whilst south of the inner Great Wall, and in the plain, the name of *Hun-ho* is applied to it. *Hun-ho* means 'Muddy River,' and the term is quite suitable. In the last century, the Emperor K'ien lung ordered the Hun-ho to be named *Yung-ting ho*, a name found on modern maps, but the people always call it *Hun-ho*." Bretschneider, *Peking*, p. 54.]

[3] Siking, Sengling, or Sengking. The hills from which the Sang-kan-ho emerges are called in Klaproth's map *Shy-king*-shan. This is perhaps the name in the text.

[4] D'Ohsson has read this passage differently: "Kúblái caused a palace to be built for him east of Kaipingfu, called Lengten; but he abandoned it in consequence of a dream."

The philosophers and architects being consulted gave their advice as to the building of this other palace. They all agreed that the best site for it was a certain lake encompassed with meadows near the city of Kaiminfu, but for this it was necessary to provide a dry foundation. Now there is a kind of stone found in that country which is used instead of fire-wood; so they collected a great quantity of that stone and likewise of wood[1], and filled up the lake and its springs with a mass of bricks and lime well shaken up together, running over the whole a quantity of melted tin and lead. The platform so formed was as high as a man. The water that was thus imprisoned in the bowels of the earth in the course of time forced outlets in sundry places, and thus fountains were produced. On the foundation formed as has been described a palace in the Chinese taste was erected, and enclosed by a marble wall. From this wall starts an outer fence of wood which surrounds the park, to prevent any one from entering, and to preserve the game. Inside the city itself a second palace was built, about a bowshot from the first; but the Kaan generally takes up his residence in the palace outside the town.

In this empire of Cathay there are many considerable cities; each has its appropriate title marking a particular rank in the scale. The relative precedence of governors is indicated by that of the cities which they administer, so that there is no need to specify their dignities in the diploma of appointment, or to enter into curious questions of precedence. You know at once [by the rank of the cities to which they are attached] which ought to make way for another or to bow the knee before him. These ranks or titles are as follows: 1. *King;* 2. *Du;* 3. *Fu;* 4. *Chu;* 5. ...; 6. *Kiun;* 7. *Hien;* 8. *Chin;* 9. *Sún*[2].

[1] *I.e.* to burn bricks and lime.

[2] 1. *King*, imperial capital, as in Pe king, Nan king; 2. *Tu*, court or imperial residence, as Tai tu, Shang tu; 3. *Fu*, a city of the first

The first of these titles designates a vast tract of country, say like *Rúm*, Persia, or Baghdad. The second is applied to a province, which is the seat of an imperial residence. The others diminish in importance in like proportion; thus the seventh indicates small cities, the eighth towns, the ninth villages and hamlets. Ports and landing places are called *Batu*[1].

A similar classification of governors according to the rank of their cities does not exist anywhere else, but the empire of Cathay is quite remarkable for the system with which it is organised.

NOTICE OF THE PRINCES, MINISTERS, AND SECRETARIES OF CATHAY, OF THEIR GRADATIONS IN RANK, OF THE RULES AND CUSTOMS AFFECTING THEM, AND OF THE NAMES THEY BEAR IN THE LANGUAGE OF THE COUNTRY.

The great princes who have the rank of Wazírs among those people have the title of *Chingsang*[2]; commanders in

class, or rather the department of which it is the head; 4. *Chau*, a city of the second class, or the district of which it is the head; 5. This is blank in Klaproth's original; Von Ham. read it *Gur*; perhaps it was *Lu*, which was a special subdivision in China under the Mongols, rendered by Pauthier *circuit* [or *tao*, a circuit]; I do not understand its relation to the others, but Duhalde says it was somewhat less than a *Fu*; 6. *Kiun*, a chief military garrison; 7. *Hien*, a city of the third order, or sub-district, of which it is the head; 8. *Chin*, a small town; 9. *Tsun*, a village. The custom of naming the dignitary by the title belonging to the class of district under him still prevails in China; "as if," says Pauthier, "we were to call our Prefects *Departments* and our Sub-Prefects *Arrondissements*" (*M.P.*, p. xcvii).

[1] Mongol pronunciation of *Matheu*, a jetty, and hence a port. See *supra*, p. 214.

[2] This title *Chingsang* represents the Chinese *Ching-siang*, a minister of state. The name of Pulad *Chingsang*, the Great Khan's ambassador to the court of the Persian Khan, occurs frequently in D'Ohsson, who also mentions that the title of *Chingsang* was conferred on Bucai, the minister of the Persian Khan Arghún, by Kúbláí (iv, 13). It is also the title which Marco Polo applies to Kúbláí's great general Bayam (or Baian) *Cinqsan*, though he strangely alleges this to mean Bayam with the Hundred Eyes (i, 62). Full particulars regarding the imperial cabinet in the time of the Mongols will be

chief of the army have that of *Thaifu*; and chiefs of ten thousand soldiers are called *Wanshi*[1].

Those Princes Wazírs and chief officers of the council who are either Tájiks[2], native Cathayans, or Ighúrs, have the title of *Fanchán*[3]. Strictly speaking the council of state is composed of four *Chingsang* or great officers, and of four *Fanchán* [*P'ing-chang*], taken from the nations of the Tájiks, Cathayans, Ighúrs, and Arkáun[4]. These latter act as inspectors on behalf of the council.

found in Pauthier's *Marc Pol*, pp. 329 *seq.* The number of the Chingsiang or chief ministers varied from two to four, and on one occasion there was but one. [See p. 265.]

[1] *Wanshi*, from *Wan*, ten thousand. The termination is Mongol according to Klaproth. *Thaifu* looks like a genuine Chinese title, though I do not find it in the books on China. It is mentioned by the merchant Suleiman (*Daifú*) as the title of the governor of a first-rate city (*Relation des Voyages*, i, 37). In the late wars against the T'aï p'ing I have seen the title *Fu-t'ai* applied to the Imperial commander [Li Hung-chang who was *fu-t'ai* (governor) of the Kiang Su province].

[2] Of Persian race.

[3] This word is read by Klaproth *Kabján*, and by Von Hammer *Tenján*. Pauthier says it should be read *Minján*, as the Mongol pronunciation of the Chinese original *P'ing-chang*. But this is arbitrary, and we find in D'Ohsson the real form of the word as used by Rashíd, viz. *Fanchán*, which differs only by dots from Klaproth's *Kabjan*. It is also written *Panchân* by Wassaf, and by Ssanang Setzen the Mongol historian, not Minján but *Bingjing*. (See *D'Ohsson*, ii, 530, 636–7.)

According to Pauthier's statement the normal composition of the Council of State was of two Chingsiang or chief ministers; four P'ing-chang, ministers of the second degree; four minister assessors called *Yeu-ching* and *Tso-ching*; and two reporting councillors, called *Thsang-ching*, the whole number making up the twelve barons of Marco Polo.

[A Samarkand man, Seyyid Tadj Eddin Hassan, ben el Khallal, quoted in the *Masâlak el Absâr*, says: "Near the Khan are two amírs who are his ministers; they are called *Djing san* (Ch'ing-siang). After them come the two *Bidjan* (P'ing Chang), then the two *Zoudjin* (Tso Chen), then the two *Yudjin* (Yu Chen), and at last the *Landjun* (Lang Chang), head of the scribes, and secretary of the sovereign. The Khan holds a sitting every day in the middle of a large building called *Chen* (Sheng), which is very like our Palace of Justice." (C. Schefér, *Cent. École Langues Orient.*, pp. 18–19. See *Marco Polo*, i, pp. 431–432.)]

[4] This is a word by which the Mongols designated the Nestorian Christians with whom they had relations. Its origin is very obscure, but from what Marco Polo says of the term (*Argon*) as elucidated in

The whole gradation of dignitaries and officers of state is as follows:—

1. The *Chingsáng* or Wazírs.

2. The great officers of the army, who make their reports to the *Chingsáng*, however exalted their rank may be.

3. The *Fanchán* or associated members of the Council of State, taken from the different nations specified.

4. *Yer Jing* or first class *Jing*.

5. *Ur Jing* or second class *Jing*.

6. *Sam Jing* or third class *Jing*[1].

7. Semi (?).

8. *Sisan Baljún*. These are book-keepers and of inferior consideration.

9. . . . .

In the time of Kúblái Kaán the Chingsáng chosen from among the princes were Haitun Noyán, Uchaar, Oljai Tarkhan, and Dáshiman. Haitun Noyán is now no more, but the others remain in office as the Chingsáng of Timúr Kaán.

Formerly the office of Fanchán was only bestowed on Cathayans, but it is now held also by Mongols, Tájiks, and Ighúrs.

The chief Fanchán is called Su Fanchán, or the Select Fanchán. In our day under the reign of Timúr Kaán the chief of the whole number is Báyán Fanchán[2], the son of

a learned and interesting note by Pauthier, it would seem to have meant properly a *half-breed*.

[Capt. Wellby writes (*Unknown Tibet*, p. 32): "We impressed into our service six other muleteers, four of them being Argoons, who are really half-castes, arising from the merchants of Turkestan making short marriages with the Ladakhi women." The Christians were called by the Mongols *Erkeun* (*Ye-li-ke-un*). Cf. *Marco Polo*, i, p. 289, Note 4.]

[1] These three ranks correspond to the Yeu-ching, Tso-ching, and T'sang-ching of the Chinese records (*Pauthier*).

[2] [The Seyyid Edjell Shams ud-Dín, also called Omar, and in Chinese *Sai tien ch'e Shan se ting*, eldest son of Ma Ha Mu, of a family coming from Bokhara, was Minister to Kúblái, and stood

the Seyid Nasr ud-Dín, who was the son of Seyid Edjell, and who bears the same title. The second, Omar Fanchán, is also a Mongol. The third, Iké Fanchán, is an Ighúr. Before him the office was filled by Lájan Fanchán, brother of his Excellency the Su Fanchán; his son is called Karmánah. The fourth Paighamísh Fanchán, whose place was formerly occupied by Timúr Fanchán, is an Ighúr.

As the Kaan generally resides at the capital he has erected a place for the sittings of the Great Council, called *Sing*. According to established custom a lieutenant is appointed to the inspection and charge of the doors, and examines all the drafts of memorials[1] that are presented.

The name of the first tribunal is *In*. All the proceedings are copied and sent with the memorials to the tribunal called *Lúsah*, which is of higher rank than the other. Thence all is carried to the tribunal called *Khalyún*, and thence to the fourth, called *Kuijún*. This is the board which has charge of all that relates to the posts and despatches. The three first mentioned tribunals are under

high in his favour; he was made a prince of Hien Yang and Governor of Tien (Yun-nan); he died in 1279, being sixty-nine years of age. His eldest son Nasr ud-Dín (*Na su la ting*), prince of Yen ngan, succeeded his father as governor of Yun nan (Karajang, *infra*, pp. 127, 131), where he died in 1292. The grandson (of Seyyid Edjell and one of the twelve sons of Nasr ud-Dín) here spoken of, Abúbakr, surnamed Báyán Fanchán, bore also the title of Seyyid Edjell which was highly respected by the Mongols (*D'Ohsson*, ii, 467, 507–8), and replaced as governor of Yun nan his uncle Hoseín, brother and successor of Nasr ud-Dín. Báyán (Poyen) was also prince of Hien Yang and of Wei ngan. (Cf. A. Vissière, in *Recherches sur les Musulmans Chinois* by Com[t]. d'Ollone, Paris, 1911.)] At least two other Báyáns are notable in the history of Kúblái's dynasty. The name *Baian* already appears as that of an Avar chief in the time of the Emperor Justin.

[Cf. Bretschneider, *Med. Res.*, i, p. 271. Vissière, *Revue du Monde Musulman*, Feb. 1908 and July–Aug. 1909.] *Marco Polo*, ii, p. 104 note.]

[1] The original word is here *Balarghúi*, which puzzled Klaproth. It is explained by Pauthier (*Marc Pol*, 331) from Schmidt's Mongol Dictionary, "*Ecrit, Mémoire peu net, avec des ratures ou phrases retranchées.*" He adds that still in China all memorials, etc., for presentation to the emperor or his council, are submitted to particular officers who correct their style.

the orders of the last; and from it business is transferred to the fifth, which bears the name of *Rusndyi*, and which has everything that concerns the army under its charge. Lastly, the business arrives at the sixth board, which is called *Siúshtah*[1]. All ambassadors and foreign merchants when arriving and departing have to present themselves at this office, which is the one which issues orders in council and passports. In our days this office is entirely under the management of the Amír Dáshiman.

When matters have passed these six boards, they are remitted to the Council of State, or *Sing*, where they are discussed, and the decision is issued after being verified by the *Khat Angusht* or "finger-signature" of all who have a right to a voice in the council. This "finger-signature" indicates that the act, to which it is attached in attestation, has been discussed and definitively approved by those whose mark has thus been put upon it.

It is usual in Cathay, when any contract is entered into, for the outline of the fingers of the parties to be traced upon the document. For experience shows that no two individuals have fingers precisely alike. The hand of the contracting party is set upon the back of the paper containing the deed, and lines are then traced round his fingers up to the knuckles, in order that if ever one of them should deny his obligation this tracing may be compared with his fingers and he may thus be convicted[2].

[1] These are the six boards of administration which still exist in China, under the names of *Kung-Pu*, *Hing-Pu*, etc. The titles given by Rashíd do not seem to attempt any imitation of the Chinese names, and are probably those in use among the Mahomedans. The third board from the top, called *P'ing pu* by the Chinese, has still authority over military affairs.

[2] [With regard to the finger print system in the Far East we shall make the following remarks: In *Nature*, Oct. 28, 1880, p. 605, Mr. Henry Faulds writing from Tokyo drew the attention to the use made by Japanese of finger prints and came to the conclusion "that the Chinese criminals from early times have been made to give the impressions of their fingers, just as we make ours yield their photo-

After the matter has thus passed through all the boards, and has been decided on by the supreme authority, it is sent back to the tribunal before which it first came.

The dignitaries mentioned above are expected to attend daily at the Sing, and to make themselves acquainted with all that passes there. And as the business to be transacted is very extensive, the Chingsáng take their part in the writing that has to be done as well as the other members of the Council whose positions we have detailed. Each takes his place, according to his degree, with a kind of table and writing materials before him. Every great officer has his seal and distinctive bearings. It is the duty of certain of the clerks to write down the names of all who attend daily, in order that a deduction may be made from the allowances of those who are absent. If any one is habitually absent from the Council without valid excuse, he is dismissed.

graphs." In the same periodical (Nov. 22, 1894, p. 77), Sir W. J. Herschel claimed to have been the first to exhibit the system of finger prints on board the P. and O. S.S. *Mongolian* in Feb. 1877; this system he had found in 1858 and communicated to Mr. Galton who made use of it in his *Finger Prints*, 1892; hence the discovery of the system was ascribed to Sir W. Herschel in a Parliamentary "Blue Book." Sir W. Herschel added in his letter that, to the best of his knowledge, the assertion that the use of finger marks in this way was originally invented by the Chinese was wholly unproved. Sir W. Herschel was entirely wrong; Mr. Faulds (*Ibid.*, Oct. 4, 1894, p. 548) protested against the claim of Sir W. Herschel, and finally a Japanese gentleman Kumagusu Minakata (*Ibid.*, Dec. 27, 1894, p. 199) proved the case for the Japanese and the Chinese. None of these writers quoted the passage of Rashíd-ud-dín which is a peremptory proof of the antiquity of the use of finger prints by the Chinese. In a note (*T'oung pao*, 1895, p. 147), G. Schlegel refers to his *Nederlandsch-Chineesch Woordenboek*, s.v. *Echtscheidingsbrief* (Letter of Divorce), which letters are authenticated by a print of the hand of the husband, and *Bezegelen*, "to confirm by the blackened palm of the hand." As we go to press we learn that Mr. B. Laufer of Chicago has just brought out a *History of the Finger Print System*, Washington, 1913, 8vo. Cf. Chavannes, *T'oung pao*, Oct. 1913, pp. 490–491, who gives additional proofs of the high antiquity of the finger print system in China. Three documents of the T'ang dynasty dated 782 and 786 bear finger prints with a formula to state "that prints of the fingers have been put on as a distinctive mark."]

It is the order of the Kaan that the four Chingsáng make all reports to him.

The Sing of Khanbaliq is the most eminent, and the building is very large. All the acts and registers and records of proceedings of several thousands of years are there preserved. The officials employed in it amount to some two thousand.

Sing do not exist in all the cities, but only in the capitals of great provinces, which, in fact, form kingdoms ranking with Baghdad, Shiraz, Iconium, and Rúm.

In the whole empire of the Kaan there are twelve of these Sing; but that of Khanbaliq is the only one which has Chingsáng among its members. The others have only dignitaries bearing the title of *Shijangi* to preside over them, aided by four Fanchán, and other members of council who have titles corresponding to their dignities.

The places where the Twelve Sing are established are, according to their respective precedence, the following:

1st Sing; that of KHANBALIQ or Daïdu. *2nd.* That of the country of the CHURCHÉ[1] and the SOLÁNGKA which is established in the city of Múnchú, the greatest town of Solángka country. Ala-uddín, the son of Husamuddín of Almáliq, and Hassan Juják are in authority there. *3rd.* That of KOLI[2] and UKOLI, a separate kingdom, the chief of which has the title of *Wang* (or king). Kúblái gave his daughter in marriage to this prince. *4th.* NAMKING. This is a great city belonging to the province of Cathay, situated on the banks of the Karamuran. It was

[1] The *Churché* are the Yu ché or Niuchen of the Chinese, the ancestors of the modern Manchus. *Solángka* is the Mongol name of the northern part of Corea, and the country through which flows the Ghirinsula or upper part of the Sungari river. (*Klap.*) The Solangas are mentioned by Rubruquis, who saw their envoys at the court of Kara Korum. The "city of Múnchú" is probably connected with the name of the *Manchu* tribes.

[2] *Kaoli* is the Chinese name of Corea. Koli and Akoli is not explained; it is probably one of those double jingles which Orientals are fond of inventing, like *Chin* and *Machin.*

once the residence of the (old) kings of Cathay[1]. *5th.* SUKCHÚ, a city situated on the frontier of Cathay towards the Turks[2]. *6th.* The city of KHINGSAI, formerly the capital of the kingdom of Manzi. Ala-uddín Fanchán, his son Saifuddín, and Taghájar Noyan Batu Kerkháhi, are its three chiefs. Omar Khwaja son of Saï, and Bik Khwaja Thusi are the Fanchāns[3]. *7th.* FÚCHÚ[4]. This is a city of Manzi. The Sing was formerly located at Zaitún, but afterwards established here, where it still remains. The chiefs there are Ran, the brother of Dáshiman, and Hhálá the brother of Báyán Fanchán. Zaitún is a great shipping-port, and the commandant there is Boha-addín Kandári. *8th.* LUKINFU, a city of Manzi, on the frontier of Tangkut[5]. *9th.* LÚMKALÍ, called by the merchants CHINKALÁN. This is a city of immense size on the sea-coast to the south of Zaitún, and has a great haven. Tukai Nám and Ruknaddín Abishári Fanchán are the chief officers there[6]. *10th.* KARÁJÁNG. This used to be an independent kingdom, and the Sing is established at the great city of Yachi. All the inhabitants are Mahomedans. The chiefs

[1] *Namking* is not our modern Nanking (which is not on the Caramuran or Hwang-ho), but K'ai fung fu in Ho nan, which was the Nanghin of Polo, the *Nan-king* or "Southern Capital" of the Kin dynasty of Cathay or Northern China. (*Klap.*)

[2] *Sukchú* is Su chau in Kan suh province, towards the Great Desert. We find it called Sukchu by Shah Rukh's ambassadors, and *Sowchick* by Anthony Jenkinson. [The first character of *Su chau* was pronounced *Suk* at the time of the T'ang; we find a *Sughčiu* in von Le Coq's MSS. from Turkestan and *Sughču* in the runnic text of W. Thomsen; cf. Pelliot, *J. As.*, Mai–Juin 1912, p. 591; the pronunciation *Suk*-chau was still used by travellers coming from Central Asia, for instance by the envoys of Shah Rukh.]

[3] Of Khingsai (Quinsai, Cansa) we have already heard and shall hear more. Note how many of these provincial governors are Mahomedans.

[4] Of Fu chau and Zaitún we have also heard in Odoric.

[5] One expects here the province of Sze-ch'wan, which is on the borders of Tangut. But the capital was *Ch'eng tu fu* (see *infra*, p. 130).

[6] On Chinkalan (Canton) also see *Odoric*, p. 179. The other name *Lumkali* is doubtful as to reading. Von Hammer read it *Kunki*.

are Noyán Takín and Yakúb Beg, son of Ali Beg the Balúch[1]. 11*th.* KENJANGFU, one of the cities of Tangkút. Ananda the son of Númúghán, resides in this country, at the place called Fanchán Náúr, where he has built a palace[2]. 12*th.* Machú or Kamkhu? is also a city of Tangkút, to which immense territories are attached. Akhtaki (or

[1] Kara-jáng is Yun-nan. In Marco Polo the modern Yun-nan is divided into two provinces, the capital of one of which is Jaci (Yach'i) as here, and the capital of the other called by the same name as the province. In Murray's edition the former province is called *Caraian*, and the latter *Karazan*, whilst in Pauthier's publication from old French MSS. *both* provinces are called *Caraian*, and the name of Karazan does not occur. But as we see that *Karajáng* was the real name of the province among the Mahomedans, it is more likely that Caraian was miswritten for Karazan than *vice versâ*. Klaproth indeed says that Yun-nan is still called *Karaian* by the people of central Asia, but gives no authority. The connection of this name with the *Karens* of Burma is, I suspect, as unfounded as M. Pauthier's derivation of the *Talaings* of Pegu from Tali-fu. According to Pauthier Yachi is Li-Kiang fu in the north-west of Yun-nan, and the other capital (Karaian or Karazan) is Tali-fu. But this makes Marco's *ponent* bear the interpretation of *south*, that being nearly the direction from one city to the other. In another passage of his great work (quoted by *Quatremère*, p. xc–xcv) Rashíd describes Karajáng as a country of vast extent, situated between Tibet, Tangut, the mountains of India, Mongolia, Cathay, and the country of the Zar dandán or Gilt-Teeth, of whom Polo also speaks. "The Chinese called it *Dai-lui* (Tali?), the Hindus *Kandar*, and the Persians *Kandahár*." [See *Marco Polo*, ii, pp. 72–73.]

[The actual Yun-nan fu was built in 1382 under the reign of Hung Wu, the first Ming Emperor; south-east of it was Shan Shan, capital of the Mong Dynasty (Nan Chao Kingdom), which was also the name of the capital of the Yun-nan province when it was called Chung K'ing in 1276 by the Mongols.]

[2] This is *King-chao*, now *Si-ngan fu* in Shensi, the Quengian and Kenjang of Polo and Kansan of Odoric (*supra*, II, p. 246). [*Marco Polo*, ii, pp. 27–29.] [Kenjang seems to be an alteration of King chao; when the Chinese knew Kenjang as the Mahomedan name of Si-ngan, they rewrote it Kin chang. Cf. Pelliot, *J. As.*, Mai–Juin 1912, p. 594.] According to Klaproth it was not Numughan, the fourth son of Kúblái, but Mangala, his third son, who ruled in Kenchangfu, and Ananda was the son of the latter. He succeeded his father Mangala in 1280, and was put to death in 1308, having claimed the throne on the death of Timúr Khan. Marco himself mentions Mangala as ruling in Kenchangfu as king. This is strictly correct, for he had the Chinese title of *Wang* or king.

[Mangala was invested in 1272 with the title of King of Ngan-si, a territory which included King chao fu (modern Si-ngan-fu). See *Marco Polo*, ii, p. 31, n. 4.]

Achiki) dwells there. The Amír Khwaja called Yasam is chief there[1].

[1] I suspect the true reading here should be *Kamchú*, the city of Kan chau in the province of Kan suh, which Marco describes under the name of Canpicion, "chief and capital of the whole province of Tangut."

The correct division of the empire into the Twelve Sing is thus given by Pauthier and Klaproth from the Annals of the Yuen dynasty: I. The Central Province, embracing the modern Shan tung, Shan si, Pe Chihli, Ho nan north of the Hwang Ho, and part of Mongolia; capital TATU or Peking. II. Province of the Northern Mountains; cap. Ho lin or KARAKORUM. III. LIAO YANG, embracing the modern Liao tung, and a good deal more to the north. Cap. of the same name. IV. HO NAN, comprising the remainder of the modern province, with that part of Kiang nan which is north of the Kiang, and the greater part of Hu kwang north of the Kiang. Cap., P'ien liang, now K'AI FUNG FU. V. SHEN SI, comprising the modern province with the greater part of Kan suh to the right of the Hwang-ho, and part of the Ordo territory. The capital was King-chao, now SI NGAN FU. VI. SZE CH'WAN, embraced also parts of Hu kwang and Kwei chau. Cap., CH'ENG TU. VII. KAN SUH, cap., KAN CHAU. VIII. YUN NAN, the modern province with part of Kwei chau, and parts of Tibet and Burma. Cap., Ch'ung k'ing, *hod.*, YUN NAN FU. IX. KIANG CHE, embracing Che kiang, Kiang nan south of the Kiang, and the eastern part of Kiang si. Cap., HANG CHAU FU, called also KING-SZE, or Capital. X. KIANG SI, cap. Lung hing, now NAN CH'ANG FU. XI. HU KWANG, cap., WU CH'ANG (Klaproth says *Chang sha fu*). XII. CHENG-TUNG, which comprised the kingdom of Corea. A table will better show the discrepancies between Rashíd and the Chinese official statements.

THE XII SING OF THE YUEN EMPIRE.

From Pauthier.	*From Rashíd.*
1. Central Province (Tatu)	1. Khanbaliq or Daïdu
2. Northern Mountains (Mongolia)	
3. Liao yang (including Manchuria)	2. Churché and Solánka, i.e. [Manchuria
4. Ho nan	4. Nanking
5. Shen si	11. Kenjangfu
6. Sze ch'wan	8. Lukinfu?
7. Kan suh	12. Kamchu
8. Yun nan	10. Karajang
9. Kiang che	6. Khingsai
10. Kiang si (cap., Lung hing) } 11. Hu kwang }	9. Chinkalan (Canton) or Lumkali
12. Cheng tung (Corea)	3. Kaoli (Corea)
	7. Fuchu
	5. Sukchu

[The twelve *Sheng* or provinces of China were then: Cheng Tung, Liao Yang, Chung Shu, Shen Si, Ling Pe (Karakorum), Kan Suh, Sze ch'wan, Ho Nan Kiang Pe, Kiang Ché, Kiang Si, Hu Kwang and Yun Nan. See long note in *Marco Polo*, i, pp. 432–433.]

Fu kien or Fu chau was, previous to 1285, and again at a later period, a separate province, which accounts for Rashíd's making it one of the

As all these cities are widely apart from one another, there is in each a prince of the blood or other prince of eminent rank, who commands the troops and governs the people, administers public affairs and maintains the laws and regulations. The Sing of each kingdom or province is established in the chief city, and every Sing is like a little town in itself, so numerous are the buildings for the use of the various public officers, and for the multitude of attendants and slaves attached to the establishment to do petty duties under the chiefs of the subordinate offices. It is the custom in that country to remove delinquents and criminals from their houses, families and property of every description, and to employ them in carrying loads, drawing carts, or moving stones for building, according to the sentence passed upon each.

The gentlemen attached to the princes and other persons of respectability, receive each the honours which are assigned to their respective ranks, and of the ranks there are several degrees.

As for the history of former emperors since time immemorial we propose to relate it specially in the Appendix to this work, for in this place we must be brief[1].

Towards the south-east everything is subject to the Kaan except an isle of the ocean called CHIPANGU[2], which is not far from the coast of Churché and Kaoli. The people of that country are of short stature, with great bellies and heads sunk between their shoulders. Straight eastward all

Twelve Sing. Kiang Si also comprised Canton prior to 1293. His making Su chau on the desert frontier a separate province is a mistake altogether; [it was included in Kan Suh].

[The Hu kwang province, with Wu ch'ang as a capital, comprised southern Hu Pe, the whole of Hu Nan and of Kwang si and western Kwang tung, including the island of Hai Nan.]

[1] All that follows is from D'Ohsson only.

[2] The *Chipangu*, *Cipangu*, *Zipangu* of Polo, JAPAN, from the Chinese name *Jih-pên-kwé* ("kingdom of the Rising Sun," *Marco Polo*, ii, p. 256 *n.*).

is subject to him that lies between the sea-coast and the frontier of the KIRGHIZ[1].

To the south-west of Manzi, on the coast between the country of Kowelaki and Zaitún, there is a thick forest, where the son of the Emperor of Manzi has taken refuge, but he is without resources and lives in indigence[2].

To the west is the country of KAFCHÉ-KUÉ[3]. It is difficult of access, and is bounded by Karajang, by a part of India, and by the sea. It has a sovereign of its own, and includes in its territory the two cities of Lujak (?) and Jessam (?). Tugan, who commands at KWE LIN FU and is in occupation of Manzi, is also charged to watch the proceedings of these hostile people. He made an expedition into their country and got possession of the cities on the coast, but after his rule had lasted a week the forces began to come forth of a sudden, as it were from the sea, from the forests, from the mountains, and fell upon the soldiers of

[1] There seems to be here some indication of an idea of the coast of China and Eastern Asia as running *west and east* rather than north and south, and I think there are traces of the same both in Polo and Odoric. The latter always goes *versus Orientem* till he reaches Cambalec.

[2] I suspect *Kowelaki* here is the same name that was previously read *Lumkali* as a synonyme of the Sin-kalan or Canton province. The two last representatives of the Sung dynasty did take refuge on the shores of that province, and there the last survivor perished in 1279. This seems to show that Rashíd sometimes wrote from old information.

[3] D'Ohsson suggests that this should be read *Kanchekué*, and that it is the Caugigu of Marco. But the mention of the sea-coast seems fatal to this, as Polo says specifically that Caugigu was far from the sea. Indeed there can be no question that *Kafchekuo* is Lower Tung king, *Kiao-chi-kwo* of the Chinese. D'Ohsson's own History contains an account of *three* expeditions into Tung king by Tugan (a younger son of Kúblái), in 1285, 1287 and 1288. The last ended very disastrously, the king of Tung king following his retreat into *Kwang si* and beating him there. Tugan was disgraced and forbidden the court (ii, 445, 449). Kwe lin fu would therefore appear to be the present capital of Kwang si so-called, and is perhaps the proper reading for the *Lukinfu* of p. 126, though there incorrectly placed. [See *Marco Polo*, ii, p. 131 *n.*]

The two names of cities are read by Quatremère *Luchac* and *Hasam* (*Rashid*, p. xcv); he takes them for Hainan (reading *Hainam*) and Lui chau in the peninsula opposite that island.

Tugan, who were engaged in plundering. Tugan made his escape, and he still resides at Kwe lin fu.

To the north-west is the frontier of TIBET and of the GOLDEN-TEETH[1]. Here there are no enemies excepting

[1] "*Zar-dandán*" (Pers.), the name used *literatim* by Polo for this people, and a translation of the term *Kin-chi* by which they were known to the Chinese. Polo [see long note, ii, pp. 84 seq.] places them five days *ponent* or west of the city of Caraian (or *Carazan* of some copies), which Pauthier identifies with Tali-fu. He ascribes to them the eccentric custom, found among various wild races ancient and modern, which sends the *husband* to keep his bed for a season when the wife has given birth to a child, and fixes their chief city at *Vociam* (Yung-ch'ang). [*Couvade*; cf. *Polo*, ii, p. 91.] Passages nearly but not quite identical with one another, which Quatremère has quoted from the history of *Benaketi* and from another part of the *Jamí'-ut-Tawáríkh* of *Rashíd*, speak of this people. "To the south-west of Cathay," they say in substance, "lies *Kara-Jang*, an extensive country lying between Tibet, Tangut, the mountains of India, Mongolia, Cathay, and the *Country of the Gold Teeth*. The Indians call it *Kandar*, and we (Persians, etc.) *Kandahar*, the Chinese *Dailiu* (Tali?). The king is called *Mahara* or Great Prince; the capital *Yachi* (*Jaci* of Polo). Among its people part are black (whence *Kara-Jang* or Black Jang), part white, called *Chaghan-Jang* or White Jang"...It is not improbable that the Kara-Jang and Chaghan-Jang (compare with Karazan of Polo) represent Black *Sháns* and White *Sháns*, and that the colours refer not to complexion but to dress. We always knew the Shans at Amarapura by their coats of *black calico*. "North-west of China is the frontier of Tibet and of the *Gold-Teeth*, who lie between Tibet and Kara-Jang. These people cover their teeth with a gold case which they take off when they eat." There is another passage of Rashíd among Elliot's extracts in which this people is mentioned, a passage which would be most interesting if the names were not so mangled. Speaking of Maabar, the historian says that two ways to China diverge thence. The first is by *Sarandíp* (Ceylon), *Lámúri*, the country of *Sumatra*, and *Darband Niás*, a dependency of Java, *Champa* and *Haitam* (qu. Hainan?), subject to the Kaan, and so to *Mahachín* (Canton), *Zaitún* and *Khinsá*. "With respect to the other road which leads from Maabar by way of Cathay, it commences at the city of *Cabal* (read *Kail*), then proceeds to the city of *Gosjú* and *Sabjú*, dependencies of Cabal, then to *Tamlifatan*, then *Karoramawár*, then to *Hawaráwún*, then to *Dakli*, then to *Bijalár*, which from of old is subject to Dehli; and at this time one of the cousins of the sultan of Dehli has conquered it and established himself, having revolted against the sultan. His army consists of Turks. Beyond that is the country of *Katban*, then *Úman*, then ZARDANDAN, so called because the people have gold in their teeth. They puncture their hands and colour them with indigo. They eradicate their beards so that they have not a sign of hair on their faces. They are all subject to the Kaan. Thence you arrive at the borders of *Tibet*, where they eat raw meat and worship images, and have no shame respecting their wives (see *Polo*, i, 44, 45). The air is so impure that if they ate their dinner after noon they would all die.

on a point occupied by Kutlugh Khwaja and his army. However, the enemy is shut off from the empire in this quarter by high mountains which he cannot penetrate. Nevertheless some troops have been posted to watch this frontier.

To the north-north-west a desert of forty days' extent divides the states of Kúblái from those of Kaidu and Dua[1]. This frontier extends thirty days from east to west. From point to point are posted bodies of troops under the orders of princes of the blood or other generals, and they often come to blows with the troops of Kaidu. Five of these corps are cantoned on the verge of the Desert; a sixth in the territory of Tangut, near *Chághán Naúr* (White Lake); a seventh in the vicinity of Karakhoja, a city of the Uighúrs[2],

They boil tea and eat winnowed barley." It is clear enough that the second part of this passage indicates a route to China from Coromandel by Bengal and the Indo-Chinese countries, but the names have been desperately corrupted. Tamlifatan looks very like a misreading of *Bimlifatan*, the port of *Bimlipatam*, on the coast of the N. Circars; and *Bijalár* is certainly *Bengala*, quasi-independent under Nasir-uddín, son of the Emperor Balban, and his family. *Katban* may just possibly have been a mispronunciation of *Habang*, i.e. Silhet (see Ibn Batuta, *infra*); whilst *Uman* is probably the Chinese *U-man* or *Ho-man*, the name applied to one of the wild tribes of the Upper Irawadi region. Gosju and Sabju look like Chinese names, so entirely out of place that I suspect interpolation by someone misunderstanding the route; the remaining names I have tried in vain to solve in any consistent manner.

Pauthier quotes passages from the Chinese Annals showing that the office of "Direction of Frontier Protection" and the like for the Gold-Teeth territory was established in Kúblái's reign, at or near Tali. But it seems to me that in his map he places this people too far to the south, and that it is pretty clear from all the passages just quoted, that they are to be placed at least as high as lat. 24°–25°, corresponding in position generally to the existing *Singphos*. (*Quatremère's Rashid*, pp. lxxxvi–xcvi; *Elliot*, p. 46; *Pauthier's Polo*, pp. 391–2, 397 *seq.*)

[1] See *ante*, p. 43. For a time at least there were two Mongol dynasties in Central Asia, between the frontier of the Great Khan and the Caspian. Kaidu, great grandson of Chinghiz through his second son and successor Okkodai, and who disputed the suzerainty with Kúblái through life, represented one of these, whilst that of Chagatai was the other. See a note appended to Ibn Batuta (*infra*) "On the History of the Khans of Chagatai."

[2] There are at least two lakes in Mongolia called by the name of Chaghan-Nor; one the *Cyagannor* or *Cianganor* of Polo where

which lies between the two states and maintains neutrality. This frontier ends at the mountains of Tibet. The great Desert cannot be crossed in summer, because of the want of water; in winter they have only snow-water to drink.

Kúblái had a palace, not far from Shang tu (*supra*, II, p. 227); the other lying north-east of Kamul, about lat. 45° 45′ and east long. 96°, which appears to be that here intended, as the first is far from Tangut. Karakhoja is still a town of Eastern or Chinese Turkestan, the position of which is indicated by Timkowski as south of Turfan, and one of the districts of that province (i, 386; see also *Ritter*, vii, 432, 435). It seems to have continued to be the frontier of the Chinese rule a century later under the Ming; for Shah Rukh's ambassadors, on their arrival at Karakhoja, or a short distance east of it, met the first Chinese officials, who took down a list of the party (*Not. et Extr.*, xiv, pt. I, 389). In another passage of Rashíd, quoted by Quatremère, he says: "When you descend below the Chaghan Naur, you are near the city of Karakhoja in the Uighúr country, where they have good wine" (*Ib.* p. 235).

["The Chinese name of Karakhodjo in the Mongol period was *Huo chou* (Fire City). Sometimes the first sound is also represented by another homophonous character; sometimes the name is also written *Ho chou.* In the *Si yu ki* and also in the *Si yu lu*, Ho chou is stated to lie 500 *li* south of Bishbalik (beyond the T'ien shan), and is identified in the latter narrative with Kao ch'ang of the T'ang period. In the *Yuan shi* the same place is noticed several times under its different names. In the Annals, *s.a.* 1286, it is recorded that Kubilai ordered cattle and corn to be given to the people of *Ho-la-huo-djo* and *Ho-mi-li* (Hami), who suffered from dearth. Karakhodjo is further mentioned, chap. cxxviii, in the biography of *A-shu*, who was a grandson of the famous Subutai. A-shu had been sent in 1286 against a rebellious prince, and died in *Ha-la-ho-djou*. The city of Karakhodjo still exists, 40 versts south-east of Turfan, according to Regel, who visited this place in 1879. He writes the name *Kara-gudsha*." (Bretschneider, *Mediæval Researches*, ii, p. 31.) Karakhodja, east of Turfan, was the anterior court of Kao ch'ang in the tenth century. Sir Aurel Stein writes: "I visited the remarkable ruins of the Turfan capital of Uigur times at Karakhodja, some seven miles to the west of Toyuk. Here a cluster of populous villages surrounds, and is partly built into, the massive clay walls which enclose nearly a square mile full of imposed ruined structures now scattered amidst cultivation...the ruined town had proved a very rich mine." (*Ruins of Desert Cathay*, ii, 1912, pp. 359–360.) During the winter of 1902–1903, Grünwedel explored the ruins of Idiqut Shahri, near Kara Khodja.—Karâ-Khoja was to the east of Turfan; it was the capital of the Uighúr kingdom of Kao ch'ang subjugated by the T'ang in 640; it was visited in 981 by the Chinese Ambassador Wang Yen-te; these Uighúrs are called by the Leao Uighúrs of Huo chau. The prince of the Uighúrs of Karâ-Khoja had the title of *Yi-tu-hu*; hence the title of *Ydyqut* and *Ydyqut Shahri* the "town of the Ydyqut" for the old Karâ Khoja; the present Karâ Khoja took the place of the old city in the 14th century.—Pelliot, *Kao-tch'ang*, *J. As.*, Mai—Juin 1912.]

IV

PEGOLOTTI'S NOTICES OF THE LAND ROUTE TO CATHAY

IV

NOTICES OF THE LAND ROUTE TO CATHAY AND OF ASIATIC TRADE IN THE FIRST HALF OF THE FOURTEENTH CENTURY

BY FRANCIS BALDUCCI PEGOLOTTI

INTRODUCTORY NOTICES

THE original of the curious work from which the extracts in the following pages are derived, was first published as an appendix to an anonymous book called "*A Treatise on the* Decima *and the various other burdens imposed on the community of Florence ; also on the currency and commerce of the Florentines up to the Sixteenth Century.* (In four vols., 4to.) Lisbon and Lucca, 1765–66." (*Della Decima*, etc.[1]) The imprint is fictitious, as the work was really published at Florence, and the author was Gian Francesco Pagnini del Ventura of Volterra[2].

[1] Della//Decima//e di varie gravezze//imposte dal Comune//di Firenze//Della Moneta//e//della Mercatura//de' Fiorentini//fino al Secolo XVI.//...//Lisbona, MDCCLXV.//&//Lucca, 4 vol. 4to, 1765–1766, pp. viii–268–xii, tables; vi–355; xxiv–380; xxxvj+1 f. n. ch. +pp. 284.

[2] *Canonico Moreni, Bibliografia Storico-Ragionata della Toscana*, ii, pp. 144–5. Pagnini was born at Volterra in 1715, and studied law at Rome. He filled a succession of considerable offices connected with Finance and Agriculture under the Tuscan Government [and among these offices that of *Cancellière della Decima*], and died in 1789. There is a monument and bust erected by his friends in the cloister of S. Annunziata and S. Pier Maggiore at Florence. Besides the work named above he published in cooperation with Angelo Tavanti (1751) a translation of Locke upon Interest and the Value of Money, with a dissertation of his own on the True Price of Things, on Money, and on the commerce of the Romans. He also published

The work of Pegolotti occupies the whole of the third volume. It was taken by Pagnini from a MS., apparently unique, in the Riccardian Library at Florence, called by the author (*Libro di Divisamenti di Paesi*, etc.[1]) "*The Book of the Descriptions of Countries*[2]," etc., though Pagnini gave it the more descriptive title of *Pratica della Mercatura*[3]. Baldelli Boni, writing some forty years ago, says that the manuscript could no longer be found in the Riccardiana. However it is to be found there now and I have examined it. It is a handsome paper folio, purporting to have been transcribed by the hand of Filippo di Nicolaio di Frescobaldi at Florence in the year 1471, and bears the No. 2441 in the collection.

Nothing is known of the author, Francesco Balducci Pegolotti, except what is gathered from his own book. From it we learn that he was a factor in the service of the Company of the Bardi of Florence. In various incidental statements also he lets us know that he was at Antwerp in their service from 1315 (and probably earlier) to 1317, when he was transferred to London[4]; and that he was

letters on agricultural subjects, and was the editor of *Applausi Poetici per la gloriosa Esaltazione all' Augusto Trono Imperiale di Francesco III, Granduca di Toscana*, Firenze, 1745. (See *Scritt. Class. Ital. di Economia Politica, Pte. Moderna*, tom. II; and *Moreni*, u.s.)

[1] ["Questo Libro è chiamato Libro de divisamenti di paesi, e di misure di mercatanzie"... Pref.]

[2] I imagine this to be the proper translation of *Divisamenti* here, as Marco Polo's book is in some copies termed "*Divisement des Diversités*," etc. (*Pauthier*, p. 33.)

[3] [Della//Decima//e delle altre gravezze &c.//Tomo terzo//contenente la Pratica//della Mercatura//scritta da//Francesco Balducci Pegolotti//E copiata da un Codice manoscritto esistente in Firenze//nella Biblioteca Riccardiana.//— Lisbona, e Lucca//—MDCCLXVI.//E si vende da Giuseppe Bouchard Librajo Francese in Firenze.

On the last page 380, at foot: "Per mano di me Filippo di Niccolajo Frescobaldi in Firenze questo di XVIIII. di Marzo MCCCCLXXI."

Count of Mas Latrie has shown the numerous mistakes of Pagnini in editing the manuscript, in his paper: "Le Manuscrit de la *Prattica della Mercatura* de B. Pegolotti," inserted at pp. 181–186 of *Notices et Documents publiés pour la Société de l'Hist. de France à l'occasion du Cinquantième Anniversaire de sa fondation*, 1884, 8vo.]

[4] *Pegolotti*, p. 257.

employed in Cyprus from May 1324 to August 1327, for at those and intermediate dates he made sundry applications to the King of Cyprus for the reduction of duties payable by his countrymen, who had previously been liable to heavier duties than the Pisans, and had consequently been obliged to employ their agency. Balducci, indignant at the conduct of the Pisans, who treated the Florentines, he says, "like Jews or slaves of theirs," made these successful efforts to get rid of this obligation[1].

In 1335 the author was still at Cyprus, or had returned thither, and obtained in that year from the King of Lesser Armenia a grant of privileges to the company which he served for their trade at Aiazzo or Aias, the port of that kingdom on the Gulf of Scanderoon[2].

[1] P. 71.

[2] P. 45. Aiazzo, or Aias, the ancient Ægæ, opposite Issus, is mentioned several times by Marco Polo as *Laias*. [See *Marco Polo*, i, p. 17 *n.* and plan, p. 41.] Whilst Persia was in the hands of the Mongols a great part of the Indian trade came by Baghdad to Tabriz, and thence by the route detailed in Pegolotti's chapter vi to Aiazzo [which was the chief port of Cilician Armenia, on the Gulf of Scanderoon] for shipment. The port was in the hands of the Christian princes called the Kings of Little Armenia, whose dynasty was founded in the mountains of Cilicia in the year 1080, by Rupen, a kinsman of the last King of Armenia Proper of the race of the Bagratidæ. Rupen's ninth successor, Leon II, got the title of king from Pope Celestine III and the Emperor Henry VI in the end of the twelfth century, and the line continued till 1342. The kingdom endured thirty-three years longer under kings of the house of Lusignan. In the time of Haiton or Hethum I [1224], when it was perhaps most flourishing, it embraced all Cilicia, with many cities of Syria, Cappadocia, and Isauria. The institutions of this country were a curious compound, uniting an Armenian church and nationality with Greek legislation and the feudal institutions and social gradations of the Franks. The capital was at *Sis* [or Sîsîyah], where there are still an Armenian population and an Armenian monastery and patriarch. (See papers by Dulaurier in *Jour. As.*, sér. v, tom. xvii and xviii; *Ib.*, v, 262; D'Ohsson, ii, 310; St. Martin, *Mém. sur l'Arménie*, vol. i.)

[Sis is on the site of the Roman city of Flaviopolis; the population includes 2500 Armenians, 700 Mohamedans, and 300 inhabitants belonging to various cults. Cf. Vital Cuinet, *Turquie d'Asie*, Vilayet d'Adana, ii, p. 92; the monastery built on the ruins of the palace of the "Takavors" (kings) is to-day inhabited by the *Catholicos*, great Armenian Patriarch of Cilicia.]

The Bardi[1] failed in 1339, owing to their unprofitable dealings with the King of England (Edward III). They and the Company of the Peruzzi were the "king's merchants," or as we should now say, bankers and agents, receiving all his rents and incomings in wool and the like, whilst meeting all his demands for cash and stores. But these last so much exceeded the receipts on his account that there was a balance due from him of 180,000 marks sterling to the Bardi, and 135,000 marks to the Peruzzi, each mark being equal to four and a half gold florins, so that the bad debt amounted on the whole to 1,365,000 florins, "che valeano un reame," as the Florentine chronicler says. Much of the money advanced consisted of the deposits of citizens and foreigners (including English), and the stoppage of payment was a great blow to Florentine commerce and to credit generally. The Bardi however seem to have got on their legs again sufficiently to fail a second time in 1345, for the sum of 550,000 florins[2]. Whether they recovered from this second failure I do not know, but other circumstances referred to by the author of the *Decima* fix the date of Pegolotti's book to about 1340. It could not of course have been written earlier than the last year of residence in Cyprus to which he makes the reference quoted above, and it must have been written before the death of King Robert of Naples, of the house of Anjou, whom he speaks of in one passage as still reigning[3]. That event occurred in 1343.

Pegolotti's Handbook, for it is just such, is purely mercantile in its bearings, and even in those parts which

[1] This house gave a husband to Dante's Beatrice; and a heroine to George Eliot in *Romola*!

[2] *Della Decima*; Giov. Villani, *Istoria Fiorentina*, bk. xi, ch. 87. The English gold florin was coined in 1343 to weigh 2 Florentine florins, and to be worth 6*s*. (See Akermann's *Num. Manual*, p. 267.) Hence 4½ Fl. florins = 13*s*. 6*d*., or a little over a mark. But 13*s*. 6*d*. represented three times as much silver as now.

[3] "*Questo Re Uberto*," p. 186.

are not mere lists or figured statements is written in the dryest and most inartificial style, if style it can be called. Devoting successive chapters to the various ports and seats of traffic of his time, and proceeding from the Asiatic coasts of the Mediterranean westward, he details the nature of the exports and imports, the duties and exactions, the customs of business appropriate to each locality, as well as the value of the moneys, weights and measures of each country in relation to those of the places with which they chiefly had to deal. Rude essays on various practical matters are interspersed and appended.

The book might have slept as undisturbed under the unattractive title of Pagnini's quartos, as it had done for centuries in manuscript on the shelves of the Florentine libraries, had not the Germans Forster and Sprengel got scent of it and made it the subject of some comment in their geographical works[1].

Their comments refer to the first two chapters of Pegolotti, the most interesting of the whole, and which I shall give unabridged. I shall also give one or two chapters that follow, having more or less bearing on our subject, and a few additional extracts where the matter seems of sufficient interest.

The notices of Sprengel seem to have furnished the source from which nearly all the later writers who have touched on Pegolotti have derived their information, as is shown by their copying an error of the press which makes him in Sprengel's book *Pegoletti*. Even Humboldt, Rémusat, and Ritter do this, and the latter assumes besides that Pegolotti had himself made the journey to Cathay, which

[1] See Forster, *Hist. des Découvertes et des Voyages dans le Nord* (Fr. Trans.), Paris, 1788, pp. 242 *et seq.*; and *Geschichte der Wichtigsten Geog. Entdeckungen*, etc., von *M. C. Sprengel* (2nd ed.), Halle, 1792. I suppose that Sprengel's first edition preceded Forster, as the former says (p. 253) that no one had yet made use of Pegolotti in the history of the Chinese trade. The original of these two chapters is given in Appendix, p. 172.

he describes. For this assumption there is not the slightest ground[1]. It is evident indeed from the terms of the account that the road to Cathay was not unfrequently travelled by European merchants in his day, and from some of these Pegolotti had obtained the notes which he communicates, as he himself in one passage distinctly intimates[2].

The fourth volume also of Pagnini's work is occupied by a later book of character similar to that of Pegolotti's, written in 1440 by Giovanni di Antonio da Uzzano, under the name of *Libro di Gabelli e Pesi e Misure di più e diversi Luoghi*, etc.[3]. At that date direct intercourse with Eastern Asia had long been interrupted, and the book has nothing of interest to extract for this collection. It contains, however, among other matters, some curious lists of the duties on a vast variety of wares at the different Italian marts, and a treatise containing sailing directions for the Mediterranean.

[1] See *Erdkunde*, ii, 404, and posthumous *Lectures on the Hist. of Geography*, Berlin, 1861, p. 220. These errors are probably derived from Malte Brun (see *D'Avezac*, p. 423). Even the *Biographie Universelle* speaks positively of Pegolotti's having visited all the places mentioned by him on the route to Cathay, and adds: "Independent of the route which he followed in going to China, Pegolotti describes also that of the caravans which without doubt he followed in returning from the Indies to the Mediterranean." This is grievous inaccuracy. Pegolotti never was in China, and describes no such return route as is here indicated. The nearest approach to it is the list of tolls between Aiazzo and Tabriz in his chapter vi.

[2] "*Secondo che si conta per gli mercatanti che l' hanno usato*," is his expression with regard to the road in question.

[3] [Della//Decima//e delle altre gravezze &c.//Tomo quarto//contenente la Pratica//della Mercatura//scritta da//Giovanni di Antonio da Uzzano//Nel 1442.//—Lisbona, e Lucca//—MDCCLXVI.//E si vende da Giuseppe Bouchard Librajo Francese in Firenze.

P. 1: "Comincia il Libro di Gabelle, e pesi, e misure di più, e diversi luoghi; e come pesi, e misure tornano di un luogo ad un' altro."

P. 284, at foot: "Finito per infino quì per me Giovanni di Bernardo d' Antonio da Uzzano nel 1440 a dì 8 di Novembre, che Iddio ci dia grazia farne qualche frutto, di che pel cattivo temporale ne dubito, e per più altri rispetti."]

Pegolotti's book begins as follows:

IN THE NAME OF THE LORD, AMEN!

THIS book is called the Book of Descriptions of Countries and of measures employed in business, and of other things needful to be known by merchants of different parts of the world, and by all who have to do with merchandize and exchanges; showing also what relation the merchandize of one country or of one city bears to that of others; and how one kind of goods is better than another kind; and where the various wares come from, and how they may be kept as long as possible.

The book was compiled by Francis Balducci Pegolotti of Florence, who was with the Company of the Bardi of Florence, and during the time that he was in the service of the said Company, for the good and honour and prosperity of the said Company, and for his own, and for that of whosoever shall read or transcribe the said book. And this copy has been made from the book of Agnolo di Lotti of Antella, and the said book was transcribed from the original book of the said Francesco Balducci.

This is followed by several pages of [the contents and] explanations of abbreviations and technicalities of different countries, which are used in the book. Thus:

Tamunga in Tauris[1], and throughout Persia, at Trebizond, at Tana, at Caffa, and throughout all the cities of the

[1] *Tunizi* is printed in the *Decima*, but unquestionably it should be *Torizi*. *Tamungha* no doubt stands for *Tamgha*, a name which was applied to all customs and transit duties under the Mongol Khans of Persia. (See *D'Ohsson*, iv, 373, 386.) The word meant *a seal*, and going still further back was the term applied to the distinguishing brands of cattle among the Mongols. (V. Hammer, *Gold. Horde*, 220.) When Sultan Baber was engaged in a holy war with the Rajput Rana Sanga, he made one of his abjurations of wine, and vowed that he would renounce the *Tamgha* if victorious. Accordingly he published a firman, solemnly announcing his repentance, and declaring that in no city or town, on no road or street or passage should the *Tamgha* be received or levied. The translators render it *stamp-tax*, but the passages in D'Ohsson, as well as Baber's words, seem to show that it was a transit duty. (*Baber*, p. 356.)

Tartars: *Pesadone* in Armenia[1]; *Doana*[2], in all the cities of the Saracens, in Sicily, in Naples, and throughout the kingdom of Apulia; *Piazza, Fondaco*[3], *Bindanajo*, also throughout all Sicily and the kingdom of Apulia; *Comerchio* in all the cities of the Greeks, and in Cyprus[4]; *Dazio* at Venice; *Gabella* throughout Tuscany; *Spedicamento* and *Pedaggio* at Genoa: *Chiaveria*[5] throughout Provence; *Lelda*[6], in part of Provence and in France; *Malatolto*[7], *Pedaggio*,

[1] Among documents of the kingdom of Lesser Armenia quoted in Dulaurier's papers referred to above, we find *Pasidum* and *Pasidonum*, with the meaning of *Customs*, custom-house, and *Capitaneus Pasidoneus de Ayacio*, as the appellation of the chief of the custom-house in that port. (*J. As.*, sér. v, tom. xviii, 326, 327.) *Pasidonum* is a Latinization of the Armenian *Pâjdûn*, from *pâj*, toll or customs, a word still existing in that language. (St. Martin, in *Notices et Extraits*, xi, 115, 117.)

[2] *Doana*, or in modern Italian *Dogana*, is believed to be from the Arabic *Dewân*, "council, council-hall, tribunal." Giov. da Uzzano spells it Dovana, which seems somewhat to confirm this derivation. (*Della Dec.*, iv, 119.)

["Neque inferior videtur eorum opinio, qui ab Arabico *Divan* seu *Diwan* Praetorium, hocque ab Hebraeo *Doun*, Judicavit, derivant, quod in *Doana* soleat de mercimoniis judicari." Ducange.—On the Arabic etymology of the word see Marcel Devic, *Dict.*, p. 32.]

[3] Some of these seem to be names of particular payments, not of *duties* or *customs* in general: *piazza*, probably a market tax; *fondaco*, payment for warehousing, which he elsewhere calls *fondacaggio*. *Alfandega*, however, is custom-house in Portuguese.

[4] Κομμέρκιον and κουμέρκιον, *Tributum, Vectigal pro mercimoniis exsolvi solitum* will be found in Ducange. (*Gloss. Græcitatis*, etc.) From the Greeks the word passed to the Turks and Arabs, see in *Freytag's Lexicon* قمرق. We also find in the Genoese version of a treaty with the Tartars of Gazaria, A.D. 1380, *Comerho* and *Comerha* for customs and custom-house. (*Not. et Ext.*, xi, 54, 57.)

[5] Some of these are probably slang. *Chiaveria*, key-money?

[6] Perhaps should be *Leuda*, which we find mentioned by Giovanni da Uzzano (p. 162) as the name of a tax at Barcelona paid by buyers or sellers not being freemen of the city. *Leuda, Lesda*, or *Ledda*, according to Ducange, is any duty, especially one paid on merchandize.

[7] *Malatolta*, according to the same authority, is an arbitrary exaction forcibly taken under the name of duty or customs. ["Maltota, Tributum quodvis, quaelibet exactio." Ducange.] He quotes [s.v. *Tolta*] among other examples a charter of Philip the Fair to the people of Bordeaux, which speaks of "*Assisiam seu coustumam, quæ in illo loco et locis circumvicinis* Malatolta *vulgariter nuncupatur*"; and one also of Peter of Castille which introduces the terms in the text preceding and following: "*Sint immunes ab omni* pedagio, leudâ, costumâ, maletotâ, *seu aliis quibusvis impositionibus*." The

and *Bara*[1] throughout all France; *Toloneo*[2] throughout Flanders; *Foveo* (?) throughout Brabant; *Costuma* throughout the Island of England; *Fedo*[3] at Tunis in Barbary; *Munda* in Friuli; *Mangona* and *Talaoch* in Spain[4];

All these names mean *duties* which have to be paid for goods and wares, and other things, imported to or exported from, or passed through the countries and places detailed in this paragraph.

Mercato in Tuscan; and *Piazza*[5] in several tongues; *Bazarra* and *Raba* in Genoese[6]; *Fondaco* in several languages; *Foda* in Cyprus; *Alla*[7] in Flemish; *Sugo* in Sara-

original for taxes and customs at p. 92 *supra* is *truuaiges et malestoultes.* The term shows just the same state of feeling that led the people in the North-West Provinces of India to apply to the tolls that used to be levied on the Grand Trunk Road, the terms *Lút* (plunder) and *Zulm* (oppression).

[1] Tolls were called *Barræ*, especially such as were levied at the gates and *barriers* of towns (*Ducange*).

[2] "Telon, Teloneum, *Toloneum*, Toll, Tolnetum, etc., *Tributum* de mercibus *marinis circa littus acceptum*" (*Ducange*). Our English word *Toll.*

[3] *Arab.* "*fadá*, Res quâ aliquis redimitur et liberatur" (Freytag). In a treaty between the Genoese and the Soldan of Babylon (Egypt) in 1290, we find the following: "*Item quod Jannenses non compellantur nec compelli debeant ad solvendum...nec* feda *nec aliquid aliud*," etc. (*Notices et Extraits*, xi, 39.) The word may have had a specific application in the custom-houses which has escaped the lexicographers.

[4] On *Talaoch* my friend Mr. Badger says: "This is probably from the Arabic اطلاق (*Itláq*), meaning *releasing*, setting free. It might have been applied to the stamp or certificate by which goods were declared to be free after payment of customs. I am not aware that the word is used in that sense now." This suggestion is strengthened by the analogous use of *Fadá* in the preceding note, and by the fact that Pegolotti in a later passage calls it *Intalacca*, an export duty levied in the ports of Morocco. By *Spain* he means the Moorish ports on both sides of the strait, as his details show (pp. 278 *seqq.*).

[5] *Piazza* is commonly used for *mercato* in Palermo, where this note is written.

[6] *Raba* must be the Arabic Rahbah "Amplum spatium loci; area ampla" (Freytag). It is used by Ibn Jubair in his description of Palermo for "an esplanade." (*Journ. Asiat.*, Jan. 1846, p. 222.)

[7] The French *Halle.*

cenesque[1]; *Fiera* in Tuscan and several other tongues; *Panichiero* in Greek[2];

All signify the place where goods are sold in cities, and where in towns and villages all manner of victuals and necessaries for the life of man are brought for sale, with corn and cattle which are brought there continually at certain fixed times of the week, or month, or year.

These may suffice as specimens.

Then some doggerel verses to the following purport introduce the body of the work.

"Honesty is always best
And to look before ye leap:
Do ever what thou promisest;
And, hard though it may be, still keep
Fair chastity. Let reason tell
Cheap to buy and dear to sell,
But have a civil tongue as well.
Frequent the church's rites, and spare
To Him who sends thy gains a share.
So shalt thou prosper, standing by one price,
And shunning pest-like usury and dice.
Take aye good heed to govern well thy pen,
And blunder not in black and white! AMEN!"

CHAPTER I.

Information regarding the journey to Cathay, for such as will go by Tana and come back with goods.

IN the first place, from TANA to GINTARCHAN[3] may be twenty-five days with an ox-waggon, and from ten to twelve days with a horse-waggon. On the road you will find

[1] *Arab. Súq.*

[2] This must be *πανηγύριον*, which has the meaning of a fair or market in Byzantine Greek (*Ducange*).

[3] [Ibn Batuta, marching on the frozen river, reached Sarai in three days from Astrakhan. Cf. *Marco Polo*, i, p. 6 *n.*] *Gintarchan*, or as below less incorrectly *Gittarchan*, is Astrakhan, though according to Sprengel the old city destroyed by Timúr in 1395 was further from the Caspian than the present one. It is mentioned by Rubruquis in the preceding century as Summerkeur or Summerkent, most probably a clerical error for *Sittarkent*, and in this century it was the seat of a

plenty of *Moccols*, that is to say, of *gens d'armes*[1]. And from Gittarchan to SARA may be a day by river, and from Sara to SARACANCO[2], also by river, eight days. You can do this either by land or by water; but by water you will be at less charge for your merchandize.

From Saracanco to ORGANCI may be twenty days' journey in camel-waggon. It will be well for anyone travelling with merchandize to go to Organci, for in that city there is a ready sale for goods. From Organci to OLTRARRE[3] is thirty-five to forty days in camel-waggons. But if when you leave Saracanco you go direct

Minorite convent. The original name was *Haj-*, or *Hajji-Tarkhan*. Ibn Batuta says it was so called after a devout Haj who established himself there, in consideration of which the prince exempted the place from all duties, *Tarkhan*, he says, signifying a *place free from duties*. This is a mistake, however, for *Tarkhan* among the Mongols denoted a *person*, the member of an order enjoying high privileges, such as freedom from all exactions, the right to enter the sovereign's presence unsummoned, and exemption from punishment for crime till a ninth time convicted. D'Ohsson quotes the mention of this title by a Greek author as old as the time of the Emperor Justin. (*Ibn Batuta*, ii, 410, and Editor's note, 458; *D'Ohsson*, i, 45, etc.) In the *Carta Catalana* and *Portulano Mediceo* the place appears as *Agitarcham*; in Fra Mauro's Map as *Azetrechan*; by Barbaro and others, up to the middle of the sixteenth century, we find it called *Citracan*.

[1] *Moccoli* are in another passage explained by Pegolotti to be *Tartari scherani*, bandits or troopers. The word is, I suppose, simply *Mongols*, or rather as called in Western Asia *Moghols*, which will be almost the Tuscan pronunciation of *Moccol*. Indeed the word is called by the Armenians *Muchal* (*Neumann's Chron. of Vahram*, p. 88).

[2] On *Sarai* see *supra*, p. 82. Saracanco appears to be unquestionably *Sarachik*, on which, and on *Organci* or Urghanj, see pp. 82, 84, 85.

[3] Oltrarre is Otrár, previously called Faráb, a city of Turkestan, of which it was once considered the capital. It stood on a tributary of the Sihun or Jaxartes, about two leagues from that river, about lat. 44° 30′, some distance west of the town called Turkestan in the maps. Its capture by Chinghiz in 1219 was the commencement of his Western conquests; and it was at Otrár that the great Timúr died, 17th February, 1405. Hayton calls the city *Octorar*, the greatest city of Turkestan. It stood on the frontier, between the Khanates of Kapchak and Zagatai.

[According to Lerch (*Archæol. Journey in Turkestan*), quoted by Bretschneider (*Mediæval Res.*, ii, p. 57), the ruins of ancient Otrár are still to be seen a little to the north of the mouth of the river *Arys*, an eastern affluent of the Syr Daria.—In 1903, two Russians, Tcher-

to Oltrarre, it is a journey of fifty days only, and if you have no merchandize it will be better to go this way than to go by Organci.

From Oltrarre to ARMALEC[1] is forty-five days' journey with pack-asses, and every day you find Moccols. And from Armalec to CAMEXU[2] is seventy days with asses, and from Camexu until you come to a river called ...... is forty-five days on horseback; and then you can go down the river to CASSAI[3], and there you can dispose of the *sommi*[4] of silver that you have with you, for that is a most

kasov and Claret, made plans of the citadel and environs of Otrár and published a report on their exploration in the "Turkestan News." See No. 4, March, 1905, of the *Bul. de l'Association int. pour l'Exploration...de l'Asie Centrale*, St. Petersburg, p. 9.]

[1] See p. 87.

[2] Camexu (i.e. *Camechu*) is considered by Forster to be Hami or Kamil, with the Chinese *chu* added. But there can be no doubt that it is the Chinese frontier city *Kan chau* in Kan Suh. That city is called by Rashíddúddin and by the author of *Masálak-al-Absár Kamchu*, so that the Western Asiatics called it just as Pegolotti does. Moreover the latter author allows only forty days from Almáliq (Armalec) to Kamchu, showing that the time named by Pegolotti is most ample allowance. The same author allows forty days from Kamchu to Khanbaliq (*Notices et Extraits*, xiii, 226).

[Kan chau is the Campichu of Marco Polo: "It is the capital and place of government of the whole province of Tangut." It fell under the Tangut dominion in 1208. Cf. *Marco Polo*, i, p. 219 and 220 *n.*]

[3] Forster chooses to consider Cassai to be a place called Kissen, on the Hwang Ho. It is not worth while to look if there is such a place, for Cassai is obviously Quinsai, Cansai, Kingszé, the commercial city of China at that time, *hod.* Hang-chau fu. It is called Cassai in the *Portulano Mediceo* and *Cassay* in the "Livre du Grant Caan" (*supra*, p. 97). [Cf. *Odoric*, p. 192 *supra* and *Marco Polo*, ii, pp. 193 *seq.*]

The river reached in forty-five days from Kan-chau is most probably the Great Canal. Forster, according to Baldelli Boni (I presume in some later edition of his work than that used by me), supplies the blank with *Karamuren* from a MS. that belonged to Sprengel. But this is of no authority, for the blank exists in the original MS. in the Riccardian library.

[4] *Sommi* of silver is written in the MS. *sonmi*, and is so printed by Pagnini. But it is a mere fashion of writing. Pegolotti writes also *channino*, *chanmello*, *fenmina*, but Pagnini does not print these so. Indeed Giovanno da Uzzano (p. 188) writes *sommi*. The *sommo*, as explained in the next chapter, was a silver ingot weighing eight and a half Genoese ounces. Ibn Batuta mentions these as current among the Tartars under the name of *saum*, sing. *saumah*. He says the

active place of business. After getting to Cassai you carry on with the money which you get for the *sommi* of silver which you sell there; and this money is made of paper, and is called *balishi*[1]. And four pieces of this money are worth one *sommo* of silver in the province of Cathay[2]. And from Cassai to Gamalec [Cambalec], which is the capital city of the country of Cathay, is thirty days' journey.

weight of each saumah or sommo was five ounces, i.e., I suppose, five-twelfths of a *rithl* (ii, 412, 414). Von Hammer says that the *súm* (as he terms it) was in the form of an octahedron, and quotes from the Persian historian Wassaf a passage which shows that the term was applied also to ingots of gold (*Geschichte der Gold. Horde*, pp. 223, 224).

[1] [The printed text has *babisci*.]

[2] Here Pegolotti speaks of the celebrated paper money of China, once deemed a fable of Marco Polo's, though before his time even it had been distinctly mentioned by the intelligent friar Rubruquis. [See Rockhill, *Rubruck*, p. 201.]

Its use was of great antiquity, for traces at least of leather representatives of money are found as far back as B.C. 118. [Mr. Rockhill (*Rubruck*, 201 note) says: "As early as B.C. 118, we find the Chinese using 'leather-money' (*p'i pi*). These were pieces of white deer skin, a foot square, with a coloured border. Each had a value of 40,000 cash. (*Ma Twan-liu*, Bk. 8, 5.)."] In the reign of Hien Tsung of the T'ang dynasty (A.D. 806–821), copper being scarce, notes were issued on deposits from the public treasury, and were current for some years. These issues were renewed under the Sung (A.D. 960), and some sixty years later amounted in nominal value to 2,830,000 ounces of silver. These were followed by further issues of real paper money, issued without reference to deposits (? so says Klaproth), and payable every three years. The business at this time was managed by sixteen chief houses, but these becoming bankrupt, the emperor abolished private notes, and established a government bank, the issues of which in 1032 amounted to 1,256,340 ounces. Such banks were established in several parts of the empire, the notes of one province not being current in another.

In 1160, in the reign of Kao Tsung, a new paper was issued, the amount of which rose in six years to 43,600,000 ounces. There were local notes besides, so that the empire was flooded with paper, rapidly depreciating in value.

When the invaders who formed the *Kin* or "Golden" Dynasty had established themselves in Northern China they also speedily took to paper, notwithstanding their name. Their notes had a course of seven years, after which new notes were given by government with a deduction of 15 per cent.

The Mongols did like their predecessors. Their first notes were issued in 1236, but on a small scale compared to the issues of Kúblái and his successors. Kúblái's first issue was in 1260; and consisted of notes of three classes; viz. notes of *tens*, i.e. of 10, 20, 30, and 50 *tsien* or cash; notes of *hundreds*, of 100, 200, and 500 *tsien*; and notes of *strings* or *thousands* of cash, viz. of 1000 and 2000. This money, however, was worth only half its nominal value, so that two notes of 1000 cash went for an ouncé of pure silver. There were also notes printed on silk, for 1, 2, 3, 5 and 10 ounces each, valued at par in silver; but these would not circulate. In 1277 Kúblái made a new issue of very small notes; and a complete new currency in 1288. One of these new notes was as before worth half its nominal value in silver, but was to be exchanged against *five* of equal nominal value of the old notes!

In 1309 a new issue took place with a like valuation; i.e. one ounce note of this issue was to exchange against five of Kúblái's last issue, and therefore against twenty-five of his older notes! And it was at the same time prescribed that the new notes should exchange at par with metals, which of course it was beyond the power of government to enforce, and so the notes were abandoned.

Issues continued from time to time to the end of the Mongol dynasty, but according to the Chinese authors with credit constantly diminishing. This depreciation might easily escape Odoric, but it is curious that it should be so entirely ignored by Pegolotti, whose informants must have been mercantile men. In fact he asserts positively that there was no depreciation. (*See below.*)

The remarks of MaTwan-lin, a mediæval Chinese historian, on this subject are curiously like a bit of modern controversy: "Paper should never be *money*; it should only be employed as a representative sign of value existing in metals or in produce, which can thus be readily exchanged for paper, and the cost of its transport avoided. At first this was the mode in which paper currency was actually used among merchants. The government, borrowing the invention from private individuals, wished to make a real *money* of paper, and thus the original contrivance was perverted."

The Ming dynasty for a time carried on the system of their predecessors, and with like results, till in 1448 the *chao*, or note, of 1000 cash, was worth but 3! Barbaro still heard of the paper money of Cathay from travellers whom he met at Azov about this time, but after 1455 there is said to be no more mention of it in Chinese history.

Though the government of China has not issued paper money since then, there has been considerable local use of such currency among the people, even in our own time. In Fu chau some years ago it had almost displaced bullion, and in that city the banking houses were counted by hundreds. Though the system was under no efficient control, few notes were below par, and failures of any magnitude were rare. The notes were chiefly from copper plates (and such notes were engraved in China as early as 1168) and ranged in value from 110 cash to 1000 dollars.

Kaikhátu Khan of Persia was persuaded to attempt the introduction of a paper currency under the Chinese name (*chao*) in 1294. After most expensive preparations in erecting offices in every province, etc., the scheme utterly failed, the shops and markets of Tabriz were deserted, and the *chao* had to be given up. Mahomed Túghlák of Dehli fared no better in a somewhat similar project in 1330–31. In Japan bank-notes were introduced about 1319–27, but in that country they always represented considerable sums. They continued to exist in the last century, and perhaps do still.

The notes of the Sung, Kin, and Mongol dynasties were all made

CHAPTER II.

Things needful for merchants who desire to make the journey to Cathay above described.

In the first place, you must let your beard grow long and not shave. And at Tana you should furnish yourself with a dragoman. And you must not try to save money in the matter of dragomen by taking a bad one instead of a good one. For the additional wages of the good one will not cost you so much as you will save by having him[1]. And besides the dragoman it will be well to take at least two good men servants, who are acquainted with the Cumanian

with the bark of the paper mulberry. Those of the first two were only printed with characters and sealed; the last were also ornamented.

[Marco Polo writes: "[The Emperor makes the notes] of the bark of a certain tree, in fact the Mulberry Tree, the leaves of which are the food of the silkworms."—Dr. Bretschneider (*Hist. Botan. Disc.*, i, p. 4) makes the following remarks on the subject: "He [Polo] seems to be mistaken. Paper in China is not made from mulberry-tree but from the *Broussonetia papyrifera*, which latter tree belongs to the same order of Moraceæ."]

A note of the Ming dynasty is figured in *Duhalde*, ii, 168. It is for 1000 cash, and bears the following inscription: "On the request of the Board of Treasurers, it is ordered that paper money thus impressed with the imperial seal have currency the same as copper money. Forgers shall lose their heads, and informers shall receive a reward of 250 *taels*, with the criminal's goods. In such a year and month of the reign of Hung-Wu." [A note of the Ming is reproduced in facsimile in Vissering's *Chinese Currency*, also in *Marco Polo*, i, p. 426.] (Klaproth in *Mém. Rel. à l'Asie*, i, 375–388; Biot, in *J. A.*, sér. iii, tom. iv; Parkes, in *J. R. A. S.*, xiii, 179; *D'Ohsson*, iv, 53; Elphinstone's *Hist. of India*, ii, 62.) Another and probably more exact account of the history of paper-money under the Mongols will be found in Pauthier's new *Marco Polo*. [See long note in our *Marco Polo*, i, pp. 426–430.]

Regarding the *balish*, see note to *Odoric*, p. 196.

[1] ["Primieramente conviene che si lasci crescere la barba grande, e non si rada. E vuolsi fornire alla Tana di Turcimanni, e non si vuole guardare a rispiarmo dall cattivo al buono, che il buono non costa quello d' ingordo che l' uomo non se ne megliori via più."] The Italian here is very obscure and probably defective, but this seems the general sense; or perhaps, "so much as the greed of the other will cause you loss."

tongue. And if the merchant likes to take a woman with him from Tana, he can do so; if he does not like to take one there is no obligation, only if he does take one he will be kept much more comfortably than if he does not take one. Howbeit, if he do take one, it will be well that she be acquainted with the Cumanian tongue as well as the men[1].

And from Tana travelling to Gittarchan you should take with you twenty-five days' provisions, that is to say, flour and salt fish, for as to meat you will find enough of it at all the places along the road. And so also at all the chief stations noted in going from one country to another in the route, according to the number of days set down above, you should furnish yourself with flour and salt fish; other things you will find in sufficiency, and especially meat.

The road you travel from Tana to Cathay is perfectly safe, whether by day or by night, according to what the merchants say who have used it. Only if the merchant, in going or coming, should die upon the road, everything belonging to him will become the perquisite of the lord of the country in which he dies, and the officers of the lord will take possession of all[2]. And in like manner if he die in Cathay. But if his brother be with him, or an intimate friend and comrade calling himself his brother, then to such an one they will surrender the property of the deceased, and so it will be rescued.

And there is another danger: this is when the lord of the country dies, and before the new lord who is to have the lordship is proclaimed; during such intervals there

[1] The Cumanian was apparently a Turkish dialect. [Cf. *Codex Cumanicus* bibliothecae ad templum Divi Marci Venetiarum Primum ex integro edidit prolegomenis notis et compluribus glossariis instruxit comes Géza Kuun...Budapestini, 1880, 8vo.] See p. 83.

[2] This custom seems to have prevailed very generally (see *Sto. Stephano* in *India in the Fifteenth Century*, p. 7). It was also the law of Lesser Armenia unless a subject of the kingdom was left heir. (*J. As.*, sér. v, tom. xviii, 346.)

have sometimes been irregularities practised on the Franks, and other foreigners. (They call *Franks* all the Christians of these parts from Romania westward[1].) And neither will the roads be safe to travel until the other lord be proclaimed who is to reign in room of him who is deceased.

Cathay is a province which contained a multitude of cities and towns. Among others there is one in particular, that is to say the capital city, to which is great resort of merchants, and in which there is a vast amount of trade; and this city is called Cambalec. And the said city hath a circuit of one hundred miles, and is all full of people and houses and of dwellers in the said city.

You may calculate that a merchant with a dragoman, and with two men servants, and with goods to the value of twenty-five thousand golden florins, should spend on his way to Cathay from sixty to eighty *sommi* of silver, and not more if he manage well; and for all the road back again from Cathay to Tana, including the expenses of living and the pay of servants, and all other charges, the cost will be about five *sommi* per head of pack animals, or something less. And you may reckon the *sommo* to be worth five golden florins[2]. You may reckon also that each ox-waggon will require one ox, and will carry ten cantars Genoese weight; and the camel-waggon will require three camels, and will carry thirty cantars Genoese weight; and the horse-waggon will require one horse, and will commonly carry six and half cantars of silk, at 250 Genoese pounds

[1] Romania means Greece, or nearly so. By Giov. da Uzzano the Morea and the isle of Scio are both spoken of as belonging to Romania (pp. 89 and 160). And the expression in the text *tutti i Cristiani delle parte di Romania innanzi in verso il Ponente* seems to *include* Romania. Yet I do not think the Greeks were or are regarded as Franks.

[2] Taking the gold florin or ducat at 9*s.* 6*d.*, the value of the goods will be nearly £12,000 and the cost of the merchant's journey from £140 to £190 going, and nearly £12 a head on his beasts coming back.

to the cantar. And a bale[1] of silk may be reckoned at between 110 and 115 Genoese pounds.

You may reckon also that from Tana to Sara the road is less safe than on any other part of the journey; and yet even when this part of the road is at its worst, if you are some sixty men in the company you will go as safely as if you were in your own house.

Anyone from Genoa or from Venice, wishing to go to the places above-named, and to make the journey to Cathay, should carry linens[2] with him, and if he visit Organci he will dispose of these well. In Organci he should purchase *sommi* of silver, and with these he should proceed without making any further investment, unless it be some bales of the very finest stuffs which go in small bulk, and cost no more for carriage than coarser stuffs would do.

Merchants who travel this road can ride on horseback or on asses, or mounted in any way that they list to be mounted.

Whatever silver the merchants may carry with them as far as Cathay the lord of Cathay will take from them and put into his treasury. And to merchants who thus bring silver they give that paper money of theirs in exchange. This is of yellow paper, stamped with the seal of the lord aforesaid. And this money is called *balishi*[3]; and with this money you can readily buy silk and all other merchandize that you have a desire to buy. And all the people of the

[1] *Scibetto.* I cannot trace this word in any dictionary, but it looks like Arabic. The nearest thing I can find is *sibt*—hides of ox leather (*Freytag*). It is possible that the silk may have been packed in such. From India and China now it is generally packed in mats. Pegolotti writes it in another place in the plural *iscibetti*, with *fardelli* as synonymous (p. 131). The Genoese pound of twelve ounces was equal to about $\frac{5}{7}$ of the London pound ($\frac{100}{142}$), as we learn from Pegolotti in another part of his book.

[2] *Tele.*

[3] The Riccardian MS. has here *palisci*, as in the previous chapter [and in the printed text] *babisci*. No doubt in both places the original had *balisci*.

country are bound to receive it. And yet you shall not pay a higher price for your goods because your money is of paper. And of the said paper money there are three kinds, one being worth more than another, according to the value which has been established for each by that lord[1].

And you may reckon that you can buy for one *sommo* of silver nineteen or twenty pounds of Cathay silk, when reduced to Genoese weight, and that the *sommo* should weigh eight and a half ounces of Genoa, and should be of the alloy of eleven ounces and seventeen deniers to the pound[2].

You may reckon also that in Cathay you should get three or three and a half pieces of damasked silk[3] for a *sommo*; and from three and a half to five pieces of *nacchetti*[4] of silk and gold, likewise for a *sommo* of silver.

[1] This seems to allude to three *classes* of notes, as in Kúblái's issue of 1260 mentioned above.

[2] *I.e.* 7 pennyweights of alloy to 11 oz. 17 dwts. of pure silver. Giov. da Uzzano in the next century speaks of the *sommi* from Caffa as being of both gold and silver, the alloy of the latter being 11 oz. 13 to 15 dwt. (p. 188).

[3] The word is *cammocca*. This the dictionaries generally are good enough to tell us means "a kind of cloth." Mr. Wright on Mandeville says it is "a rich cloth of silk mentioned not unfrequently in medieval writers," but this is still very unprecise. I had arrived at the conclusion that it must be *damasked silk*, and I now find this confirmed by Ducange (*Gloss. Græcitatis*, etc.): "καμουχᾶς, *Pannus sericus more damasceno confectus.*" Moreover the word is almost certainly the Arabic كمخوا *kimkhwá*, "Vestis scutulata Damascena" (*Freytag*). I suppose that the *kimkhwáb* of Hindustan, now applied to a gold brocade, is the same word or a derivative.

[*Camocato* (*camocan*, *camocas*) originally from China, hence *Kincha* or *Kimcha*, brocade; manufactured at Herat, Nishapur, Tabriz under the name of *Kimkhā* or *Kamkhā*; known among the Greeks as καμουχᾶς. Cf. Heyd, ii, pp. 697–8 and *Hobson-Jobson*, s.v. *Kincob*, "Gold brocade."]

[4] In a later chapter describing the trade at Constantinople, our author details "silk velvets, *cammucca*, *maramati*, gold cloth of every kind, *nacchetti* and *nacchi* of every kind, and likewise all cloths of gold and silk except *zendadi* (gauzes)." [*Zendado* (cendal), a silk taffeta. Cf. Heyd, ii, p. 701.] The *nacchi* and *nacchetti* appear to have been cloths of silk and gold. The former (*nakh*) is so explained by Ibn Batuta, who names it several times. It was made, he tells us,

CHAPTER III.

Comparison of the weights and measures of Cathay and of Tana.

				lbs.	ozs.
The maund[1] of	Sara =	in Genoa weight		6	2
"	Organci	"	"	3	9
"	Oltrarre	"	"	3	9
"	Armalec	"	"	2	8
"	Camexu	"	"	2	0

Tana on the Black Sea.

At Tana, as shall next be shown, they use a variety of weights and measures, viz.:

The *cantar*, which is that of Genoa.

at Nisabur in Khorassan, and in describing the dress of the princess of Constantinople he says she had on "a mantle of the stuff called *nakh*, and also *nasíj*." These two, however, were apparently not identical, but corresponded probably to the *nacchi* and *nacchetti* of Pegolotti. For Polo in the Ramusian version has "panni d' oro *nasiti* (*nasici ?*) fin, e *nach*, e panni di seta." And in the old version printed in Baldelli Boni's first volume this runs "*nasicci*, drappi dorati"; whilst Rubruquis mentions *nasic* as a present given him by Mangu Khan. [Marco Polo, i, p. 63, writes: "In Baudas they weave many different kinds of silk stuffs and gold brocades, such as *nasich*, and *nac*, and *cramoisy*, and many another beautiful tissue richly wrought with figures of beasts and birds." Among the articles sent from Baghdad to Okkodai Khan, mentioned in the *Yüan ch'ao pi shi* (made in the 14th century), quoted by Bretschneider (*Med. Res.*, ii, p. 124), we note: *Nakkut* (a kind of gold brocade), *Nachidut* (a silk stuff interwoven with gold), *Dardas* (a stuff embroidered in gold). Bretschneider (p. 125) adds: "With respect to *nakhut* and *nachidut*, I may observe that these words represent the Mongol plural form of *nakh* and *nachetti*.... I may finally mention that in the *Yüan shi*, chap. lxxviii. (on official dresses), a stuff, *na-shi-ki*, is repeatedly named, and the term is explained there by *kin kin* (gold brocade)." Cf. *Marco Polo*, i, p. 65.] I know not what *maramati* is, unless it should rather be *maramali* for *makhmal*, velvet. [*Maramoto* or *Maramanto*, from the Arabic *mahremah*, a gold brocade. Cf. Heyd, ii, p. 698.] (*Ibn Batuta*, ii, 309, 388, 422; iii, 81; *Polo* in *Ramus.*, pt. i, c. 53; *Il Milione*, i, 57; *Rub.*, p. 317.)

[1] *Mena*, representing the Arabic *man*, I suppose from Greek and Lat. *mina*, diffused over all the East with an infinite variety of values from below two pounds up to one hundred pounds. We have Anglicized it in India into *maund*. The *man* of Ghazan Khan, which may be meant here, was of 260 drachms.

The *great pound*[1] = 20 lbs. Genoese.
The *ruotolo*[2], of which 20 = 1 great pound.
The *little pound*, which is the Genoese pound.
The *tocchetto*, of which 12 = 1 great pound.
The *saggio*, of which 45 = 1 sommo.
The *picco*[3].

Wax, ladanum[4], iron, tin, copper, pepper, ginger, all coarser spices, cotton, madder, and suet, cheese, flax, and oil, honey, and the like, sell by the great pound.

Silk, saffron, amber wrought in rosaries and the like, and all small spices sell by the little pound.

Vair-skins by the 1000; and 1020 go to the 1000.

Ermines by the 1000; 1000 to the 1000.

Foxes, sables, fitches and martens, wolfskins, deerskins, and all cloths of silk or gold, by the piece.

Common stuffs, and canvasses of every kind sell by the *picco*.

Tails are sold by the bundle at twenty to the bundle.

Oxhides by the hundred in tale, giving a hundred and no more.

Horse and pony hides by the piece.

Gold and pearls are sold by the *saggio*[5]. Wheat and

[1] This should be equal to thirty, not twenty, Genoese pounds, as is shown by passages at pp. 31, 37, of Pegolotti. Is this *great pound* the origin of the Russian *pood*?

[2] The *cantaro* and *ruotolo* both survive in Southern Italy and Sicily, the former derived from the *kantár* and the latter from the *rithl* of the Arabs, though the first of these words, and perhaps both, must have come to the Arabic from the Latin.

[3] The *pik* is still the common cloth measure in the Levant. It seems generally to be about twenty-eight inches.

[4] *Ladanum* or *labdanum* (the *ládin* of the Arabs) is a gum resin derived from the *Cistus creticus*, which grows in the Islands of the Levant. It is exported in solid pieces of cylindrical and other forms. A long description of the mode of collecting it, etc., will be found in Tournefort, *Voyage du Levant*, i, 84, *et seq.* [Cf. Heyd, ii, p. 631.] According to Herodotus ladanum was derived "from a most inodorous place," viz. the beards of he-goats, which collected it from the bushes in browsing. (Rawlinson's *Herod.*, bk. iii, 113.)

[5] The saggio in Italy was $\frac{1}{72}$ of a pound, *i.e.* $\frac{1}{6}$ of an ounce. (*Pegol.*

all other corn and pulse is sold at Tana by a measure which they call *cascito*[1]. Greek wine and all Latin wines are sold by the cask as they come. Malmsey and wines of Triglia and Candia are sold by the measure.

Caviar is sold by the *fusco*, and a *fusco* is the tail-half of the fish's skin, full of fish's roe[2].

CHAPTER IV.

Charges on merchandize which are paid at Tana on things entering the city, nothing being paid on going forth thereof.

Gold, silver, and pearls at Tana pay neither *comerchio*, nor *tamunga*, nor any other duties.

On wine, and ox-hides, and tails, and horse-hides, the Genoese and Venetians pay four per cent., and all other people five per cent.

What is paid for the transit of merchandize at Tana.

Silk 15 aspers per pound.

All other things, at...aspers for 3 cantars.

At Tana the money current is of *sommi* and aspers of silver. The *sommo* weighs 45 *saggi* of Tana, and is of the alloy of 11 oz. 17 dwt. of fine silver to the pound. And if

p. 31). Here it was a little more, as may be deduced from its relation to the *sommo* opposite.

[1] *Cascito* must have been miswritten for *cafiço*. There is a measure called *kafīz* in Arabic, and specified as *cafizium* in some of the treaties (*Not. et Ext.*, xi, 30). Hammer-Purgstall mentions *kofeiz* as a standard measure at Tabriz, which is doubtless the same. (*Gesch. der Golden Horde*, etc., p. 225.) And Pegolotti himself has *cafisso* as a Moorish measure. Indeed, I need not have sought this word so far away. It is still used in Sicily as *Cafisu* for an oil measure, the fifth part of a *Cantaro*. It also exists in Spanish as *Cahiz*, and will be found in Ducange in a variety of forms, *Caffium*, *Caficium*, *Cafisa*, *Cappitius*, etc.

[2] Caviare is now exported in small kegs. *Fusco* is perhaps just *fish*. In the dialect of the Goths of the Crimea that word was *fisct* according to Busbeck. [Caffa was a great place for the caviare trade. Cf. Heyd, ii, p. 395.] The sturgeon of the Borysthenes are already mentioned by Herodotus as large fish without prickly bones, called *antacæi*, good for pickling, and according to Professor Rawlinson caviare also was known to the Greeks as τάριχος Ἀντακαῖον.

silver be sent to the Tana mint, they coin 202 aspers from the *sommo*[1], but they pay you only 190, retaining the rest for the work of the mint and its profit. So a *sommo* at Tana is reckoned to be 190 aspers. And the *sommi* are ingots of silver of the alloy before mentioned, which are paid away by weight. But they do not all weigh the same, so the ingots are weighed at the time of payment, and if the weight is less than it ought to be the balance is paid in aspers, to make up every *sommo* to the value of 45 *saggi* of Tana weight.

And there are also current at Tana copper coins called *folleri*, of which sixteen go to the asper. But the *folleri* are not used in mercantile transactions, but only in the purchase of vegetables and such small matters for town use[2].

CHAPTER V gives details as to the relation of the Tana weights and measures to those of Venice, etc.; as to the weights and measures of Caffa; and as to those of Tabriz (*Torissi di Persia*). The duties at Tabriz are called *Cammunoca*.

CHAPTER VI.

On the expenses which usually attend the transport of merchandize from Ajazzo of Erminia to Torissi, by land[3].

In the first place from AJAZZO as far as COLIDARA[4] i.e.,

[1] The *asper* must therefore have contained silver to the amount of about 0*s*. 2.8*d*.

[2] *Follero* is the Byzantine copper *Follis*, and perhaps Persian *pul*.

[3] [At the meeting of the 20th October, 1881, of the philos.-hist. section of the Prussian Academy of Sciences, Hr. Kiepert read a paper: "Über Pegolotti's vorderasiatisches Itinerar" (*Monatsb. d. kön. preuss. Ak. d. Wiss. zu Berlin*, 1881, pp. 901–913) in which he criticized both Yule, *Cathay*, ii, pp. 291–301, and Wilhelm Heyd, *Geschichte des Levantehandels im Mittelalter*, 1879, ii, pp. 113 *seq.* Heyd answered in the French edition of his work: *Histoire du Commerce du Levant*, ii, 1886, pp. 112 *seq.* We shall examine the arguments given on both sides.]

[4] Respecting Ajazzo see note, p. 139 *supra*. *Colidara* should

as far as the King of Armenia's territory extends, you pay altogether 41 taccolini and 3½ deniers (at the rate of 10 deniers to the taccolino) on every load, whether of camels or of other beasts. Now taking the taccolino to be about an asper, the amount will be about 41 aspers of Tauris per load. And 6 aspers of Tauris are equal to one Tauris bezant.

At GANDON, where you enter upon the lands of Bonsaet, i.e. of the lord of the Tartars[1], on every load	20 aspers.
At the same place, for watching, ditto .	3 „
At CASENA	7 „
At the CARAVANSERAI of the ADMIRAL[2] .	2 „
At GADUE	3 „

perhaps be Gobidar, the name of an Armenian fortress and barony in Taurus, which is mentioned in *Journ. As.*, sér. v, vol. xviii, 314.

[Dulaurier, *Rec. des Hist. des Croisades, Doc. Arméniens*, i, Int., p. ci, calls *Colidara*, "Gobidar, dans le Taurus cilicien," in his short itinerary of Pegolotti.]

[According to Kiepert, Italian caravans leaving Lajazzo, would follow the Djihan river [Pyramus] until they reached the neighbourhood of Missis (Massissa); then go northward to reach Sis, the capital of Armenia; beyond they would pass the Sarus gorges to reach the mountainous region of Kozan, the Casena of Pegolotti. Heyd, pp. 113–4, objects that there is no proof that there is a locality called Kozan, and that the passes of the Taurus, north of Sis, were avoided by travellers, on account of the tribes living of plunder. Heyd thinks that western merchants leaving Lajazzo, followed the Djihan until Anabad; then they left this river to follow its tributary the Anabad Su which led them under the walls of Geben or Gaban; there is a diploma of the emperor Leon II, dated March, 1201, stating that the Genoese paid a tax to the lord of this stronghold, to pass the Djihan; it was the place where they crossed from the right side of the river to the left; then they went along the Anabad Su, the basin of which was under the dominion of the Lord of Gaban; hence Geukoun was reached without any difficulty.—Khozan is a sandjak with Sis as a caza and chief town.]

[1] *Bonsaet* is Abu Sa'id Bahadur Khan, the last effective sovereign of the Mongol dynasty in Persia, who died 1335. He is called Busaid by some Arabic writers, and on some Mongol coins. The Pope in addressing him calls him *Boyssethan*, i.e. Busaid Khan. (*D'Ohsson*, iv, 716; *Mosheim*, 144.)

[2] *Gavazera del Amiraglio*, I suppose *Karwánsarai-ul-Amír*. The same word is used at each place rendered caravanserai.

At the CARAVANSERAI of CASA JACOMI[1] .	3 aspers.
At the entrance to SALVASTRO[2] from Ajazzo	1 „
Inside the city	7 „
Leaving the city on the road to Tauris .	1 „
At DUDRIAGA[3]	3 „
At GREBOCO[4]	4 „
At MUGHISAR[5]	2½ „
At ditto, as *tantaullaggio*[6] for the watch	0½ „
At ARZINGA[7], at entrance to the town .	5 „
Ditto, inside the city	9 „
Ditto, for the watchmen, on leaving.	3 „

1 [*Gavazera di Casa Jacomi.*]

2 Sebaste, now Sivas. [Cf. *Marco Polo*, i, pp. 43, 44 *n.*]

3 The proper reading is probably *Duvriaga*, viz. Divrik or Τεφρικη, a place still existing between Sivas and Erzinjan.

[Heyd, p. 115, says that Dudriaga must be the present village of Todurga (Todorag), 10 leagues E.N.E. of Sivas in the upper valley of the Halys; and that the road to Erzinghian by Divrighi and the valley of the Euphrates is longer and more difficult. Kiepert is also in favour of Todurga. Divrighi is on the road from Ordu to Kharpont, near the Chatta Irmak, a tributary of the Kara Su (Western Euphrates). To go from Sivas to Erzinghian, the road instead of turning to the S.E. to the Euphrates would then follow the valley of the Kizil Irmak. The Kizil Irmak (Red River, ancient *Halys*) has its source at the foot of the Kizil Dagh (Red Mountain) in the caza of Kochkiri, sandjak of Sivas, and falls into the Black Sea, at the eastern end of the bay of Sinope.]

4 [Kiepert has very cleverly discovered *Greboco* in the *Agreboce* of the Map of the brothers Pizzigani, Venice, 1367, probably the *Arauraci* of the Romans.]

5 [According to Heyd, p. 115, possibly the modern *Mushar* or *Mehar.*]

6 This was probably written *Tancaullaggio*. The *Tangauls* were guards or patrols upon the roads in Persia. An edict of Ghazan Khan, cited by D'Ohsson, illustrates these charges. He denounces the Tangauls for their exactions from travellers, and authorises them to take a fee of half an *akché* and no more, for every two camels or four mules loaded. (The *akché* was, I presume, the same as the asper, for it is named from *ák*, white, as the asper from ἄσπρον, white.) At every station of *Tangauls* there was to be a stone pillar indicating their number, the duties of their chief, and the fees due. (*D'Ohsson*, iv, 471-2.) Pegolotti, in his prefatory glossary, says *Tantaullo* in Tartaresque is applied "to people who act as guards of places and of roads for gentlemen and others," p. xxiii.

7 Erzinjan of our maps.

[According to Vital Cuinet, the distances from Erzrum to Erzinjan are the following:

At the Caravanserai on the Hill[1]	3	aspers.
At LIGURTI[2].	2	,,
At ditto, at the bridge, for *tantaullaggio*[3]	0½	,,
At the Caravanserai outside ARZERONE[4] .	2	,,
At Arzerone, at the Baths	1	,,
Ditto, inside the city	9	,,
Ditto, as a present to the lord . .	2	,,
Ditto. at the Baths towards Tauris[5] .	1	,,
At POLORBECH[6]	3	,,

From Erzrum to Seni Keuï	kilom.	49,500
,, Seni Keuï to Mama Khatum	,,	38,500
,, Mama Khatum to Palanka	,,	27,500
,, Palanka to Erzinjan	,,	60,500
Together	,,	176,000

Cf. Marco Polo, i, pp. 46–47.]

[1] [*Gavezera sulla montagna.*]

[2] [Neither Kiepert nor Heyd have identified this Ligurti.]

[3] [To-day, says Heyd, the road usually followed by the caravans, crosses the Euphrates about half-way between Erzinghian and Erzrum, at Mamakhatun, on the well-known old bridge of Korgeun. As Pegolotti's Ponte must be looked for nearer Erzrum, Kiepert rightly thinks that a more northern route then existed crossing the Euphrates not further than Aqkala. Between this bridge and the town of Erzrum, there were but two stations, a caravanserai, and a bath house.]

[4] Erzrum.

[5] In connexion with these baths at the entrance and exit from the city we read that Ghazan Khan, in building New Tabriz, caused to be erected at each gate of the city a great caravanserai, a market, and a set of baths, so that the merchants, from whatever quarter they came, found a serai and baths adjoining the custom-house where their wares were examined (*D'Ohsson*, iv, 276).

[According to Vital Cuinet, *Turquie d'Asie*, i, p. 165, the distances from Trebizond to the Persian frontier are the following:

From Trebizond to Erzrum			kilom. 314
,, Erzrum to Hassan-Kaleh	kilom.	33,000	
,, Hassan-Kaleh to Deli-Baba	,,	55,000	
,, Deli-Baba to Mollah-Suleïman	,,	49,500	
,, Mollah-Suleïman to Kara-Kilisse	,,	27,500	
,, Kara-Kilisse to Diadin	,,	66,000	
,, Diadin to Bayazid	,,	33,000	
			264
,, Bayazid to the Persian frontier	,,		16
From Trebizond to the Persian frontier			kilom. 594

[6] [*Polorbech*, in Armenian *Polorabahag*, "the round fortress," at

At ditto	$0\frac{1}{2}$	aspers.
At SERMESSACALO[1] for *tantaullaggio* . .	$0\frac{1}{2}$	"
At AGGIA, for the whole journey . . .	$0\frac{1}{2}$	"
At the middle of the plain of Aggia, for duty	3	"
At ditto for *tant.*	$0\frac{1}{2}$	"
At CALACRESTI[2], ditto	$0\frac{1}{2}$	"
At the THREE CHURCHES[3], for *tant* . .	$0\frac{1}{2}$	"
Under Noah's Ark[4], for duty	3	"
Ditto ditto for *tant.*	$0\frac{1}{2}$	"
At SCARACANTI, ditto	$0\frac{1}{2}$	"
At LOCCHE ditto	$0\frac{1}{2}$	"
At the plain of the Falconers, ditto (twice altogether)	I	"

nine hours from Erzrum on the Araxes, crossed there to-day by a bridge of seven arches called Choban-Keupri. Cf. Heyd, p. 116.]

[1] I have no doubt that this is the Sarbisacalo of Odoric; see note at p. 101.

[2] Probably the place called *Kara-Kilisse* (the Black Church).

[Kara-Kilisse, on the road from Erzrum to the Persian frontier, is situated 165 kil. to the east of Erzrum, 66 kil. to the N.E. of Diadin, and 99 kil. from Bayazid, on a tributary of the Murad Su. Cf. Vital Cuinet, i, p. 235.]

[3] I presume that this route from Erzrum to Tabriz follows the old Genoese line between Trebizond and Tabriz, which passed to the *south* of Ararat. The *Three Churches* are not therefore those of Echmiazin, but the *Uchkilisi* of the maps in the position just mentioned.

Tre Chiese. ["This name (Tre Chiese)," writes Dulaurier, *Hist. des Croisades, Doc. arméniens*, i, Int., p. ci, "is but a translation of the Turkish name *Uch Kiliceh*, which is still given to the convent and church of Echmiazin, with the two other churches on the right and the left, under the invocation of Saint Hr'ipsimê and Saint Kaïanê."—At Uch-Kilisse, there is a monastery supposed to possess the tomb of the patriarch Noah, and with a magnificent church of the 3rd century; during the last war it was pillaged by the Kurds who destroyed the fine library. Not far from the Three Churches is Diadin, on the Murad Su (Eastern Euphrates), and on the road from Trebizond to the frontier, 33 kilom. from Bayazid. Cf. Vital Cuinet, i, p. 234.]

[4] "*Sotto Larcanöe!*" Probably at Bayazid.

[After Uch-Kilisse, the station was in the vicinity of the present town of Diadin, on a height (*Sotto Larcanoe*) where could be seen to the south-west the peak of Massis, wrongly called Ararat; not far from it was the actual town of Karakand, the Scaracanti of Pegolotti. Cf. Heyd, p. 116.]

[I do not see any good reason to think with Kiepert that Pegolotti's route does not pass through Bayazid and runs along lake Urmiah,

At the said plain, for a ticket or permit from the lord	0½ aspers.
At the CAMUZONI, for *tant*.	0½ "
At the Plains of the RED RIVER[1]. for *tant* .	0½ "
At CONDRO, for *tant*.	0½ "
At SANDODDI, ditto	0½ "
At Tauris, ditto	0½ "

And you may reckon that the exactions of the Moccols or Tartar troopers along the road, will amount to something like fifty aspers a load. So that the cost on account of a load of merchandize going by land from Ajazzo of Armenia to Tauris in Cataria[2] (?) will be, as appears by the above details, 209 aspers a load, and the same back again[3].

CHAPTER VIII.

Detail showing how all goods are sold and bought at Constantinople and in Pera, and of the expenses incurred by traders; but especially as regards Pera, because most of the business is done there, where the merchants are more constantly to be found. For the rest of Constantinople belongs to the Greeks, but Pera to the Franks, i.e. to the Genoese. And from Constantinople to Pera, 'tis five miles by land, but half a mile by water.

This is one of the longest chapters in the book, and embraces numerous particulars as to the customs of trade; as of tare, damage, garbling, samples, etc. We shall give some extracts.

Goods are sold at Constantinople in various ways.

instead of passing by Marand. Bayazid is on the road from Trebizond to the Persian frontier, at 264 kil. from Erzrum.]

[1] The Red River (*Fiume Rosso*) is mentioned in this position by the Palatine version of Odoric also. There is no Red River here, so named, but no doubt what is meant is the Araxes, or *Arás*, called by Edrisi Al *Rás*, a name sure to be Italianized into *Rosso*.

[Yule is here mistaken; this *fiume rosso* is no doubt the tributary of the Araxes, the Kizil Chaï which waters Khoi.]

[2] Tartaria?

[3] It is really 203 aspers (about £2. 8*s*. 0*d*.). Apparently he has added in the 6 aspers named at the end of the first paragraph.

The indigo called *Baccaddeo* is (sold in packages) of a certain weight, and the weight you must know should be the cantar. And if the buyer chooses to take it from the seller without weighing it, be it more or less than a cantar, 'tis to the profit or loss of the buyer. But they do almost always weigh it, and then payment is made according to the exact weight, be it more or less than a cantar. And the skin and wrapper are given with it but no tare is deducted; nor is garbling allowed; nor do they allow the indigo to be examined except by a little hole, from which a small sample may be extracted. For such is use and wont in those parts.

The following are sold by the cantar (of 150 Genoese lbs.).

Wormwood; madder, and the bag goes as madder without any allowance for tare. Alum of every kind, and even if it be Roch-alum, the sack and cord go as alum.

The following also are sold by the cantar at Constantinople and in Pera.

Ox hides Buffalo hides Horse hides	In purchasing these they are shown to the provers up the hill, i.e. in Pera; and if the hides smell damp or wet, then a fit allowance is made, and this is the system in Pera and in Constantinople, and they are not put in the sun unless they are exceedingly wet indeed.

Suet in jars[1]; iron of every kind; tin of every kind; lead of every kind. *Zibibbo*[2] or raisins of every kind, and the mats go as raisins, with no allowance for tare unless

[1] "*Sevo in* parrocie"; the latter word is to be found in no dictionary. But in a grant of trading privileges to the Genoese from Leon III, King of Armenia, we find "*Vinum possit rendere in vegetis vel in* parge." And on this St. Martin observes, "This is the common Armenian word *p'hartch*, signifying a *jar*." (*Notices et Extraits*, xi, 114.) I have little doubt that this is the word represented by *parrocie*.

[2] *Arab. zibib*; the word is still in Italian use.

they be raisins of Syria. In that case the baskets or hampers are allowed for as tare, and remain with the buyer into the bargain.

Soap of Venice, soap of Ancona, and soap of Apulia in wooden cases. They make tare of the cases, and then these go to the buyer for nothing. But the soap of Cyprus and of Rhodes is in sacks, and the sacks go as soap with no tare allowance.

Broken almonds in bags; the bag goes as almonds; only if there be more than one sack and cord it must be removed, or deducted, so that the buyer shall not have to take more than one sack and cord as almonds, but for any beyond that there shall be tare allowed; and the cord shall go to the buyer gratis.

Honey in kegs or skins; tare is allowed for the keg or skin, but it remains with the buyer gratis.

Cotton wool[1]; and the sack goes as cotton without tare. Cotton yarn; and the sack is allowed as tare, and remains with the buyer for nothing.

Rice; and the bag goes as rice, but if it be tied the cord is allowed as tare and remains with the seller. Turkey galls of every kind; and if they are in bags you weigh bag and all, and do not make tare of the bag. Dried figs of Majorca and Spain in hampers. Orpiment, and the bag goes as orpiment. Safflower[2], and you make tare of bag and cord, and after that they remain with the buyer gratis.

Henna[3]; and the bag goes as henna, only a tare of four per cent. is allowed by custom of trade. Cummin; and

1 "*Cotone mapputo.*"

2 Here the word is *Asfrole*, the identity of which with safflower will perhaps be doubted. But at p. 373, where he makes the word *affiore*, the description of the article and the way to judge of qualities appear to point to safflower. In other passages he has *astifore*, *astuffi*, but also *zaffole* (di Valenza), *zaffiore*, *zafflore* (pp. 64, 295, 211, 113, 134, 137).

3 "*Alcana*," the Cyprus of the Greeks, the *Phylleria* or Mock-privet of Gerarde, now called *Lawsonia Inermis*, used by Eastern women to tinge the nails, by men in dyeing the beard, etc.

the bag goes as cummin, and if tied with rope the rope is allowed as tare but remains with the buyer gratis.

Pistachios[1]; and the bag goes with them with no allowance for tare, unless there be more bags than one, and if there be, then the excess is weighed and allowed as tare, and the buyer has the one bag gratis.

Sulphur; and the bag or barrel in which it is, is allowed as tare, and goes to the buyer gratis. Senna; and the bag is tare and goes to the buyer. Pitch; and the mat is allowed for as tare, and goes to the buyer. *Morda sangue*[2]; the bag goes with it and no tare allowed.

The following are sold in the same way (but the particulars as to customs of sale, etc., are omitted).

Saltmeat; cheese; flax of Alexandria and of Romania; Camlet wool; washed wool of Romania; unwashed ditto; washed or unwashed wool of Turkey; chestnuts.

The following are sold by the hundredweight of 100 *Genoese pounds* (details omitted).

Round pepper; ginger; barked brazil-wood; lac; zedoary[3]; incense; sugar, and powdered sugar of all kinds; aloes of all kinds; quicksilver; cassia fistola; sal ammoniac or *lisciadro*; cinnabar; cinnamon; galbanum[4]; ladanum

[1] *Fistuchi.* Though I do not find this form in any Italian dictionary, *Macculloch's Commercial Dict.* mentions *Fastucchi* as an Italian form of *Pistacchi*, and I have no doubt this is the word. For the Arabs call pistachioes *Fustúk* and the Turks, *Fistik*. The Persian is *Pistah* with no *k*, so that the word probably was first introduced in the Arabic form. I find Gerarde calls pistachioes *Fistick-Nuts*.

[2] This perplexing word must be the Persian *Murdah-sang*, "Litharge." Burnes however renders *Moordar-sung* (as he spells it) "sulphate of copper" (*Travels*, iii, 207).

[3] *Zettoara.* This is a drug now almost disused; the root of a plant which used to be exported from Malabar, Ceylon, Cochin China, etc. (*Macculloch.*)

[4] A gum-resin derived from a perennial plant (*G. officinale*) growing in Syria, Persia, the Cape of Good Hope, etc. It is imported into England from the Levant chiefly. (*Macculloch.*)

of Cyprus; mastic; copper; amber, big, middling, and small, not wrought; stript coral; clean and fine coral, middling and small.

The following are sold by the pound.

Raw silk; saffron; clove-stalks[1] and cloves; cubebs; lign-aloes; rhubarb; mace; long pepper; galangal[2]; broken camphor; nutmegs; spike[3]; cardamoms; scammony; pounding pearls[4]; manna; borax; gum Arabic; dragon's blood; camel's hay[5]; turbit[6]; silk-gauze; sweetmeats; gold wire; dressed silk; wrought amber in beads, etc.

Sold in half scores of pieces.

Buckrams of Erzingan and Cyprus.

[1] *Fusti di Gherofani.* These, when good, are said elsewhere by Pegolotti to be worth one-third the price of good cloves. The phrase appears often in Uzzano's book, as well as *Fiori* and *Foglia di Gherofani.* Garzia, quoted by Mattioli on Dioscorides, says the *stalks* of the cloves are called *Fusti.* But old Gerarde says: "That grosse kinde of cloves which hath been supposed to be the male, are nothing else than fruit of the same tree tarrying there untill it fall down of itselfe unto the grounde, where by reason of his long lying and meeting with some raine in the mean season, it loseth the quick taste that the others have. Some have called those *Fusti*, whereof we may English them *Fusses.*" Pegolotti has also (p. 309) *Fistuchi di Gherofani*, but these seem to have been clove twigs, which were formerly imported along with cloves, and which Budaeus in a note on Theophrastus considers to have been the *cinnamomum* of the ancients. (See a passage in Ibn Batuta, *infra*; *Gerarde's Herball*, 1535; *Mattioli*, 354; *Budaeus* on *Theophrastus*, 992–3.)

[2] *Galanga*, a root imported from India and China, of aromatic smell and hot unpleasant taste. (*Macculloch.*)

[Galanga or Galangal was much used as a spice in the Middle Ages; it exists of two kinds: *Great* or *Java Galangal* and *Lesser* or *China Galangal.* Cf. *Marco Polo*, ii, p. 229 note.]

[3] *Spigo*; the spike lavender from which this was made was called *Italian Nard.* Marsden supposes the spigo of M. Polo to be spikenard.

[4] *Perle da Pestare*, mentioned also by G. da Uzzano; I suppose for use in medicine. Mattioli quotes from Avicenna and others that pearls were good in palpitations and watery eyes; but not as if they were used in his own time.

[5] *Squinanti*, the σχοῖνος of the Greek herbalists, or *Juncus Odoratus.* The name in the text is that used (and perhaps invented) by Gerarde.

[6] The cortical part of the root of a species of convolvulus from various parts of the East Indies. Like other drugs named here, it is but little used in medicine now-a-days.

By the piece.

Silk velvets; damasks; *maramati*; gold cloth of every kind; *nachetti* and *nacchi* of every kind; and all cloths of silk and gold except gauzes[1].

Sold by the hundred piks *of Gazaria*[2].

Common stuffs and canvasses of all kinds, except those of Champagne; also French and North-country broad cloths.

Then follow details of the different kinds of cloths, with the length of the pieces. And then a detail of special modes of selling certain wares, such as:

Undressed vairs, and vair bellies and backs; Slavonian squirrels; martins and fitches; goat skins and ram skins; dates, filberts, walnuts; salted sturgeon tails; salt; oil of Venice; oil of the March; oil of Apulia, of Gacta, etc.; wheat and barley; wine of Greece, of Turpia in Calabria[3], of Patti in Sicily, of Patti in Apulia[4], of Cutrone in Calabria[5], of the March, of Crete, of Romania; country wine.

Then follow details on the money in use, on the duties levied,—

(And don't forget that if you treat the custom-house officers with respect, and make them something of a present in goods or money, as well as their clerks and dragomen, they will behave with great civility, and always be ready to appraise your wares below their real value.)

[1] On the words in this passage see note, p. 155 *supra*.

[2] Gazaria, the country embracing the Sea of Azov and the Crimea, in which were the Frank factories of Tana, Caffa, Soldaia, etc.; so named from the ancient tribes of the Khozars or Chasars.

[3] Tropea, on the west coast of Calabria.

[4] Patti in Sicily is a small cathedral town west of Milazzo. The other I cannot indicate.

[5] Cotrone, the ancient Crotona, on the east coast of Calabria.

—On the preferential prices given for certain kinds of goods; as to the fees paid for weighing, garbling, brokerage, packing, warehousing, and the like; with details of the relation of the weights and measures to those of most European countries.

This may serve as a sample of the average contents of the book.

CHAP. XXIX treats of how various kinds of goods are packed, etc.

CHAP. XXX is on shipment and matters connected therewith.

CHAP. XXXV is on assays of gold and silver.

CHAP. LXII is *on London in England in itself;* but it does not contain anything of interest for extract. The chief idea connected with England in Pegolotti's mind appears to have been wool[1].

CHAP. LXIII gives a detail of the "Houses (Religious) in Scotland, in England[2], that have wool."

The list is very curious. It embraces:

Niobottoli[3], Merososso[4], Barmunacche[5], Cupero[6], Chilosola[7], Donfermellino[8], Dondarnane[9], Grenellusso[10], Balledirucco (?), Guldingamo[11], Ghelzo[12], Norbonucche[13], Sansasano (?)[14], Grideghorda (?).

But he soon passes from Scotland to England, for the

[1] Woollen cloth was one of the staples of Florentine commerce. In 1338 there were 200 *botteghe*, producing cloth to the value of 1,200,000 *zecchins*, and supporting 30,000 persons. (*Della Decima*, iv, p. 24.)

[2] "*Magioni di Scozia d' Inghilterra.*"

[3] Newbattle. [4] Melrose? or perhaps "Mary's House."

[5] Pagnini has *Barmicciacche*, but the above is from the MS. Balmerynac or Balmannac is the old name of the Abbey of Balmerino in Fifeshire.

[6] Cupar. [7] Killoss or Kynloss in Moray.

[8] Dunfermline. [9] Dundrennan. [10] Glenluce.

[11] Coldingham. [12] Kelso. [13] North Berwick?

[14] This seems like St. Susan's, but I can trace no such Scotch abbey.

following *Houses of the Cistercian Order* certainly belong to the south:

Olcholtam[1], Niomostriere[2] in Orto Bellanda, Fornace in Orto Bellanda[3], Calderea in Coppolanda[4], Salleo in Cravenna[5], Giervalese[6], Fontana[7], Biolanda[8], Bivalse[9], Miesa in Oldaraese[10], Chirchistallo[11], Laroccia[12], Il Parco di Livia[13], Chiricchistede[14], Revesbi[15], Svinsivede[16], Lavaldio[17], Rufforte in Estierenda[18], Gierondona[19].

The chapter contains many more puzzles of the same kind. But our extracts have wandered far from Cathay or the road thither, and must stop.

[1] Holm Cultrum Abbey in Cumberland.

[2] "Newminster," near Morpeth, in "Northumberland."

[3] "Furness in Northumberland," in which it is not.

[4] "Calder Abbey in Cumberland" (and this shows that the Englishman slurred his R's already).

[5] "*Sawley* Abbey in Craven."

[6] Jorvaulx.

[7] Fountains.

[8] Byland.

[9] Probably should be *Rivalse*, Rivaulx.

[10] "Meaux Abbey in Holderness."

[11] Kirkstall.

[12] Roche Abbey.

[13] Probably Louth Park, called "*de Parco lude.*"

[14] Kirkstead.

[15] Revesby Abbey in Lincolnshire.

[16] Swineshead.

[17] The Abbey of *Vaudey* or "de Valle Dei" in Lincolnshire.

[18] Rufford or Rumford Abbey in Nottinghamshire.

[19] Gerondon or Geraldon Abbey in Leicestershire. For these abbeys (which are all Cistercian) see *Tanner's Notitia Monastica.*

APPENDIX

TRANSCRIPT from the original MS. of the first two chapters of PEGOLOTTI.

CAP. I.

Avixamento del viaggio del Ghattaio per lo chanmino della Tana ad andare e ttornare chon merchatantia. Primieramente dalla Tana in Gintarchan sia XXV giornate di charro di buoi e chon carro di chavallo circa da X in XII giornate. Per chanmino si trovano moccholi assai cioe gente d arma e da Gittarchan in Sara sia una giornata per fiumana dacqua et di Sara in Sarachancho sia 8 giornate per una fiumana dacqua e puotesi andare per terra e peracqua ma vassi peracqua per meno spesa della merchatantia. E da Sarachancho in fino in Orghanci sia XX giornate di charro di chanmello e chi va chon marchantia gli conviene che vada in Orghanci pareche la è spacciativa terra di marchatantia. E d' Orghanci in Oltrarre sia da 35 in 40 giornate di chanmello chon carro e chi si partisse di Sarachanco e andasse dritto in Oltrarre si va L giornate e segli non avesse merchatantia gli sarebbe migliore via che dandare in Orghanci. E di choltrarre in Armalecchо sia 45 giornate di some dasino e ogni die truovi moccholi. E d Armalecchо infino in Chamexu sia 70 giornate dasino et di Chamexu in sino che vieni a una fiumana che si chiama... sia XLV giornate di chavallo e dalla fiumana se ne puoi andare in Chassai ella vendere sonmi dellargento che avessi, perocche la e spacciativa terra di merchantia. E di Chassai si va cholla muneta chessi trae de sonmi dellargento venduti in Chassai che è moneta di charta chessappella la detta moneta babisci che gli quattro di quella moneta vagliono un sonmo dariento per le contrade del Ghattaijo. E di Chassai a Ghamalecco che è la mastra città del paese del Ghattaijo si va 30 giornate.

CAP. II.

Cose bixognevole a Merchatanti che vogliono fare il sopradetto viaggio del Ghattaijo. Primieramente chonviene che si lasci crescere la barba grande et non si rada. E vuolsi fornire alla Tana di Turcimanni e non si vuole guardare a rispiarmo dal chattivo al buono nonchosta quella dingordo chelluomo non se ne megliori vi va piu. E oltre a Turcimanni si chonviene menare per lo meno due fanti buoni che ssapiano bene la lingua Cumanesca e sse il merchatante vuole menare dalla Tana niuna fenmina chon secho si puote e sse nolla vuole menare non fa forza mappure se la menasse sara tenuto di miglior chondizione che se nolla menasse e pero sella mena chonviene che sappia la lingua Chumanesca chome il fante. E dalla Tana infino in Gittarchan si chonviene fornire di vivanda 25 dì cioe di farina e di pesci insalati perocche charne truova assai per chanmino in tutti i luoghi. E ssimilmente in tutti i luoghi che vai da uno paexe a un altro nel detto viaggio sechondo le giornate dette di sopra si chonviene fornire di farina e di pesci insalati che altre chose truovi assai e spezialmente charne.

Il chanmino dandare dalla Tana al Ghattajo è sichurissimo e di dì e di notte sechondo che ssi chonta pergli merchatanti che lhanno uxato salvo se il merchatante che va o che viene morisse in chanmino ogni chosa sarebbe del singnore del paexe ove morisse il merchatante e tutto prenderebbono gli uficiali del singnore. E ssimilmente se morisse al Ghattajo veramente segli avesse suo fratello o stretto chompangno che dicesse che fusse suo fratello si gli sarebbe dato lavere del morto e chonperebbesi in questo modo lavere. E ancora va un altro pericholo cioe che quando lo singnore morisse insino che non fusse chiamato laltro singnore che dovesse singnoreggiare in quello mezzo alchuna volta ve stata fatta novitade a Ffranchi e ad altre stranee genti. I Franchi appellaneglino tutti i christiani delle parti di Romania innanzi in verso il ponente. E non chorre sichuro il chanmino infino che non è chiamato laltro singnore che dee regnare appresso di quelloche è morto.

Il Ghattajo si è una Provincia dove a molte terre e molte chasali in fra laltre si a una cioe la mastra cittade ove riparano merchatanti e ove si fa il forza della merchatantia la quale cittade si chiama Chambalecchо. E la detta cittade gira cento miglia ed è tutta piena di gente e di magione e di abitanti nella detta cittade.

Ragionasi che un merchatante chon uno Turcimanno e con due fanti e con avere della valuta di XXV miglia di Fiorini doro spenderebbe infino al Ghattajo da LX in LXXX sonmi dargento volendo fare masserizia e per tutto il chanmino da ttornare dal Ghattajo ala Tana chontando spese di boccha e ssalario di fanti e tutte spese intorno a cio sonmi V alla soma o meno e puote valere il sonmo da fiorini cinque doro. E ragionasi chel carro debbe menare pure uno bue e del charro X cantara di genova el charro di chanmelli mena 3 chanmeli e del charro 30 cantari di Genova e il carro de chavalli mena 1° chavallo e del charro cantara 6½ genovesche di seta communalmente da libre 250 genovesche e uno scibetto di seta si ragiona da libre 110 in 115 genovesche.

Raggionasi che dalla Tana in Sara sia meno sichuro il chanmino che non e tutto laltro chanmino ma segli fussono 60 uomini quando il chanmino è in piggiore chonditione andrebbe bene sichuro come per la casa sua.

Chi volesse muovere da Genova o da Vinegia per andare al detto luogo e viaggio del Ghattajo portasse tele e andasse in Organci ne farebbe bene e in Organci chonperasse sonmi e andasse chon essi avanti sanza investire in altra merchatantia seggià nonavesse alquante balle di tele molto sottilissime che tengono piccholo inbuglio e non vogliono piu di spesa, che vogliono altre tele piu grosse.

E possono i Mercanti cavalcare per lo chanmino o chavallo o asino o quella cavalcatura che piace loro di cavalcare.

Tutto largento che i merchatanti portano e che va al Ghattajo il Singnore del Ghattajo lo fa pigliare per se e mettelo in suo texoro e merchatanti che lui portano ne da loro moneta di pappiero cioe di charta gialla choniata della bolla del detto Singnore la quale moneta sapella paliscj della qual moneta puoi e ttruovi chonperare seta ed ognaltra merchatantia e cosa che chonperare volesse e tutti quelli del paexe sono tenuti di prenderla e gia pero non si cosi sopra chonpera la merchatantia perche sia moneta di pappiero. E della detta moneta di pappiero ne sono di tre ragioni che luna si mette per piu che laltra secondo che sono ordinate a valuta per lo Singnore.

E ragionasi che al Ghattajo arai da libre 19 in 20 di seta Ghattaja recato a peso di Genova per uno sonmo d'argento che puote pesare da once 8½ di Genova ed è di lega d once 11 e denari 17 fine per libbra.

E ragionasi che avai al Ghattajo da 3 in 3½ pezze di chanmoccha di seta per uno sonmo e da 3½ in sino in 5 pezze di nacchetti di seta e doro per uno sonmo dargento.

V

MARIGNOLLI'S RECOLLECTIONS OF EASTERN TRAVEL

V

JOHN DE' MARIGNOLLI AND HIS RECOLLECTIONS OF EASTERN TRAVEL

BIOGRAPHICAL AND INTRODUCTORY NOTICES

THESE notices of Eastern Travel are found, like unexpected fossils in a mud-bank, imbedded in a Chronicle of Bohemia, which was first printed from an old MS. in the latter half of the last century. Of the author there is not very much to be learned, except what can be gathered from these reminiscences of his. John of Florence, a Minorite, is known to the ecclesiastical biographers as the author of sundry theological works, and as Bishop of Bisignano. And a John of Florence, a Minorite, is also known, through brief notices in the Annals of Raynaldus and Wadding, as having gone on a mission to Cathay. But till the publication of the Bohemian Chronicle the identity of these Johns does not seem to have been suspected, and even since the date of that publication they have been carefully discriminated by a very learned Franciscan[1].

The two Johns were, however, one. He was a native of Florence or its neighbourhood, and came of the Marignolli of San Lorenzo, a noble family of the Republic which derived its name from a village called Marignolle, in the

[1] See *Supplementum et Castigatio ad* Scriptores Trium Ordinum S. Francisci a Waddingo, &c., *opus posthumum Fr. Jo. Hyacinthi Sbaraleæ*, Romæ, 1806, p. 436. Another John of Florence, also connected with the Eastern missions of the fourteenth century, is mentioned by Quétif; but he was a Dominican, and bishop of Tiflis in Georgia. (*Script. Ord. Prædicht.*, p. 583.)

Valley of the Arno, about two miles south-west of the city. The family of the Marignolli was, in the middle ages, one of the most influential in Florence, and its members were generally leaders in the Guelf faction. They were expelled from the Republic on the defeat of that party at Montaperti in 1260[1],

> "Lo strazio e 'l grande scempio
> Che fece l' Arbia colorata in rosso,"

but after a few years effected their return, and long continued to give many gonfaloniers and other magistrates to the city. In the seventeenth century, however, they were already quite extinct. A street in Florence near the cathedral, now called Via de' Cerretani, is still marked as having formerly borne their name (*Già de' Marignolli*)[2].

The date of John's birth is not known. But it may be guessed from the wandering garrulity of his recollections, that he was an aged man, when, some time about 1355, he put them on paper; and this is confirmed by a circumstance which will be cited below. He was therefore born, in all probability, before 1290.

He was a member of the Franciscan monastery of Santa Croce in Florence, to which he apparently refers in his story, when he tells us that on his return from the East he deposited a certain Indian garment in the sacristy of the Minorites in that city.

He is known for certain as the author of two works in Tuscan: one a *History of St. Onufrio*; the other a work called *The Acts of the Apostles*, whether a translation of Scripture or a collection of legends, I do not know. Both are said to be cited as authorities in Italian by the Della Crusca vocabulary. But he is also supposed to have been

[1] *G. Villani*, *Istoria Fiorentina*, book v, c. 79, 80.

[2] The last fact is from personal observation. Others in this paragraph are partly from *Italia Sacra* of Ughelli (Venice, 1717, i, 522), and partly from a respectable Tuscan authority the reference to which I have omitted to note.

the John of Florence who wrote a History of his Order, and a treatise on the Canonization of St. Francis, works which formerly existed in the library of Santa Croce[1]. Sbaralea also regards as probably written by Marignolli a small Italian work on *The Flowers of St. Francis*, which was printed by Nicolas Girardengo at Venice in 1480, and often reprinted; and also a Life of St. John Baptist, which is appended to the former in the MS. at Bologna.

Marignolli refers in his recollections to having at one time given lectures at Bologna[2]. And this is all that I can collect about him previous to his mission to the East.

John of Monte Corvino, the venerable Archbishop of Cambalec, died as we have already seen about 1328, and the successor appointed by Pope John in 1333 seems never to have reached his destination[3].

In 1338 however there arrived at Avignon an embassy from the Great Khan of Cathay, consisting of Andrew a Frank, and fifteen other persons. They brought two letters to the pope: one purporting to be from the Grand Khan himself, and the other from certain princes of the Christian Alans in his service[4].

1 *Sbaralea*, u.s.

2 "*Vidi etiam Bononiæ quando ibi legebam.*" (*Dobner*, p. 112.)

3 See above, p. 11.

4 ["Ineunte hoc anno pervenerunt Avenionem Legati Imperatoris maximi Tartarorum, qui se Imperatorum Imperatorem nuncupabat (erant enim in Tartaria plures Imperatores, quibus hic praecellebat) icturi foedus cum Pontifice, vel majorem conciliaturi amicitiam per frequentes & alternas, quas stabilire cupiebat legationes: eo praesertim titulo, quod Christianis omnem favorem impenderit; quibus veluti peculiaris eorumdem fautor & protector, Pontificiam deprecabatur benevolentiam. Ita etiam ipsi testati sunt, praecipue Principes Alanorum, scriptis per eosdem Legatos litteris, quibus Imperatoriam erga se depredicant beneficentiam, & gratias a Pontifice rependi deposcunt. Exhibeo ipsas eorumdem litteras, per quas constabit rei Christianae status inter Tartaros, & Minoritarum, praesertim bonae memoriae Joannis a Monte Corvino, olim Archiepiscopi Cambalien. in fide propaganda inter efferas gentes sollicitudo." Wadding, vii, p. 209.

The envoys were Andrew and William "of Nassio" and Thogay, an Alan of Cathay: "Scribitur littera salvicunductus pro Andrea et

It is not stated that Andrew was an ecclesiastic; but it is possible that he may have been our acquaintance the Bishop of Zayton[1].

D'Ohsson[2] regards the whole matter as an example of the sham embassies which on several occasions were palmed off on the European courts as coming from the Mongol princes. But he is apparently not aware of Marignolli's narrative of the return mission and its reception. And the Khan's letter looks very genuine in its haughty curtness and absence of swelling titles, the use of which Chinghiz prohibited to his successors. The preliminary phrase also seems the same that is found prefixed to the Tartar letters in the French archives; and which Rémusat states to be a mark of genuine character[3]. In any case the letter is meritoriously short and to the point, so we may give it in full[4].

"In the strength of the Omnipotent God!

"The Emperor of Emperors commandeth:

"We send our envoy, Andrew the Frank, with fifteen others, to the Pope, the Lord of the Christians, in Frankland beyond the Seven Seas[5] where the sun goes down, to

Guillelmo de Nassio et Thogay Alano de Cathayo nunciis imperatoris Tartarorum super certis fidem catholicam tangentibus ad sedem apostolicam destinatis et cum litteris sursalibus ejusdem sedis remissis. Dat. Avenione, XIII kal. julii, anno quarto." Reg. vatic. 62, f. xxxii v°, quoted by C. de La Roncière and Léon Dorez, *Lettres inédites de Marino Sanudo l'ancien* in *Bib. de l'École des Chartes*, lvi, 1895, p. 29.]

[1] See p. 28 above. [2] *Hist. des Mongols*, ii, 608.

[3] *Mém. de l'Académie des Inscript.* (Modern) vii, 367. He renders it "*Par la force du Ciel suprême.*"

[4] This and the other letters connected with this embassy are given in *Wadding*, vol. vii, pp. 209 and *seq.*; also in *Mosheim*, Append., pp. 166 and *seq.*

[5] Meinert (see below) supposes these seven seas to be the Aral, Caspian, Sea of Azov, Black Sea, Sea of Marmora, Archipelago, and the Mediterranean. It may be noted that Edrisi also reckons seven seas besides the Great Ocean, viz. Sea of China, Red Sea, Green Sea (Persian Gulf), Sea of Damascus (Mediterranean), Sea of Venice, Sea of Pontus, and Sea of Jorjan (Caspian). And the Arabian navigators of the ninth century also reckon seven seas between Basra and China. But any such

open a way for the frequent exchange of messengers between us and the Pope; and to request the Pope himself to send us his blessing, and always to remember us in his holy prayers; and to commend to him the Alans, our servants and his Christian sons. Also we desire that our messengers bring back to us horses and other rarities from the sun-setting.

"Written in Cambalec, in the year of the Rat, in the sixth month, on the third day of the Moon[1]."

The letter of the Alan chiefs, with partial omissions, runs as follows:

"In the strength of the Omnipotent God, and in the honour of our Lord the Emperor!

"We, FUTIM JOENS, CHATICEN TUNGII, GEMBOGA EVENZI, JOANNES IUCHOY (and RUBEUS PINZANUS)[2],

scientific precision is here highly improbable. The reference is more likely to be to the seven annular seas of the Buddhist cosmogony, and done into vulgar English means only that the Pope lived at the "Back of Beyond."

[1] About July 1336.

["In fortitudine Omnipotentis Dei, Imperatoris Imperatorum praeceptum. Nos mittimus Nuncium nostrum Andræam Francum cum quindecim sociis ad Papam, Dominum Christianorum in Franchiam ultra septem maria, ubi sol occidit, ad aperiendum viam nunciis saepe mittendis per nos ad Papam, & per Papam ad nos, & ad rogandum ipsum Papam, ut mittat nobis suam benedictionem, & in orationibus suis sanctis semper memoriam faciat de nobis. Et quod Alanos servitores nostros, filios suos Christianos, habeat recommendatos. Item quod adducant nobis ab occasu solis equos, & alia mirabilia. Scripta in Cambalec in anno Rati mense sexto, tertia die lunationis." Wadding, vii, p. 209.]

[2] These at first sight look like names out of *Gulliver's Travels*, such as Quinbus Flestrin and the like. They are several times repeated in the copies of different letters from the Pope that have come down to us, and the forms vary considerably. We have the following:

Futim Joens, Fodim and Fodin Jovens;
Chaticen Tungii [and Ghaticen Tungy], Chyansam and Chyausam Tongi;
Gemboga Evenzi, Chemboga Vensii or Vense [and Venz];
Ioannes Jukoy, Iochoy, or Yathoy [and Yotkoy];
Rubeus Pinzanus or Puizanus.

The last name occurs in two of the Pope's letters, but not in that of the Alans as we have it.

with our heads in the dust salute our Holy Father the Pope. ...For a long time we received instruction in the Catholic faith, with wholesome guidance and abundant consolation, from your Legate Friar John, a man of weighty, capable, and holy character. But since his death, eight years ago, we have been without a director, and without spiritual consolation. We heard, indeed, that thou hadst sent another legate, but he hath never yet appeared. Wherefore

I cannot venture to say what these names are meant to represent, but the following suggestions may at least show the sort of explanations that are practicable. I have a suspicion that the first six words form two names only instead of three. Assuming this we have for the first, Futim Joens (i.e. Yoens) Chyansam. To reduce Yoens or Yovens to a rational form it must be remembered that these names were probably transferred from Persian, or some analogous character. Transfer Yovens *back* into Persian it becomes يونس, which when read properly into Roman letters is *Yúnus* or Jonas, no doubt the name of the personage in question; whilst *Futim* may represent the Chinese title *Fu t'ai*, and *Chyansam* that of *Chingsang*, the designation of the great ministers of state which often occurs in the Mongol history, and has already occurred in the extracts from Rashid. (*D'Ohsson*, ii, 636; *Journ. Asiat.*, sér. ii, tom. vi, pp. 352–3; *supra*, p. 119.)

The next name will be *Tungii Gemboga Vensii*. *Tungii* looks like the *Dankji* of Shah Rukh's Embassy, in the narrative of which we find it applied to the Chinese governors of the frontier provinces, perhaps as a corruption of the Chinese *Tsiang kiun*, a general. *Gemboga* or Chambuca is the proper name, a name quite Tartar in character, for scores of *Boghas* will be found in the histories of the Mongols and of Timur (from Turki *Bugha*, an army leader). We find *Jamuca*, which is perhaps the same name, as one of the rivals of Chinghiz (*D'Ohsson*, i, 70). And Vensii is almost certainly *Wan shi*, a commandant of ten thousand.

The *Yukoy*, which appears to be the title of Joannes, the next of the Alans, is perhaps *Yeukie*, which according to Visdelou (*Suppt. to Herbelot*) is a rank equivalent to colonel, or as Pauthier calls it, "*chef de bataillon*" (*Chine Mod.*, 221). [Couvreur gives *Iou ki*, Lieut.-Colonel, and Mayers, *Yeo ki*, Major; but the title did not exist at the time of the Mongols.] Lastly we have in the title of *Rubeus Pinzanus*, the *Fanchán* or *Panchán* of the Persian historians of the Mongol dynasty (*D'Ohsson*, vi, 530, 637, etc.; Ext. from Rashid, *supra*, p. 120) representing the Chinese title of an under minister of state. *Rubeus* is probably a translation of the original name, *Kizil* or the like, meaning *Red*.

[This note of Yule might perhaps have been suppressed; for the names somewhat altered, of Futim, and others, however strange they look, are genuine; the first three: Fodim = Fou ting, Chiansam = Hiang chan, Gemboga = Tchŏ-yen-p'ou-houa (J̌ayanbogha), have been found by Pelliot in the *Yuen Shi* and no doubt the others will be discovered in the same work.]

we beseech your Holiness to send us a legate, wise, capable, and virtuous, to care for our souls. And let him come quickly, for we are here a flock without a head, without instruction, without consolation.... And it has happened on three or four different occasions that envoys have come on thy part to the aforesaid Emperor our Master, and have been most graciously received by him, and have had honours and presents bestowed upon them; and although all of them in turn promised to bring back thine answer to our Lord aforesaid, never yet hath he had any reply from thee or from the Apostolic See. Wherefore let your Holiness see to it that this time and henceforward there may be no doubt about a reply being sent, and an envoy also, as is fitting from your Holiness. For it is cause of great shame to Christians in these parts, when their fellows are found to tell lies." (Date as above.)[1]

[1] ["In fortitudine omnipotentis Dei, & in honore Imperatoris Domini nostri.

"Nos Futim Juens, Caticen Tungii, Gemboga Evenzi, Joannes Juckoy, sanctum Patrem Dominum Papam nostrum, capitibus ad terram positis, pedes osculantes, salutamus, petentes benedictionem suam & gratiam, & quod in orationibus suis sanctis faciat de nobis memoriam, & numquam obliviscatur nostri. Hoc autem sanctitati vestrae sit notum, quod longo tempore fuimus informati in fide Catholica, & salubriter gubernati, & consolati plurimum per Legatum vestrum fratrem Joannem, valentem, sanctum, & sufficientem virum, qui tamen mortuus est ante octos annos, in quibus fuimus sine gubernatore, & sine spirituali consolatione, licet audierimus, quod providistis de alio legato, ille tamen nondum venit. Quare supplicamus Sanctitati Vestrae, quod mittatis nobis bonum, sufficientem, ac sapientem Legatum, qui curam habeat de animabus nostris, & quod cito veniat, quia male stamus sine capite, sine informatione, & sine consolatione, supplicamus etiam sapientiae vestrae, quod Domino nostro Imperatori respondeatis gratiose, ita quod aperiatur via, sicut & ipse petit, expedita & apta nunciis saepe mittendis a vobis ad ipsum, & ab ipso ad vos, & ad conferendam inter vos & ipsum amicitiam: quia si hoc feceritis magnum bonum subsequetur pro salute animarum, & pro exaltatione fidei Christianae, quia favor ejus in imperio suo facere potest innumera bona, & indignatio ejus innumera mala, & ideo recommendetis nos sibi, filios vestros, & fratres, & fideles alios, qui sunt in imperio ejus, quia si ita feceritis, bono maxima facietis, cum ita factum fuerit, quod ex parte vestra diversis temporibus tres vel quatuor nunc iverunt ad praefatum Imperatorem Dominum nostrum, a quo gratiose recepti fuerunt, & honorati & remunerati; & ex tunc dictus Imperator nullum a vobis, vel a Sede

The position of these Alans in China suggests a curious and perplexing problem. We shall find that Marignolli speaks of them as "the greatest and noblest nation in the world, the fairest and bravest of men"; as those to whose aid Chinghiz owed all his great victories; and who in the writer's own day were to the number of thirty thousand in the service of the Great Khan, and filled the most important offices of state, whilst all were, at least nominally, Christians.

The Alans were known to the Chinese by that name, in the ages immediately preceding and following the Christian era, as dwelling near the Aral, in which original position they are believed to have been closely akin to, if not identical with, the famous Massagetæ. Hereabouts also Ptolemy (vi, 14) appears to place the Alani-Scythæ, and Alanæan Mountains. From about 40 B.C. the emigrations of the Alans seem to have been directed westward to the lower Don; here they are placed in the first century by Josephus and by the Armenian writers; and hence they are found issuing in the third century to ravage the rich provinces of Asia Minor. In 376 the deluge of the Huns on its westward course came upon the Alans and overwhelmed them. Great numbers of Alans are found to have joined the conquerors on their further progress, and large bodies of Alans afterwards swelled the waves of Goths, Vandals, and Sueves, that rolled across the Western Empire. A portion of the Alans, however, after the Hun invasion retired into the plains adjoining Caucasus, and into the lower valleys of that region, where they maintained the name and nationality which the others speedily lost. Little is heard of these Caucasian Alans for many centuries,

Apostolica responsum accepit, licet singuli promiserunt se a vobis responsa ad praefatum Dominum reportare. Quare provideat Sanctitas vestra, quod hac vice, & deinceps habeat certum a vobis responsum & nuncium, sicut decet Sanctitatem vestram, quia magna verecundia est Christianis in partibus istis, quando mendacia inveniuntur in ipsis. Scripta in Cambalec in anno Rati, mense sexto, tertia die lunationis." Wadding, vii, pp. 209–210.]

except occasionally as mercenary soldiers of the Byzantine emperors or the Persian kings. In the thirteenth century they made a stout resistance to the Mongol conquerors, and though driven into the mountains they long continued their forays on the tracts subjected to the Tartar dynasty that settled on the Volga, so that the Mongols had to maintain posts with strong garrisons to keep them in check. They were long redoubtable both as warriors and as armourers, but by the end of the fourteenth century they seem to have come thoroughly under the Tartar rule; for they fought on the side of Toctamish Khan of Sarai against the great Timur.

The Chinese historians of the Mongol dynasty now call this people ASU, and by that name (Aas and the like) they were also known to Ibn Batuta and to the Frank travellers, Carpini, Rubruquis, and Josafat Barbaro. This and other reasons led Klaproth to identify them with the *Ossethi*, still existing in Caucasus. Vivien de St. Martin however has urged strong reasons against this identification, though he considers both tribes to have been originally members of one great stock of *Asi*, who by routes and at times widely separated, severally found their way from Central Asia to the region of Caucasus. According to the same authority the Georgians, who always distinguished between the *Alanethi* and *Ossethi*, still recognize a people of the former branch in the interior of the Abaz country where no traveller has penetrated.

We now come to the difficulty of accounting for the appearance of numerous Alans in the armies and administration of the Yuen dynasty, a difficulty which perhaps led Klaproth to suggest that those were really of a Mongol tribe bearing that name, and had nothing in common with the Caucasian people of whom we have been speaking[1].

[1] *Klaproth, Magazin Asiatique*, i, p. 199.

This suggestion has not met with acceptance. And there are notices to be found which account to some extent for the position ascribed to the Alans in China, though the records on the subject seem to be imperfect. Chinghiz Khan, in the course of his western conquests, is recorded to have forced many of the inhabitants of the countries which he overran to take service in his armies. The historian Rashíduddín, in speaking of the Christianity of the Keraits, and especially of the mother and the minister of Kuyuk-Khan, who were Christians of that tribe, says that they summoned to the court of Karakorum numerous priests of Syria, Asia Minor, *the Alan country*, and Russia. And Gaubil, without apparently being aware of the identity with the Alans of the Asu (or Aas) who are spoken of in the text of the Chinese history which he follows, observes in a note that the country of the Asu, after its conquest, furnished many valuable officers to the Mongols, and that it could not have lain far from the Caspian. The same narrative states that Kúblái Khan, when despatching an army against the Sung dynasty of Southern China, desired his general to select the best possible officers, and that there were consequently attached to the army many chiefs of the Uighúrs, Persians, Kincha, *Asu*[1], and others. The

[1] [See Marco Polo, ii, p. 179 *n.* Mr. Rockhill writes (*Rubruck*, p. 88 *note*): "The Alans or Aas appear to be identical with the An-ts'ai or A-lan-na of the *Hou Han Shu* (bk. 88, 9), of whom we read that 'they led a pastoral life N.W. of Sogdiana (K'ang-chü) in a plain bounded by great lakes or swamps, and in their wanderings went as far as the shores of the Northern Ocean.' (Ma Twan-lin, bk. 338.) *Pei-shi* (bk. 97, 12) refers to them under the name of Aorsi living to the north but contiguous to the Albani, whom some authors confound with them, but whom later Armenian historians carefully distinguish from them. (De Morgan, *Mission*, i, 332.) Ptolemy (vi, 14) speaks of this people as the 'Scythian Alans' ('Αλανοὶ Σκύθαι); but the first definite mention of them in classical authors is, according to Bunbury (ii, 486), found in Dionysius Periergetes (305), who speaks of the ἀλκήεντες 'Αλανοί (see also De Morgan, i, 202, and Deguignes, ii, 279, *et seq.*)." According to the *Yuen shi* and Devéria, *Journ. Asiat.*, Nov.–Dec. 1896, p. 432, in 1229 and 1241, when Okkodaï's army reached the Country of the Aas (Alans), their chief submitted at once and a body of one thousand Alans was kept for the private guard of

anecdote which Marco Polo relates of the massacre of a body of Christian Alans during this very war, may also be called to mind[1].

Still the numbers and very prominent position ascribed by Marignolli to the Alans in the Mongol-Chinese empire, are, after all allowance for natural exaggeration of the importance of his co-religionists, rather startling. The history of these later princes of the Yuen dynasty does not seem to be accessible in any great detail, but it is easily conceivable that as the spirit of the Mongols degenerated, their princes, as in so many similar cases, came to lean more and more on their foreign auxiliaries, and that these may have been often found in occupation of the highest posts of the empire. Indeed it was one of the complaints against Tocatimur or Shun Ti, the Emperor reigning at this time, that he gave too much authority to "foreigners of ill-regulated morals[2]."

Returning to the embassy of 1338, we find that it was graciously received by the Pope, Benedict XII, one mark of his favour being to create one of the Tartar envoys sergeant-at-arms to himself[3]; that in due time his Holiness delivered answers to the letters from Cathay; and that shortly afterwards he appointed legates to proceed on his own part to the court of Cambalec, with a charge which

the Great Khan; Mangu enlisted in his bodyguard half the troops of the Alan prince, Arslan, whose younger son Nicholas took a part in the expedition of the Mongols against Karajang (Yunnan). This Alan imperial guard was still in existence in 1272, 1286 and 1309, and it was divided into two corps with headquarters in the Ling pei province (Karakorúm). See also Bretschneider, *Mediæval Researches*, ii, pp. 84-90.]

[1] [See *Marco Polo*, ii, pp. 178–179. This massacre is confirmed by Chinese Sources.]

[2] See a learned article by *Vivien de St. Martin*, in *Ann. des Voyages* for 1848, iii, 129; also *Rubruquis*, pp. 242, 243, 252, 381; *Carpini*, pp. 709, 729; *Ramusio*, ii, 92; *St. Martin* in *Journ. Asiat.*, sér. ii, tom. v, 175; *Klaproth* in ditto, p. 389; *Jacquet* in ditto, vii, 417–433; *St. Martin, Mém. sur l'Arménie*, ii, 280; *Ibn Batuta*, ii, 448; *Gaubil, Hist. de Gentchis Can.*, pp. 40, 147; *Deguignes*, iv, 215, etc.

[3] *Baluzius, Vitæ Pap. Avenion.*, i, 242.

combined the reciprocation of the Khan's courtesies with the promotion of missionary objects.

The letters addressed by the Pope in reply to the Khan and the Alan Princes are of no interest[1]. They were accompanied by letters also to the Khans of Kipchak and Chagatai, and to two Christian ministers of the latter sovereign, expressing the Pope's intention speedily to send envoys to those courts. With these letters the eastern envoys departed from Avignon in July 1338, bearing recommendations from the Pope to the Doge and Senate of Venice, and to the Kings of Hungary and Sicily[2].

Some months later the Pontiff named the legates, and addressed a letter to them under date II Kal. Novemb., in the fourth year of his Popedom, *i.e.*, 31st October, 1338. Their names were Nicholas Bonet S.T.P., Nicholas of Molano, JOHN OF FLORENCE, and Gregory of Hungary[3].

But for the disinterment of Marignolli's reminiscences in the Bohemian Chronicle, this is all that we should know of the mission, excepting what is conveyed by a few brief lines in Wadding's Annals of the Order under 1342, as to the arrival of the party at the Court of Cambalec, and eleven years later as to the return of its surviving members to the headquarters of the Church at Avignon.

It does not appear with what strength or composition the mission actually started, but probably there were a good many friars in addition to the legates. Indeed, a contemporary German chronicler says, that fifty Minorites were sent forth on this occasion; but it is evident that he had no accurate knowledge on the subject; and, indeed,

[1] The letter to the Khan from this James Fournier, Bishop of Rome under the name of Benedict XII, commences without any mincing of the matter: "*Nos qui, licet immeriti,* LOCUM DEI TENEMUS IN TERRIS."

[2] *Wadding*, l. c.

[3] ["Dilectis filiis Nicolao Boneti sacrae Theologiae Professori, Nicolao de Molano, Joanni de Florentia, & Gregorio de Hungaria Ordinis Fratrum Minorum." Wadding, vii, p. 214.]

his notice is accompanied by one of the fabulous statements, so frequent in that age, as to the conversion of the Grand Khan to Christianity, and by other palpable errors[1]. Marignolli mentions incidentally that the party, during their stay at Cambalec, consisted of thirty-two persons, but with no further particulars. Nor do we even know what became of his colleagues in the legation. Though Marignolli's name comes only third in the Pope's letters, he speaks throughout his narrative as if he had been the chief, if not the sole, representative of the Pontiff. And it is him alone that Wadding mentions by name in his short notices of the proceedings and return of the mission.

One of the four indeed, Nicholas Bonet, must have returned speedily if he ever started for the East at all. For in May 1342 he is recorded to have been appointed by Clement VI to the Bishopric of Malta[2].

Marignolli's notices of his travels have no proper claim to the title of a narrative, and indeed the construction of a

[1] Under the year 1339: "The King of the Tartars is reported to have been converted through the agency of a certain woman who had been brought to the Catholic faith by the Minor Friars dwelling in that country for the purpose of preaching Christ's Gospel. And he sent ambassadors with a letter to Pope Benedict, to beg that he would deign to send teachers, preachers, and directors of the orthodox faith to convert the people, to baptize the converted, and to confirm the baptized in their new faith. And the Pope, joyfully assenting, arranged the despatch of fifty Minor Friars (because men of that order had been the instruments of the king's conversion), all men of good understanding and knowledge of life. But as to what progress they have made, or how much people they have won to the Lord Jesus Christ, up to this present time of Lent in the year 1343 no news whatever hath reached Suabia." (*Joannis Vitodurani* (of Winterthur) *Chron.* in *Eccard*, i, col. 1852.)

[2] *Wadding*, An. 1342, § iv. This annalist says of Nicholas, as if knowing all about his return, "*qui tamen ob graves causas ex ipso reversus est itinere.*"

["*Supremae dignitatis*, II Kalend. Jun. fratre Nicolao Boneti, Viro docto, sacrae Theologiae Magistro, (quem superius, diximus destinatum Legatum ad Tartaros, qui tamen ob graves causas ex ipso reversus est itinere) ad Milevitanum, sub Archiepiscopo Panormitano, per obitum Henrici etiam Minoritae." Wadding, vii, p. 253. According to Gams' *Series Episcoporum*, Nicolas was elected to the see of Malta on the 27th of the eleventh month of 1342 and died in 1360.]

narrative out of them is a task something like that of raising a geological theory out of piecemeal observations of strata and the study of scattered organic remains. It is necessary, therefore, to give a short sketch of the course of his travels, such as the editor has understood it, unless readers are to go through the same amount of trouble in putting the pieces together. But in doing so I shall anticipate as little as possible the details into which our author enters.

The party left Avignon in December 1338, but had to wait at Naples some time for the Tartar envoys, who had probably been lionizing in the cities and courts of Italy. Constantinople was reached on the 1st May, 1339, and there the party halted till midsummer. They then sailed across the Black Sea to Caffa, and travelled thence to the Court of Uzbek, Khan of Kipchak, no doubt at Sarai. The winter of 1339 was passed there; and, supposing the party to start about May and to take the usual commercial route by Urghanj, they would get to Armalec (or Almaliq), the capital of the Chagatai dynasty or "Middle Empire," about September. The stay of the mission at Almaliq was prolonged. They did not quit it till 1341, and perhaps not till near the end of that year. They must also have spent some considerable time at Kamul[1], so that probably they did not arrive at Peking till about May or June 1342. It was, however, almost certainly within that year; for both Wadding's notice, and a curious entry in the Chinese Annals, agree in naming it[2].

[1] See Marignolli's Recollections of Travel, *infra*, near the end.

[2] *Wadding*, vii, p. 258, and note, *infra*, on the horses conveyed to the Khan by Marignolli.

[1342. "XI. Magnus erat sub hoc tempore in Tartaria Christianorum numerus, & frequentes Fratrum missiones, quorum & domicilia multa, & opinio magna. Habebant domum prope magni Chami palatium, & convescebantur ei, a quibus etiam dum iret cubitum, volebat benedici. In magna Tartaria, prope regionem Millescorte plura habebant domicilia, in civitate Seitin aliud, in Armalech alterum quod Alisolda, uti diximus, destruxit; in Iberia duo immobilia, & quinque ad tentorii modum mobilia; in Taurisio

The time spent by Marignolli at Cambalec extended to three or four years, after which he proceeded through the empire to the port of Zaytún, where there were houses of his Order. He sailed from Zaytún for India on the 26th December, either in 1346 or 1347, probably the latter. Of this voyage unluckily he says not one word, except to record his arrival at Columbum (Quilon) in Malabar, during the following Easter week. He remained with the Christians of Columbum upwards of a year, and then, during the south-west monsoon of 1348 or 1349, set sail for the Coromandel Coast to visit the shrine of Thomas the Apostle. After passing only four days there he proceeded to visit Saba, a country which he evidently means to be identified with the Sheba of Scripture, and which he finds still governed by a queen.

As this Saba and its queen offer the most difficult problem in all the disjointed story of Marignolli's wanderings, and as his notices of it are widely dispersed, I will bring together the substance of all in this place, hoping that some critic may have learning and good luck enough to solve a knot which I have given up in something like despair.

This Saba, then, is the finest island in the world; the Arctic Pole is there, as was pointed out to Marignolli by Master Lemon of Genoa (I suppose after his return to

duo; in Masserica alia duo, & alibi plura. Horum numerum auxerunt, & Fratribus majorem advexerunt opinionem frater Joannes de Florentia, & socii. Legati missi a Benedicto ad magnum Chamum Imperatorem, qui a Principibus Orientis honorifice habiti, pervenerunt hoc anno ad civitatem Cambaliensem. Ita prudenter & modeste egerunt, ut summam invenerint gratiam in Principis conspectu, & novo edicto licentiam fecerit fidem Christianam, in suo Imperio praedicandi. Reliquis praeibat frater Joannes exemplo, magnam crucem manu portans, hinc inde, tamquam scintilla discurrens, multos ad Christi fidem convertens, intrepide Christi nomen omnibus inculcans. Erectae tunc multae Christianorum Ecclesiae; & diffusa per multas partes fides Romana. Tamdem post aliquot annos eumdem fratrem Joannem remisit Imperator ad Innocentium VI. Pontificem honorifice functurum legatione, uti sub anno MCCCLIII. referemus." Wadding, vii, pp. 257–8.]

Europe), six degrees below the horizon, and the Antarctic as much above it, whilst many other wonderful astronomical phenomena are visible; women always or very generally administer the government; the walls of the palace are adorned with fine historical pictures; chariots and elephants are in use, especially for the women; there is a mountain of very great height called *Gybeit* or The Blessed, with which legends of Elias and of the Magi are connected; the queen treats the traveller with great honour and invests him with a golden girdle, such as she was wont to bestow upon those whom she created princes; there are a few Christians there; and finally when Marignolli has quitted Saba he is overtaken by a series of gales, which drive his ship (apparently contrary to intention) into a port of Ceylon.

Meinert, the first who commented on Marignolli, is clear that Java is intended by him; Kunstmann as clear that he speaks of the Maldives. The latter idea also occurred to me before I had the pleasure of seeing Professor Kuntsmann's papers, but I reject it for reasons which seem insuperable.

It is true and certainly remarkable that both Mas'udi in the end of the ninth century, and Edrisi in the eleventh, speak of the *Dabihat* or *Robaihat* (which are apparently errors of transcription for *Dibaját*, and mean the Maldives) as more or less under female government; and when Ibn Batuta was in the same islands a short time before Marignolli's return from China, there actually reigned a female sovereign, Kadija by name, the daughter of the deceased sultan, and who had been set upon the throne in place of a brother whom the people had deposed. Her husband exercised the authority in fact, but all orders were issued in her name. Edrisi also mentions the queen as going on "state occasions with her women mounted on elephants, with trumpets, flags, etc., her husbands and vizirs following at an interval[1]." This is striking; but it is impossible to accept the evidence about the elephants without strong corroboration. These would at all times have been highly inconvenient guests upon the little Maldive Isles, and we gather from Ibn Batuta that in his time (and Marignolli's) there were but one horse and one mare on the whole metropolitan island. Nor could our author with any show of reason call these little clusters, with their produce of cowries and coco-nuts, "the finest *island* in the world." We might perhaps get over the statement about the latitude, as wiser men than Marignolli made great mistakes in such matters. But where are we to find a "very lofty and almost inaccessible mountain" in the Maldives? You might as well seek such a thing on the Texel.

We may remember that Odoric in his quaint idiom terms Java "the second best of all islands that exist," whilst the historic pictures on the palace walls of Saba rather strikingly recall what the same friar tells us about the like in the palace of the Kings of Java, and I should be quite content to accept Java with Meinert, if we could find there any proof of the frequency of female sovereignty. I quote below the only two traces of this that I have been enabled to discover[2]. Though I do not think it so probable,

[1] Jaubert's *French Trans.*, vol. i, pp. 67, 8.

[2] The chronology of Javanese history up to the establishment of Islam is very doubtful, and it is difficult to say how far either of the following instances of female rule might suit the time of Marignolli's voyage:

1. An ineffectual attempt having been made by Ratu Dewa, a native of Kuningan in the province of Cheribon, who had been entrusted with the administration of Gálu, to maintain an authority independent of Majapahit, he lost his life in the struggle, and his widow Torbita, *who persevered and was for a time successful*, was at length overcome and went over to Majapahit.

2. Merta Wijaya, fifth prince of Majapahit, left two children, a daughter named Kanchana Wungu, and a son, Angka Wijaya, who according to some authorities ruled jointly. The *princess, however, is better known as an independent sovereign*, under the title of Prabu Kanya Kanchana Wungu (See Raffles, *Hist. of Java*, ii, 107 and 121).

it is just possible that some province of Sumatra may be meant. We know that island to have been called Java by the Mahomedan navigators, as may be seen in Marco Polo, Ibn Batuta, and the Catalan Map, in which last the great island named *Jana* (for Java) seems certainly to represent Sumatra. And, curiously enough, in this map we find towards the north end of the island *Regio Feminarum*, with the effigy of a queen. Also Ida Pfeiffer, during her wanderings in Sumatra, heard that there existed round the great Lake Eier Tau, a powerful people under female rule. *Valeant quantum!*

It is worth while, however, to note what Nikitin the Russian, in the succeeding century, says about a place called Shabat or Shabait, which he heard of in India. It was a very large place on the Indian seas, two months' voyage from Dabul, one month's voyage from Ceylon, and twenty days from Pegu. It produced abundance of silk, sugar, precious stones, sandal wood and elephants. The Jews called the people of Shabait Jews, but they were in truth neither Jews, nor Mahomedans, nor Christians, but of a different religion. They did not eat with Jews or Mahomedans, and used no meat. Everything was cheap, etc. If we could identify this place, perhaps we should find the Saba[1] of Marignolli.

Though the latitude assigned to Saba applies correctly

This second instance seems the most pertinent, and as the fifth prince of Majapahit, according to Walckenaer's correction of the chronology, came to the throne in 1322, the time appears to suit fairly. (See *Mém. de l'Acad. des Inscript.*, xv (1842), pp. 224 *seqq.*)

The stories of Elias (or Khidr) would be gathered from the Mahomedan settlers here as those of Adam and Cain were gathered (as we shall see) by our traveller in Ceylon.

[Female rule in a state of the South Seas (1349) is confirmed in the *Ta yi chi lio.*]

[1] ["On the whole, it seems most nearly to answer to some region of Java or Sumatra, and the Blessed Mountain Gybeit of which he talks so much, corresponds admirably in title and description to the *Great S'lamat*, or 'Hill of Peace,' near the northern coast of Central Java." (Beazley, *Dawn of Modern Geog.*, iii, 1906, p. 301.)]

to Java and not to Sumatra, we must remember that Marco Polo there speaks with wonder of the country's lying so far to the south that the Pole Star could not be seen. And in a very curious contemporary reference to Polo[1], the author says of the Magellanic cloud: "In the country of the ZINGHI there is seen a star as big as a sack. I know a man who saw it, and he told me that it had a faint light like a piece of cloud, and is always in the south. I was told of this and other matters also by Marco the Venetian, the most extensive traveller and the most diligent inquirer whom I have ever known. He saw this same star under the Antarctic; he described it as having a great tail, and drew a figure of it, *thus*. He also told me that he saw the Antarctic Pole at an altitude above the earth, apparently equal to the length of a soldier's lance, whilst the Arctic Pole was as much depressed. 'Tis from that place, he said, that they export to us camphor, lign-aloes, and brazil. He says the heat

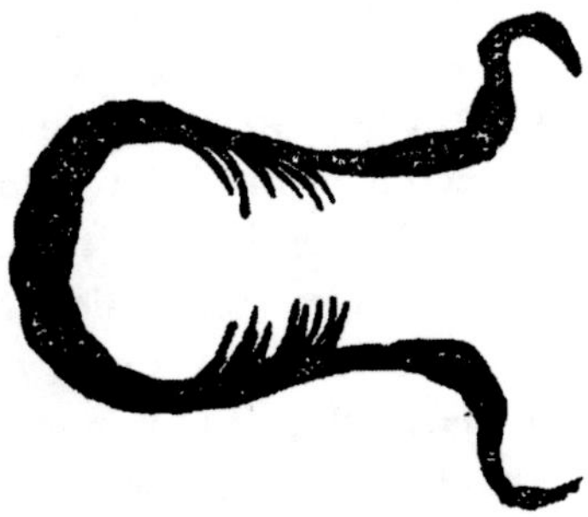

there is intense, and the habitations few. And these things he witnessed in a certain island at which he arrived by sea; ...and there was no way of getting at this place except by sea." There can be no doubt that this reported oral relation

[1] *Petri Aponensis Medici ac Philosophi Celeberrimi*, *Conciliator*, Venice, 1521, fol. 97. This Peter, physician and astrologer, born in 1250 at Abano, near Padua, was Professor of Medicine at the University in that city. He was twice brought up by the Inquisition on charges of sorcery, and the second time he only escaped their hands by death in 1316. He was posthumously condemned, but the magistrates objected to further proceedings, and his body was burnt in effigy only.

This curious passage was first pointed out by Zurla (quoted by *Baldelli Boni*, *Il Milione*, ii, 486). But I do not think he notices the woodcut, which is omitted in some editions. It has been thought worth copying here, as an approach at least to an autograph drawing by Marco Polo! [See *Marco Polo*, i, p. *120*, and notes.]

of Marco referred to Sumatra, and the wording of the passage in regard to the Poles, as well as the description of the "other wonderful things in regard to the stars," lead me strongly to suspect that it was from this very passage of Peter of Abano that Master Lemon of Genoa pointed out those facts to Marignolli.

In quitting Saba our author took ship again, probably to return to Malabar on his way towards Europe, and was driven into Ceylon in the manner mentioned above. Here he fell into the hands of a Mussulman buccaneer, who had at this time got possession of a considerable part of the island; and was by him detained for some four months, and stript of all the Eastern valuables and rarities that he was carrying home.

Notwithstanding these disagreeable experiences, Marignolli appears to recur again and again with fascination to his recollections of Ceylon, and they occupy altogether a considerable space in these notices. The Terrestrial Paradise, if not identified in Marignolli's mind with a part of the island (for his expressions are hazy and ambiguous), is at least closely adjacent, and sheds a delicious influence over all its atmosphere and productions. This idea is indeed so prominent that a short explanatory digression on the subject will not be inappropriate.

It was in the west that the ancients dreamed of sacred and happy islands, where the golden age had survived the deluge of corruption. But it was to the opposite quarter that the legends of the middle ages pointed, building as they did upon that garden which was planted "eastward in Eden"; and though it was in sailing west that Columbus thought he had found the skirts of Paradise near the mouths of Orinoco, it must be remembered that he was only seeking the "far East" by a shorter route.

What has been written on the Terrestrial Paradise would probably fill a respectable library. Marignolli's idea of it was evidently the same as that which seems to have been generally entertained in his age, viz., that of a great mountain rising in ineffable tranquillity and beauty far above all other earthly things, from which came tumbling down a glorious cataract, dividing at the foot into four great rivers, which somehow or other, underground or over, found their several ways to the channels of Hiddekel and Euphrates, and of such other two streams as might be identified with Gihon and Phison. This mountain was frequently believed to rise to the sphere of the moon, an opinion said to be maintained even by such men as Augustine and Bede[1].

The localities assigned to Paradise have been infinitely various. Old oriental tradition was satisfied to place it in Ceylon; but western belief more commonly regarded it as in the more extreme east, where John of Hese professes to have seen it. Cosmas, again, considered it to lie with the antediluvian world beyond the ocean which encompasses the oblong plateau of the earth that we inhabit. Father Filippo the Carmelite thinks it lay probably in the bosom of Ararat, whilst Ariosto seems to identify it with Kenia or Kilimanjaro,—

> "Il monte ond' esce il gran fiume d' Egitto
> . . . .
> Ch' oltre alle nubi e presso al ciel si leva;
> Era quel Paradiso che terrestre
> Si dice, ove abitò già Adamo ed Eva."—(xxxiii, 109, 110.)

The map of Andrea Bianchi, at Venice, agrees with Marignolli, for it shows *Paradiso Terrestre* adjoining Cape

[1] "*Joannes Hopkinsonius*," however, who has disserted upon Paradise, judiciously stigmatizes this as a manifest figment. For, quoth he, is not the height of the moon according to Ptolemy and Alphraganus, seventeen times the earth's diameter; and would not such a mountain therefore require for a base *at least* the whole superficies of the terrestrial hemisphere, and deprive us of a great part of the sun's light? Joannes Tostatus therefore is more reasonable when he says that Paradise does not quite reach the moon, but rises into the third region of the air, and is higher than all other mountains of the earth by twenty cubits! (The same John thinks Paradise was or

Comorin, whilst the four rivers are exhibited as flowing up the centre of India,—one into the north of the Caspian, near *Agrican* (Astracan, viz., the Volga); a second into the south of the Caspian, near Jilan (Araxes?); a third into the Gulf of Scanderoon (Orontes?); and the fourth, Euphrates[1].

Some other old maps and fictitious voyagers, such as John of Hese, assign a terrestrial position also to Purgatory. Dante, it will be remembered, has combined the sites of Purgatory and of the earthly Paradise, making the latter the delightful summit of the mountain whose steep sides are girt with the successive circles of purification.

And to conclude this matter in the words of Bishop Huet of Avranches: "Some have placed the terrestrial Paradise...under the arctic pole; some in Tartary, on the site occupied now by the Caspian; some at the extreme south, in Terra del Fuego; many in the East, as on the banks of the Ganges, in the island of Ceylon, in China, beyond the sun-rising, in a place no longer habitable. Others in America, in Africa, in the equinoctial orient, under the equator, on the Mountains of the Moon. Most have set it in Asia; but of these, some in Armenia Major, some in Mesopotamia, in Assyria, in Persia, in Babylonia, in Arabia, in Syria, in Palestine. Some even would stand up for our own Europe; and some, passing all bounds of

is about twelve miles long, and some thirty-six or forty in compass.) Of his mind is Ariosto when he speaks of

"La cima
Che *non lontana* con la superba balza
Dal cerchio della Luna esser si stima."—(xxxiv, 48.)

(See *Hopkinsonius*, etc., in *Ugolini*, as quoted below, vii, pp. dcxi–xiii–xiv.)

[1] "The summit of Meru is the city of Brahma...The holy river of Ganges issuing from the foot of Vishnu and washing the moon, falls here from the skies, and after encircling the city of Brahma divides into four mighty rivers, flowing in opposite directions. These are on the north the Indus...on the east the Sanpo or Brahmaputra..., on the west the Sutlej..., on the south the Karnali...". (C. A. Sherring, *Western Tibet*, Lond., 1906, pp. 44–45.).

nonsense, have placed it at Hesdin in Artois, urging the resemblance to *Eden*[1]."

How, or in what company, Marignolli quitted Ceylon, he leaves untold. We only gather from very slight and incidental notices that he must have sailed to Hormuz, and afterwards travelled by the ruins of Babylon to Baghdad, Mosul, Edessa, Aleppo, and thence to Damascus, Galilee, and Jerusalem. The sole further trace of him on his way to Italy, is that he seems to have touched at Cyprus.

In 1353, according to Wadding, he arrived at Avignon, bringing a letter from the Khan to the Pope (now Innocent VI), in which the monarch was made to express the greatest esteem for the Christian faith, to acknowledge the subjection of his Christian lieges to the Pope, and to ask for more missionaries.

It was probably during the visit of the Emperor Charles IV[2] to Italy in 1354, to be crowned by the Pope at Rome, that he became acquainted with Marignolli, and made him one of his domestic chaplains. To this he was perhaps induced by curiosity to hear at leisure the relations of one who had travelled to the world's end; for, though mean in moral character, Charles was a man of intelligence, and an encourager of learning and the useful arts[3].

In 1354 also the Pope rewarded our traveller with the

[1] *F. D. Huetii, Episc. Abrinc. Tract. de Situ Paradisi Terrest.* in *Ugolini, Thesaurus Antiq. Sacr.*, Venet., 1747, vii, p. dii. Also Cosmas in *Montfaucon, Coll. Nova Patrum*, ii, 131; *Peregrin. Joannis Hesei*, etc., *Antv.*, 1565, etc.

[2] Charles, son of John of Luxemburg, King of Bohemia, the blind warrior who fell at Crecy, was born on [16th May] 1316, and on [19th July] 1346 was elected emperor in place of the excommunicated Lewis of Bavaria.

[3] Dobner was not able to find the appointment of Marignolli among the archives of Charles's court at Prague, though he found several other nominations to that dignity, viz., as "*consiliarius, capellanus, familiaris et commensalis domesticus.*"

bishopric of Bisignano in Calabria[1]. The bishop, however, seems to have been in no hurry to reside there; thinking perhaps that a man who had spent so many years of his life in travelling to Cathay and back, might well be excused from passing the whole of those that remained to him in the wilds of Calabria. He seems to have accompanied the Emperor on his return from Italy to his paternal dominions[2]; whilst in 1356 we find him at Avignon, acting as envoy to the Pope from the republic of Florence; and in 1357 he is traced at Bologna by his grant of indulgence privileges to one of the churches in that city[3].

It was, no doubt, during Marignolli's visit to Prague that the Emperor desired him to undertake the task of recasting the *Annals of Bohemia*. Charles would have shewn a great deal more sense if he had directed his

[1] 12th May, 1354 (*Ughelli, Italia Sacra*, as above). ["12. Fr. JOANNES ex nobili Marignolla familia satus, patria Florentinus, professione Franciscanus, Christophoro in Episcopatu successit ann. 1354. 4. idus Maij ut ex regesto Vatic. eruitur. Hic insignis S. Crucis monasterii Florentini alumnus extitit, ob doctrinae famam, familiaeq; claritatem ad hunc Episcopatum evolavit; quanto postea tempore vixerit me latet...." (*Ughelli, Italia Sacra*, i, col. 522, *Bisinianenses Episcopi*.)] The small episcopal city of Bisignano, supposed to have been the ancient Besidiæ, stands on a hill to the east of the post-road between Castrovillari and Cosenza. It gives the title of prince to the Sanseverino family (*Murray*). Wadding notices the appointment of a Friar John to this bishopric, but seems not to have known that it was the legate whose return from Cathay he had recorded.

[2] Marignolli's most distinct mention of having been at Prague is found at p. 136 (of Dobner), in introducing a chapter entitled "*Miraculum de Incisione digiti Sancti Nicolai.*" He says this finger was sent to the Emperor with other reliques by the Pope, "and it will not be irrelevant to state," he proceeds, "a new miracle which mine own eyes have seen and mine own hands have handled," etc.; and then tells his story about blood flowing when the Emperor pricked the finger, etc. Now, according to Dobner, Hagecius a Bohemian chronicler ascribes this story to 1353. This is probably wrong, otherwise the Emperor must have called Marignolli to Prague previous to his own visit to Italy.

[3] *Sbaralea*, as above. In the grant of indulgence he speaks of himself as administering for Richard Archbishop of Nazareth, a brother of his order. The diocese of Nazareth, created in honour of the name, had a scattered jurisdiction chiefly in the kingdom of Naples. (*Ughelli*, vol. vii.)

chaplain to write a detailed narrative of his own eastern experiences. However, let us be thankful for what we have. The essential part of the task set him was utterly repugnant to the Tuscan churchman. He drew back, as he says himself, "from the thorny thickets and tangled brakes of the Bohemian chronicles"; from "the labyrinthine jungle of strange names, the very utterance of which was an impossibility to his Florentine tongue." And so he consoled himself under the disagreeable duty imposed on him, by interpolating his chronicles, *à propos de bottes*, with the recollections of his Asiatic travels, or with the notions they had given him of Asiatic geography. It might have been hard, perhaps, to drag these into a mere chronicle of Bohemia; but in those days every legitimate chronicle began from Adam at latest, and it would have been strange if this did not afford latitude for the introduction of any of Adam's posterity.

Chronicle and reminiscences alike slept in Prague cloister dust for some four centuries. During all that time Marignolli's name as a Bohemian chronicler is only twice alluded to, and that by authors strange to nearly all beyond Bohemian boundaries; one of whom, moreover, does not seem to have read him[1]. It was not till 1768 that he became accessible to the world in the second volume of unpublished monuments of Bohemian history, edited by the Reverend Gelasius Dobner, member of an educational order[2]. Dobner's qualifications for dealing with Bohemian history were probably superior to what he

[1] These are, according to Dobner, Hagecius, and Matthias Bolesluzky, a historian of the seventeenth century.

[2] *Monumenta Historica Boemiæ nusquam antehac edita*, etc., *Collegit*, etc., P. Gelasius Dobner a S. Catharina, *e Clericis Regularibus Scholarum Piarum*, tom. i, Prague, 1764; tom. ii, *ib.*, 1768, 4to.

Observationes praeviae in Chronicon Marignolae, ii, pp. 68–78.

Chronicon Reverendissimi Joannis dicti de Marignolis de Florentia Ordinis Minorum Bysinianensis Episcopi, gloriosae memoriae Imperatoris Caroli IV. Imperialis Aulae Capellani, ii, pp. 79–282.

exhibits in commenting on Asiatic travels and geography. His notes on the latter subjects are often astonishing indeed, and are calculated amply to justify the foresight of his godfathers and godmothers in the name they gave him.

But though the account of Marignolli's journeys became thus *accessible* to the world, it only transferred its sleep from manuscript to type; for no one seems to have discovered these curious interpolations in a Bohemian chronicle till 1820, when an interesting paper on the subject was published by Mr. J. G. Meinert in the Transactions of the Scientific Society of Bohemia[1]. He adopted the plan of extracting from Dobner all that bore upon Marignolli's travels, and then rearranging the passages in as orderly and continuous a form as they admitted of, accompanying the whole with an intelligent commentary.

An essay on Marignolli's travels has also been published by Professor Kunstmann in his series of papers already alluded to[2]. To both of these articles I have been indebted for occasional suggestions, and especially for indications of some of the illustrative sources which I have followed up. But my work was far advanced before I met with Kunstmann[3].

The time when Marignolli digested the chronicles, and salted them with his recollections, cannot be precisely determined. All that can be said positively is, that it was *after* his nomination as bishop (for that dignity is specified

[1] *Abhandl. der K. Böhm. Gesellschaft der Wissenschaften*, vol. vii. "Johannes von Marignola minderen Bruders und Päbstlichen Legaten Reise in das Morgenland v. J. 1339–1353.—Aus dem Latein übersetzt, geordnet und erläutert von J. G. Meinert." Prag, 1820, 8vo, pp. 108.

[Cf. Notice sur la relation du frère Jean de Marignola, par M. le Baron de Férussac. (*Bul. Soc. Géog.*, ii, 1824, pp. 115–120.)]

[2] See p. 88.

[3] [Another essay on Marignolli has been written by Mr. R. Beazley, *Dawn of Modern Geog.*, iii, 1906, pp. 288–309, with quotations from, and references to the text in the *Fontes Rerum Bohemicarum* (1882), vol. iii, pp. 492–604.]

in the title and body of the chronicle, see p. 209), and *previous* to the death of Innocent VI, of whom he speaks in the last paragraph of his book as still reigning; *i.e.*, between May 1354 and September 1362. But there can be little doubt that he wrote the book during his visit to Prague in 1354 or 1355.

It has been already said that Marignolli must have been an old man when he wrote these recollections; and I think readers will assent to this, though it has been found impossible in the translation to avoid softening his peculiarities. There are often vivid remembrance and graphic description of what he has seen; but these are combined with the incontinent vanity of something like second childhood, and with an incoherent lapse from one subject to another, matched by nothing in literature except the conversation of Mrs. Nickleby. His Latin is of a bad sort of badness. The Latin of Jordanus is bad in one sense. When he says "*istud ales quod vocatur rhinocerunta*," he utters almost as many blunders as words; but he is nearly always perfectly and vividly intelligible. The Latin of Marignolli is bad because it is the hazy expression of confused thoughts[1]. The supposition that Marignolli was at

[1] As an example of Marignolli's incoherence take the original of a passage in Dobner, p. 100 (see below, in chapter *Concerning Clothing of our First Parents*):

"Ideo videtur sine assercione dicendum, quod non pelliceas tunicas est legendum, sed *filiceas*. Nam inter folia *nargillorum*, de quibus supra dictum est, nascuntur fila ad modum tele, staminis quasi grossi, et rari sicci, de quibus eciam hodie fiunt apud illos et apud Judeos vestes pro pluvia rusticorum, qui vocantur camalli, portantes seu onera, et eciam homines et mulieres portant super scapulas in lecticis, de quibus in Canticis; ferculum fecit sibi *Salomon* de lignis *Lybani*, id est lectulum portatilem, sicut portabar ego in *Zayton*, et in India. Unam talem vestem de filis illis camallorum, non camelorum, portavi ego usque *Florenciam*, et dimisi in sacristia Minorum similem vesti *Johannis baptiste*. Nam pili camelorum sunt delicacior lana, que sit in mundo post sericum. Fui enim aliquando cum infinitis camelis et pullis camelorum in deserto vastissimo descendendo de *Babilon* confusionis versus *Egiptum* per viam *Damasci* cum *Arabibus* infinitis. Nec in *Seyllano* sunt cameli, sed elephantes innumeri, qui licet sint ferocissimi, raro tamen nocent homini peregrino. Ego equitavi super

this time advanced in years, and moreover not looked on as very wise in his generation, is confirmed by a curious letter bearing to be addressed to him by a Bishop of Armagh, which Dobner turned up among the records of the Emperor Charles's time in the Metropolitan chapter library at Prague. It may be gathered from the letter that some intention had been intimated, on the part of higher ecclesiastical authorities, of sending Marignolli to Ireland in connexion with questions then in debate with the writer. The wrath of the latter seems to have been sorely stirred at this intimation, and he turns up the lawn sleeves and brandishes the shillelagh in the following style of energetic metaphor. We can hardly read the letter without a feeling that it ought to have been dated from Tuam rather than Armagh. But the writer turns out to have been one who had high claims to respect[1].

"Reverend Father and very dear Friend!

"What those honourable gentlemen — De —, and — De — have told of your behaviour is anything but fitting in a man of your grey hairs and superior pretensions. And the message which your Reverence sent me by them is a poor sample of your prudence.

"By the help of the Lord and the right that was on my side did not I exterminate ———, the flower of your Order? Have not I bate him already in fair fight, and am I going to stand in fear of any of the rest of ye? Sure nothing is deficient in the present conjuncture, but that the conquering

unum Regine *Sabe*, qui videbatur habere usum racionis, si non esset contra fidem."

[1] Some local colour has seemed necessary to do justice to this letter in translation, so I subjoin the latter part as a sample of the original:—"...Veniat igitur inveteratus ille Bisanensis Episcopus, veniat: quis ille, qui se Apostolum Orientis in Curiâ Cesaris ampulose denominat, ut experiatur in opere, quid sompnia sua sibi prodesse valeant. Nam si canum latrancium juventuti intersit vincula, nostre provisionis industria facile quidem palpitantem senio molossum ligare curabimus, cui jam neque vocis claritas, neque sciencie habilitas suffragantur." [Dobner, ii, p. 74.]

hero should receive the prize, and that by the blessing of God the crown of victory should descend to decorate his troyumphant brows!

"A rich recompense must abide the pen which eradicated the briars and thorns from the garden of Holy Church, which sent the ugly faction of error to the right-about, and cleared the street for Catholic Truth to walk in!

"*I* am not afraid of your Reverence's coming. 'Tis not likely that the prospect of having you for antagonist would frighten *me;* me, who tore to rags the sophistries of the Englishmen, Okkam[1] and Burley[2], and the like, when they tried to spread a flimsy veil over the web of lies that they were weaving; me who had stopped their bootless barking with the words of piety and truth! Let him come on then (say we), that old beggar of a Bisignano Bishop! Let him come on! We'll take the measure of him, though he does paycock about the Kaisar's Court and call himself (save the mark) the Aposthle of the East! We'll let him find out what good his doting dreams will do him in a practical question. 'Twill be a pity if I, who have muzzled a whole pack of yelping hounds, find it a hard matter to put a collar on a poor old wheezing tyke, who has scarcely a bark left in him, and never had the least repute for brains!"

1 William Ockham or Occam, an English Franciscan, very eminent among the schoolmen [born in Surrey]. He was provincial of his order in England, and as such took a prominent part at a council held at Assisi in 1322 in support of the strict obligation to poverty. It was perhaps on this question that he had been at war with the Archbishop of Armagh. Ockham took part with Corbarius the Antipope, and was excommunicated by John XXII [in 1330]. He took refuge with the Emperor Lewis the Bavarian, who was under the like ban, and died at an advanced age at the convent of his order in Munich [on the 7th April] 1347. (*Cave*, App., p. 28; *Biog. Universelle.*)

["His death cannot have occurred before 1349, but it is unlikely that he long survived that year." (*Dict. of Nation. Biog.*)]

2 Walter Burley, another eminent English Schoolman, and tutor to the Black Prince, born at Oxford 1275, died 1357 (some say 1337).

["Burley was certainly alive later than 1337, as he wrote his treatise on Aristotle's 'Politics' at the request of Richard Bentworth, bishop of London (1338–9), who was not consecrated till July 1338." (*Dict. of Nation. Biog.*)]

Dobner does not identify the writer of this letter, but there can be no doubt that it was Richard Fitz Ralph, Archbishop of Armagh, a strenuous adversary of the Franciscans and other mendicant orders, who however proved too strong for him at last, and brought him into trouble which he did not survive[1].

This is the last that we can trace of Marignolli. The time of his death is unknown; nor has even the date of his successor's nomination to Bisignano been recovered, so as to fix it approximately[2].

[1] A native of Dundalk; he was held in high esteem by Edward III, and became successively Professor of Theology at Oxford, Chancellor of the University (1333), Dean of Lichfield (1337), and Archbishop of Armagh (8th July 1347). In his constant war against the friars we are told that "*eorum vanam et superbam paupertatem Oxonii in lecturis theologicis* salse vellificare solebat; *episcopus vero factus* acriori calamo confixit"; statements which from the style of his letter can be well believed. They also appear to disprove the allegation of Wadding that Fitz Ralph's enmity to the friars first arose out of the resistance of the Franciscans of Armagh to a piece of injustice on the part of the archbishop.

Some sermons which he preached in London in 1356 against the friars and the profession of voluntary poverty gave great offence. They accused him of heresy, and had him cited to Avignon (1357) where he was long detained. The questions perhaps involved very serious consequences to those who rashly stirred them, for only four years before, two Franciscans, for holding wrong opinions concerning the principle of poverty (though probably in a direction opposite to Fitz Ralph's) had been burnt to death in the Pope's own city of Avignon. So the archbishop seeing that the authorities were going against him, retired (according to Wadding) to Belgium, probably on his way to England, and died there 16th December, 1359 or 1360; (Cave says, however, that he died at Avignon, 13th November, 1360 [and the *Dict. of Nat. Biog.*, probably 16 Nov. 1360]).

It is pleasant to see that when Luke Wadding the Franciscan annalist treats of this worthy, the Irishman is stronger in him than the Friar. "Some," he says, "have counted Fitz Ralph a heretic, but undeservedly; he sinned more from exuberant intellect than from perversity of will." He was deemed a saint in Ireland. His best title to the respect of posterity rests on his claim to have translated the Scriptures into Irish; the whole, according to Fox; the New Testament, according to Bale. He left many other works, chiefly controversial, of which some have been printed. One discourse which he delivered at Avignon in defence of his sermons against the friars may be seen in the *Monarchia Sacri Rom. Imperii* of Goldastus. (*Wadding, An. Min.*, viii, an. 1357, § 4–9; *Cave, Script. Eccl.*, Oxon., 1743, in *Append.*); *Baluzii Vit. Pap. Avenion*, i, 323; *Goldasti*, etc., ii, p. 1392; *Dict. of Nat. Biog.*)

[2] *Ughelli*, u. s.

It only remains to say a word about the MSS. of Marignolli's chronicle. That from which Dobner edited the work is described as a paper folio, written partly at the end of the fourteenth century and partly at the beginning of the fifteenth. It was then in the Library of the Brethren of the Cross, or Passionists, in the old town of Prague; but when Meinert wrote his essay it had been transferred to the Royal University Library. This MS. was supposed to be unique, but in the St. Mark's Library at Venice I have seen a partial copy, apparently of the fifteenth century, embracing all the most important part of the Asiatic notices[1]. Its differences from Dobner's edition were very trifling, and it contained the same error as to the date of the legation's departure from Avignon. But it has given distinctly the reading of a few names which had probably been misread by Dobner, such as *Manci* and *Mangi* where he read *Maugi*, *Mynibar* where he read *Nymbar*, *Thana* for *Chana*, with a very few other differences of more doubtful character.

[1] Bibl. Marciana, Class. x, Codd. Latt. clxxxviii, ff. 243–263. It ends with that chapter of the second book which treats of Roman history. The volume contains a variety of other transcripts connected with Papal and Bohemian history.

BIBLIOGRAPHY.

—Monumenta Historica Boemiae nusquam antehac edita...Collegit ...P. Gelasius Dobner a S. Catharina e Clericis Regularibus Scholarum Piarum. i, Pragae, 1764; ii, 1768, 2 vols. 4to.

—Johannes von Marignola minderen Bruders und Päbstlichen Legaten Reise in das Morgenland v. J. 1339-1353. Aus dem Latein übersetzt, geordnet und erläutert von J. G. Meinert....Für die *Abhandlungen der K. böhm. Gesellschaft der Wissenschaften*. Prag, 1820, in 8vo, pp. 108.

Abstract Vol. vii, *Abhandlungen der Königlichen Böhmischen Gesellschaft der Wissenschaften*, Historischer Theil. Prag, 1822.

—Notice sur la relation du frère Jean de Marignola, par M. le Baron de Férussac. (*Bull. de la Soc. de Géog.*, ii, 1824, pp. 115-120.)

—Die Missionen in Indien und China im vierzehnten Jahrhundert. (*G. Phillips, und G. Görres, Historisch-Politische Blätter für das Katholische Deutschland*, München, 1856, I Bd.)—I. Die Mission in Meliapor und Tana, pp. 25-38.—II. Die Mission in Columbo, pp. 135-152.—III. Die Mission in China, pp. 225-252.—(*Ibid.*, 1856, II Bd.)—IV. Der Missionsbericht des Odoricus von Pordenone, pp. 507-537.—V. Der Reisebericht des Johannes Marignola, pp. 701-719, 793-813.—(*Ibid.*, 1859, I Bd.) Die Mission in China, pp. 677-681.

By Prof. F. Kunstmann.

—Dal Chronicon boemorum di Giovanni de' Marignolli Fiorentino vescovo di Bisignano. (Angelo de Gubernatis, *Storia dei Viaggiatori italiani nelle Indie orientali*, 1875, pp. 142-150.)

Rep. by Marcellino da Civezza, pp. 372-383 of his *Saggio di Bibliografia Sanfrancescana*, 1879.

—Amat di S. Filippo. *Studi biografici e bibliografici*. Edizione seconda. Roma, 1882, i, pp. 103-109.

—R. Beazley. *Dawn of Modern Geography*, iii, 1906, pp. 288-309.

RECOLLECTIONS OF TRAVEL IN THE EAST, BY JOHN DE' MARIGNOLLI,

PAPAL LEGATE TO THE COURT OF THE GREAT KHAN, AND AFTERWARDS BISHOP OF BISIGNANO

THE author begins by announcing his intention of dividing his work into Three Books, viz. I. *Thearchos*, or the History of the World from the Creation to the Building of Babel; II. *Monarchos*, or the History of Kings, from Nimrod down to the Franks and Germans, and so to the Kingdom of Bohemia; III. *Ierarchos*, or the Ecclesiastical History, from Melchizedek to Moses and Aaron, to the Foundation of Christianity, and so to the Roman Pontiffs and the Bishops of Bohemia in order.

After speaking of the Creation the author comes to treat of Paradise, "Eastward in the place called Eden, beyond India," and this launches him at once on his reminiscences as follows:

And now to insert some brief passages of what I have seen myself. I, Friar John of Florence, of the order of Minors, and now unworthy Bishop of Bisignano, was sent with certain others, in the year of our Lord one thousand three hundred and thirty [eight][1], by the holy Pope Benedict the Eleventh[2], to carry letters and presents from the

[1] In both MSS. this is *tricesimo quarto*, but beyond question from a clerical error, as there is no doubt about the true year. Probably in the original MS. VIII was taken for IIII.

[2] *Undecimo* in the Venice MS.; Dobner has *duodecimo*. This Pope is sometimes XI, sometimes XII; Benedict X being in the latter case an antipope. [Benedict X, antipope (1058–1059); B. XI, Saint, Nicolas Bicassini (1303–1304); B. XII, Jacques de Novelles, called Fournier (1334–1342).]

apostolic see to the Kaan or chief Emperor of all the Tartars, a sovereign who holds the sway of nearly half the eastern world, and whose power and wealth, with the multitude of cities and provinces and languages under him, and the countless number, as I may say, of the nations over which he rules, pass all telling.

We set out from Avignon in the month of December, came to Naples in the beginning of Lent, and stopped there till Easter (which fell at the end of March), waiting for a ship of Genoa, which was coming with the Tartar envoys whom the Kaan had sent from his great city of Cambalec to the Pope, to request the latter to despatch an embassy to his court, whereby communication might be established, and a treaty of alliance struck between him and the Christians; for he greatly loves and honours our faith. Moreover the chief princes of his whole empire, more than thirty thousand in number, who are called Alans, and govern the whole Orient, are Christians either in fact or in name, calling themselves *the Pope's slaves*, and ready to die for the *Franks*. For so they term us, not indeed from France, but from Frank-land[1]. Their first apostle was Friar John, called De Monte Corvino, who seventy-two years previously, after having been soldier, judge, and doctor in the service of the Emperor Frederic, had become a Minor Friar, and a most wise and learned one[2].

[1] "*Non a Francia sed a Franquia.*"

["Summi eciam principes sui Imperii tocius, plus quam triginta millia, qui vocantur *Alani*, & totum gubernant imperium orientis, sunt *Christiani*, re vel nomine, & dicunt se *Sclavos Pape*, parati mori pro *franquis*, sic enim vocant nos, non a *francia*, sed a *franquia*." Dobner, ii, p. 85.]

[2] "*Qui primo miles, judex et doctor Friderici Imperatoris post* lxxii *annos factus frater Minor.*" A perplexing passage, owing to some error of the author's. Montecorvino could have been but three years old when Frederick II died in 1250. Dobner and Meinert assume that Marignolli *meant* John de Plano Carpini, who went on a mission from Pope Innocent IV to Tartary in 1246; but *he* was no apostle of Cathay; nor does there seem reason for believing that he was ever soldier or judge. No doubt one takes a liberty in rendering

Howbeit on the first of May we arrived by sea at Constantinople, and stopped at Pera till the feast of St. John Baptist[1]. We had no idle time of it however, for we were engaged in a most weighty controversy with the Patriarch of the Greeks and their whole Council in the palace of St. Sophia. And there God wrought in us a new miracle, giving us a mouth and wisdom which they were not able to resist; for they were constrained to confess that they must needs be schismatics, and had no plea to urge against their own condemnation except the intolerable arrogance of the Roman prelates[2].

Thence we sailed across the Black Sea, and in eight days arrived at Caffa, where there are Christians of many sects. From that place we went on to the first Emperor of the Tartars, Usbec, and laid before him the letters which we bore[3], with certain pieces of cloth, a great war-horse,

"post lxxii annos" by "seventy-two years previously"; but if it does not mean that, *what* does it mean? In 1266, which would be seventy-two years previous to 1338, John of Montecorvino was about twenty years old and might have become a friar. The Venice MS. has "*pts* lxxii *annos*," but I find no light in that.

[1] 24th June 1339.

[2] Five years before this two bishops had come from Rome to argue the point with the Patriarch. The latter was in great trouble, for the public mind was excited on the matter, and he was himself "unaccustomed to public speaking," whilst he knew most of his bishops to be grossly ignorant and incapable. (*Nicephori Gregoriæ* Hist. Byzant., x, 8.) No wonder that Marignolli carried all before him with antagonists so painted by their own friends.

Mandeville relates how, to Pope John XXII's invitations to come under his authority, the Greeks "sent back divers answers, amongst others saying thus: 'We believe well that thy power is great upon thy subjects. We may not suffer thy great pride. We are not in purpose to fulfil thy great covetousness. The Lord be with thee; for our Lord is with us. Farewell!' And no other answer might he have of them." (P. 136.) Many efforts were made to unite the churches from the time of Michael Palæologus, whose ambassador at the Council of Lyons in 1274 acknowledged the Pope's supremacy, to the time of John Palæologus, who in 1438 made a like acknowledgment. But these acts were never accepted by the Greek Church or people.

[3] The legates had letters from the Pope for Uzbek himself, for his eldest son Tanibek, and to a certain Franciscan, Elias the Hungarian, who was in favour with the latter. (See *Wadding* as before; and Append. to *Mosheim*, Nos. 81, 85, 86.)

some strong liquor[1], and the Pope's presents. And after the winter was over, having been well fed, well clothed, loaded with handsome presents, and supplied by the King with horses and travelling expenses, we proceeded to ARMALEC [the capital] of the Middle Empire. There we built a church, bought a piece of ground, dug wells[2], sung masses and baptized several; preaching freely and openly, notwithstanding the fact that only the year before the Bishop and six other Minor Friars had there undergone for Christ's sake a glorious martyrdom, illustrated by brilliant miracles. The names of these martyrs were Friar Richard the Bishop, a Burgundian by nation, Friar Francis of Alessandria, Friar Paschal of Spain (this one was a prophet and saw the heavens open, and foretold the martyrdom which should befall him and his brethren, and the overthrow of the Tartars of Saray by a flood, and the destruction of Armalec in vengeance for their martyrdom, and that the Emperor would be slain on the third day after their martyrdom, and many other glorious things); Friar Laurence of Ancona, Friar Peter, an Indian friar who acted as their interpreter, and Gillott [Gilottus], a merchant[3].

[1] The word in Dobner is *Cytiacam*, which I can trace nowhere. That editor's note is: "Seu *zythiacam*, i.e. liquorem causticum, vulgo *rosoglio*," etc. But ζῦθος means drink of the beer genus. The Venice MS. has *Tyriacam*, probably for *Theriacam*. I imagine however that Dobner is substantially right, and that something strong and sweet is meant. Rubruquis, nearly a century before, took with him for Uzbek's ancestors *vinum muscatel*.

[2] "*Ubi fecimus ecclesiam, emimus. aream*, fecimus fontes, *cantavimus missas*, etc." The *fontes* are not very intelligible. Prof. Kunstmann suggests *fonticum* (Ital. *fondaco*) for fontes, which is possible, as that word is blundered in another passage of this MS.

[3] On these Armalec martyrs see *ante*, p. 31 *seqq*. The statement of Marignolli that their death took place the year before his arrival, appears to fix it to 1339, instead of 1340 or later as stated by ecclesiastical chroniclers. Dobner goes eminently astray here, confounding these Franciscans, martyred in Turkestan in the fourteenth century, with those Franciscans who were martyred in Japan in the seventeenth, and whose formal canonization lately made so much noise. Accordingly he thinks it probable that Armalec was one of the Islands of Japan, and Saray another!

Towards the end of the third year after our departure from the Papal Court, quitting Armalec we came to the CYOLLOS KAGON, i.e. to the Sand Hills thrown up by the wind. Before the days of the Tartars nobody believed that the earth was habitable beyond these, nor indeed was it believed that there was any country at all beyond. But the Tartars by God's permission, and with wonderful exertion, did cross them, and found themselves in what the philosophers call the torrid and impassable zone[1]. Pass it however the Tartars did; and so did I, and that twice. 'Tis of this that David speaketh in the Psalms, '*Posuit desertum*,' &c.[2] After having passed it we came to CAMBALEC, the chief seat of the Empire of the East. Of its incredible magnitude, population, and military array, we will say nothing[3]. But the Grand Kaam, when he beheld the great horses, and the Pope's presents, with

[1] It is not quite clear whether he intends that *Cyollos Kagon* (or *Kagan* in Ven. MS.) *signifies* Sandhills. ["*Cyollos Kagon*, id est, ad montes arene, quos faciunt venti, ultra quos ante Thartaros nullus putavit terram habitabilem, nec putabatur ultra aliquam terram esse." Dobner, ii, p. 86.] Their position is evidently to be sought on the northern verge of the Gobi, which is his Torrid Zone, and probably among those to the north-east of Kamul. Hereabouts indeed, in a Chinese work on Turkestan, we find repeated mention of the *Sha-Shan* or "Sand Mountains," from which flows one source of the Barkul Nur, north of Kamil. (See *Julien* in *N. Ann. des Voyages*, 1846, iii, 37–44.) One of the reports translated in *The Russians in Central Asia* (London, 1865, p. 111), speaking of the desert says: "From this region (about Yarkand) it gradually widens as it runs eastward, where it forms the vast Gobi, devoid of all vegetation... where the sand is heaped up in such lofty ridges that the inhabitants give them the name of '*Gag*' (mountain)." If this be no misprint we have here perhaps one element of the name used by Marignolli, and in the Turkish and Persian *Chûl*, a desert, written by Vambery *Tchöl* and *Tchöle*, we have perhaps the other.

[2] "*Posuit Desertum in stagna*" (*Ps.* cvi, our cvii, 35). Probably his twice having passed the Torrid Zone is explained rightly by Meinert's suggestion that Marignolli regarded the Syrian desert, which he crossed on his return to Europe, as only another part of the same belt of desolation. That the Torrid Zone was uninhabitable was maintained, as is well known, by Aristotle and many other philosophers.

[3] The author's expression is, "*de cujus magnitudine incredibili et populo*, ordine militum sileatur," of which I greatly doubt my having given a correct interpretation.

his letter, and King Robert's too, with their golden seals, and when he saw us also, rejoiced greatly, being delighted, yea exceedingly delighted with everything, and treated us with the greatest honour[1]. And when I entered the Kaam's presence it was in full festival vestments, with a very fine cross carried before me, and candles and incense, whilst *Credo in Unum Deum* was chaunted, in that glorious palace where he dwells. And when the chaunt was ended I bestowed a full benediction, which he received with all humility[2].

And so we were dismissed to one of the Imperial apartments which had been most elegantly fitted up for us; and two princes were appointed to attend to all our wants. And this they did in the most liberal manner, not merely as regards meat and drink, but even down to such things as paper for lanterns, whilst all necessary servants also were detached from the Court to wait upon us. And so they tended us for nearly four years[3], never failing to treat us

[1] It is pleasing to find that though our legate has no place in the Chinese Annals, the "great horses" (*dextrarii*), which he took with him, have. Under our year 1342 it is recorded that there were presented to the emperor horses of the kingdom of Fulang (*Farang*, Europe), of a race till then unknown in China. One of these horses was eleven feet six inches in length and six feet eight inches high, and was black all over, except the hind feet, which were white. This present was highly esteemed. (*De Mailla*, ix, 579, and *Gaubil*, *Hist. de Gentchis Can*, etc., p. 279.) Indeed Gaubil tells us in another work, "In the Imperial Palace is preserved with care a picture in which Shun Ti, the last emperor of the Yuen dynasty, is represented on a fine horse, of which all the dimensions are detailed. It is remarked that this horse was presented to Shun Ti by a foreigner of the kingdom of France" (! No, Père Gaubil, *non a Francia sed a Franquia*!) See *Tr. de la Chronol. Chin.*, p. 186. This vast animal was surely the prototype of the Destrier, which Mr. Millais painted under Sir Ysenbras some years ago.

[Prof. Pelliot has a good many documents drawn from Chinese sources about this great horse, and he can trace the picture in the Imperial Palace up to the beginning of the nineteenth century.]

[2] [From Chinese sources, Pelliot has come to the conclusion that Marignolli's audience took place on the 19th August, 1342.]

[3] *Annos quasi quatuor*, whilst a little below he speaks of residing in Cambalec *annis quasi tribus*. It is possible that the first expression includes the whole time up to his embarking for India, but it cannot be determined.

with unbounded respect. And I should add that they kept us and all our establishment clothed in costly raiment. And considering that we were thirty-two persons, what the Kaam expended for everything on our account must have amounted, as well as I can calculate, to more than four thousand marks. And we had many and glorious disputations with the Jews and other sectaries[1]; and we made also a great harvest of souls in that empire.

The Minor Friars in Cambalec have a cathedral church immediately adjoining the palace[2], with a proper residence for the Archbishop, and other churches in the city besides, and they have bells too, and all the clergy have their subsistence from the Emperor's table in the most honourable manner.

And when the Emperor saw that nothing would induce me to abide there, he gave me leave to return to the Pope, carrying presents from him, with an allowance for three years' expenses, and with a request that either I or some one else should be sent speedily back with the rank of Cardinal, and with full powers, to be Bishop there[3]; for the office of Bishop is highly venerated by all the Orientals, whether they be Christians or no. He should also be of the Minorite Order, because these are the only priests that they are acquainted with; and they think that the Pope is always of that Order because Pope Girolamo was so who sent them that legate whom the Tartars and Alans venerate as

[1] Of the ancient settlement of Jews in China, said to have taken place in the third century B.C., though others name a later date, some notice will be found in the *J. R. G. S.*, xxvii, 297. See also *Silv. de Sacy* in *Notices et Extraits*, vol. iv, and *Alvaro Semedo, Rel. della Cina*, 1643, p. 193, etc. [See a bibliography of the Jews in China in Cordier's *Bibliotheca Sinica*, col. 1354–1360, and an article by the same author in the *Jewish Encyclopedia.*]

[2] See the building of this mentioned by Archbishop John in his letter at p. 55.

[3] A cardinal never came to China till the early part of the eighteenth century (Mezzabarba), and his mission did not prosper. [Mezzabarba was not a cardinal when he went out to China.]

a saint, viz., Friar John of Monte Corvino of the Order of Minorites, of whom we have already spoken[1].

We abode in Cambalec about three years, and then we took our way through MANZI[2], with a magnificent provision for our expenses from the Emperor, besides about two hundred horses; and on our way we beheld the glory of this world in such a multitude of cities, towns, and villages, and in other ways displayed, that no tongue can give it fit expression.

And sailing on the feast of St. Stephen[3], we navigated the Indian Sea until Palm Sunday, and then arrived at a very noble city of India called COLUMBUM[4], where the

[1] By Pope Girolamo he means Friar Jerome Musci, Bishop of Palestrina, elected Pope as Nicholas IV, and who sent John of Monte Corvino on his distant mission. Dobner, having taken up the notion that Carpini is meant, says "*legendum Innocentius*"; but he is quite wrong. The Tartars looked on the Pope as the people of India (according to the common story) used to look on John Company, viz. as in a manner immortal. "*Quærebant enim de Magno Papâ*," says Rubruquis, "*si esset ita senex sicut audierunt*" (p. 278).

[2] Dobner's book has here and afterwards *Mauzi*, but this is probably from ignorance only. The Venice MS. has *Manci* and *Manzi* plainly enough.

[3] Here the chronology of the journey calls for remark. The last precise date afforded was St. John's Day, 1339. The succeeding winter is passed at the court of Uzbek. Supposing the party to quit Sarai in May 1340, they would reach Armalec about September (see *Pegolotti*, pp. 285–6), and they did not quit that city till near the end of the third year from their leaving Avignon, viz., late in 1341. The journey from Armalec to Peking would occupy four or five months, but probably much more, as they appear (see *infra*, near the end) to have spent some time at Kamul. Hence perhaps they did not arrive at Peking earlier than the latter part of 1342, but not later than that, as the Chinese record about the horses fixes the year. The St. Stephen's day (26th December) on which he sailed from Zaytún could not have been *earlier* than that of 1346, but might have been later. Meinert takes the day for 2nd August (*Stephen I, Pope and Martyr*), but as Kunstmann justly points out, that would be no season for sailing from China. The latter fixes the date to 1347, as Easter fell late in 1348, and more time is thus allowed for the voyage to Malabar. We will assume it so.

[4] Ritter over hastily identifies Marignolli's Columbum with Columbo in Ceylon, and deduces that pepper was then a staple of that island (*Erdkunde*, v, 688), though as the author says that the "whole world's pepper" was produced there, this interpretation would imply that none was produced in Malabar, the Pepper Metropolis from time imme-

whole world's pepper is produced. Now this pepper grows on a kind of vines, which are planted just like in our vineyards. These vines produce clusters which are at first like those of the wild vine, of a green colour, and afterwards are almost like bunches of our grapes, and they have a red wine in them which I have squeezed out on my plate as a condiment. When they have ripened, they are left to dry upon the tree, and when shrivelled by the excessive heat the dry clusters are knocked off with a stick and caught upon linen cloths, and so the harvest is gathered.

These are things that I have seen with mine eyes and handled with my hands during the fourteen months that I stayed there[1]. And there is no roasting of the pepper, as authors have falsely asserted, nor does it grow in forests, but in regular gardens; nor are the Saracens the proprietors but the Christians of St. Thomas. And these latter are the masters of the public steel-yard, from which I derived, as a perquisite of my office as Pope's legate, every month a hundred gold *fan*, and a thousand when I left[2].

morial. Even Dobner is more judicious here, and concludes that Columbo is *not* meant, as the place is clearly placed by Marignolli on the continent. But then he continues, entirely losing this gleam of judgment, that it was in *Nimbar* (see note further on), and so could not be in *Malabar*, "*adeoque in regno* Indostan. *An fortassis urbs* Lahor *sit, judicium penes lectorem esto.*" One can only say with Friar Jordanus, "Wonderful!" For further remarks on Columbum, see note to *Odoric*, p. 129.

Probably the name should be rendered *Columbus* as in the only nominative I can find, viz. in Jordanus's letter at p. 77. But I have followed the French editor of Jordanus's *Mirabilia* in calling it Columbum, and it is not worth while to alter what may have authority which I have overlooked.

[1] Our author afterwards calls this time a year and four months.

[2] As to the pepper, *Fr. Jordanus*, p. 27, and *Ibn Batuta*, iv, 77. Marignolli's denial of its growing in forests is probably a slap at the Beato Odorico (see p. 132 *ante*); yet up to the present century there was a tract on the Malabar coast called "the Pepper Jungle" (Buchanan's *Christ. Resear.*, p. 111). Father Vincenzo Maria (Rome, 1672) still speaks of the Christians of St. Thomas as having the pepper chiefly in their hands. Dobner, Meinert, and Kunstmann all strangely misunderstand "*qui habent* stateram *ponderis totius mundi*," as if it meant something about the Christians having a right to an export tax on the pepper. Yet in this very Chronicle (*Dobner*,

There is a church of St. George there, of the Latin communion, at which I dwelt[1]. And I adorned it with fine paintings, and taught there the holy Law. And after I had been there some time I went beyond the glory of Alexander the Great, when he set up his column (in India). For I erected a stone as my landmark and memorial, in the corner of the world over against Paradise, and anointed it with oil! In sooth it was a marble pillar with a stone cross upon it, intended to last till the world's end. And it had the Pope's arms and my own engraved upon it, with inscriptions both in Indian and Latin characters. I consecrated and blessed it in the presence of an infinite multitude of people, and I was carried on the shoulders of the chiefs in a litter or palankin like Solomon's[2].

p. 164–5) they might have found a passage in which *statera* can mean nothing but a steelyard. It is in fact used for the Italian *stadera*. So in a correspondence quoted further on, one of the Florentine demands on the Sultan of Egypt is "*che possino tenere* stadere *nelli loro fondachi*," that they may have an authorized steelyard in their factories. The value of the *fanam* (Marignolli's *fan*) has varied so much that it is difficult to estimate what the legate received in this way. Marsden makes the *fanam* 2½*d*. (*Marco Polo*, p. 656). In the beginning of last century, Visscher says the *fanam* of Cochin was about 1½*d*., that of Calicut 6*d*., and that of Quilon 15*d*. Late in the same century Friar Paolino states the Paliacat *fanam* at 9 *sous* or 4½*d*., that of Tanjore or Calicut at 6*d*. or 7*d*., and that of Madura at 3½*d*. And Ibn Batuta (iv, 174) tells us that 100 *fanams* were equal to 6 *dinars*, which would make the *fanam* nearly 8*d*. This last may be taken as probably about the value of our author's *fan*. So his monthly perquisite would be about £3. 6*s*., and the present he received at parting £33. If we may judge from the calculations based on Ibn Batuta's statement of prices at Delhi in his time, the money would represent at least ten times as much wealth as at present.

[1] This church "*Latinorum*" was probably founded by Jordanus, and was possibly the same old church *fatto al modo nostro mediocre* which the Portuguese were taken to see on their first visit to *Colom*, though that was then entitled S. Maria (*Ramusio*, i, f. 146). Day indeed (*Land of the Permauls*, p. 4) mentions a church dedicated to St. George, within which may be seen a painting representing God the Father. But this is at Curringhacherry, ten miles from Cochin, and could scarcely have been the church of our author. If Jordanus or any successor in the episcopate had survived at Columbum surely Marignolli would have alluded to the fact? He says below in quitting the place "*valefaciens fratribus*," which perhaps implies that there were friars there.

[2] The Column or Columns of Alexander formed the subject of

So after a year and four months I took leave of the brethren, and after accomplishing many glorious works

some legend that grew out of the memory of the altars on the Hyphasis. In the Pseudo-Callisthenes, edited by Müller, we are told that Alexander got to Serice where the Seres produce silk, and there erected a stone pillar and wrote upon it: *Alexander, King of the Macedonians, got as far as this spot* (p. 102). Imagination was dissatisfied with Alexander's turning back from India scarcely entered—(does not one still feel disappointment every time the story is read?)—and in defiance of history prolonged his expedition to the ends of the earth. We have seen before that the cave temples of Western India were ascribed to him (*ante*, p. 114); Tennent cites a Persian poem describing his journey to Ceylon and Adam's Peak (*Ceylon*, i, 605); whilst Friar Mauro's Map attributes to Alexander the chains that still aid pilgrims in climbing that mountain. John of Hese likewise, in his imaginary travels, finds within a mile of the Mountain of Paradise another mountain, on which Alexander is said to have stood when he claimed tribute also from Paradise. Earlier than these the versifying geographers in their apparent identification of *Kolis* (the *idea* of which is Cape Comorin, though the name may have belonged to a more eastern promontory) with Aornos, seem to indicate that in their notions Alexander had attained the furthest extremity of India.[1] Thus Dionysius—

"παρὰ τέρματα Κωλίδος αἴης
Ἡ δ' ἤτοι προνένευκεν ἐπ' Ὠκεανὸν βαθυδίνην
Ἠλίβατος ταχινοῖσι δυσέμβατος οἰωνοῖσιν
Τοὔνεκά μιν καὶ φῶτες ἐπικλείουσιν Ἄορνιν."
(*Orb. Descrip.*, v. 1148.)

Dobner indeed refers to a passage in the same author as speaking of the columns erected by Alexander on the ocean, but though otherwise appropriate, it is of Bacchus that the geographer speaks; it runs in the paraphrase of Festus Avienus:

"Oceani Eoi prætenti denique Bacchus
Littore, et extremâ terrarum victor in orâ
Ducit laurigeros post Indica bella triumphos,
Erigit et geminas telluris fine columnas."—(V. 1380.)

But the most appropriate illustration is in a passage of Mandeville quoted by Meinert from a German edition, but which I do not find in Wright's: "So he set up his token there as far as he had got, like as Hercules did on the Spanish Sea towards the sunset. And the token that Alexander set up towards the sunrising, hard by Paradise, hight Alexander's Gades, and that other hight Hercules's Gades: and these be great Pillars of Stone, that stand upon lofty mountains, for an eternal Sign and Token that no man shall pass beyond those pillars."

Was this pillar of Marignolli's that which the Dutch chaplain Baldæus thus mentions: "Upon the rocks near the sea shore of Coulang stands a Stone Pillar, erected there, as the inhabitants report, by St. Thomas; I saw the Pillar in 1662"? Three hundred years of tradition might easily swamp the dim memory of John the Legate in that of Thomas the Apostle. Mr. Day (*Land of the Permauls*, p. 212) tells us that this pillar still exists, but Mr. Broadley Howard in a recent book (*Christians of St. Thomas*, p. 9) says in

I went to see the famous Queen of SABA. By her I was honourably treated, and after some harvest of souls (for there are a few Christians there) I proceeded by sea to SEYLLAN, a glorious mountain opposite to Paradise. And from Seyllan to Paradise, according to what the natives say after the tradition of their fathers, is a distance of forty Italian miles; so that, 'tis said, the sound of the waters falling from the fountain of Paradise is heard there[1].

CHAPTER CONCERNING PARADISE.

Now Paradise[2] is a place that (really) exists upon the earth surrounded by the Ocean Sea, in the regions of the Orient on the other side of Columbine India, and over against the mountain of Seyllan. 'Tis the loftiest spot on the face of the earth, reaching, as Johannes Scotus hath proven, to the sphere of the moon; a place remote from all strife, delectable in balminess and brightness of atmosphere, and in the midst whereof a fountain springeth from the ground, pouring forth its waters to water, according to the season, the Paradise and all the trees therein. And there grow all the trees that produce the best of fruits; wondrous fair are they to look upon, fragrant and delicious for the food of man. Now that fountain cometh down from the mount and falleth into a lake, which is called by the philosophers EUPHIRATTES. Here it passes under another water which is turbid, and issues forth on the

reference to the passage of Baldæus just quoted: "Mr. D'Albedhyll, the Master Attendant at Quilon, told me that he had seen the pillar, and that it was washed away a few years ago." I wish some one would still look for it!

[1] A MS. of the fifteenth century in the Genoese Archives, from which extracts are given by Gräberg de Hemso, says that the Four Rivers flow down from Paradise with such a noise that the people who inhabit round about those parts are born deaf! (*Annali di Geografia e di Statistica*, ii, App.) Akin to this is the myth of the dwellers in the extreme east hearing a tremendous noise made by the sun in rising (*Carpini*, p. 661).

[2] See Introductory Notice to Marignolli, p. 197.

other side, where it divides into four rivers which pass through Seyllan; and these be their names[1]:

[1] Considering how rarely in reality a plurality of rivers have a common source, so rarely that in the discussions arising out of Captain Speke's great journey it has even been denied that such a thing exists in nature, it is remarkable how frequent is the phenomenon in the traditions of many nations, and there must be something in the idea attractive to man's imagination.

The interpretation of the four rivers of Eden as literally diverging from one fount has long been abandoned by Catholics as well as Protestants; but in the Middle Ages, meeting perhaps that attraction to which allusion has been made, it was received to the letter, and played a large part in the geography both of Christendom and Islam; the possible traces of which remain stamped on the map of Taurus in the names of Sihun and Jihun given to the *Sarus* and the *Pyramus*. (See *Mas'udi*, i, 264, 270.) The most prominent instance of the tradition alluded to is that in both Brahmanical and Buddhist cosmogony which derives four great rivers of India, the Indus, the Sutlej, the Ganges, and the Sardha from one Holy Lake at the foot of Kailas. It is also firmly believed by the Hindus that the Sone and the Nerbudda rise out of the same pool near Amarkantak. The natives were so convinced that there was a communication between the Jumna and the Saraswati, which flows towards the Sutlej, that an officer of the Revenue Survey reported it to government as a fact, and my then chief (afterwards Major-General W. E. Baker) was desired to verify it. We found that the alleged communication was supposed to take place *gupti gupti*, i.e., in a clandestine manner! Hiuen Tsang relates that from the Dragon Lake on the high lands of Pamir one stream descends to the Oxus, another to the Sita, which Ritter supposes to be the river of Kashgar, but which perhaps is the mystic source of the Hwang-Ho. In a later form of the same tradition, reported by Burnes, the Oxus, Jaxartes, and Indus are all believed to rise in the Sirikul on Pamir. The rivers of Cambodia, of Canton, of Ava, and a fourth (perhaps the Salwen) were regarded by the people of Laos as all branches of one river; a notion which was probably only a local adaptation of the Indian Buddhist tradition. A Chinese work mentioned by Klaproth describes the river of Siam as being a branch of the Hwang-Ho. Even in the south of New Zealand we find that the Maoris have a notion that the three chief rivers known to them issue from a common lake. These legendary notions so possessed travellers and geographers that they seemed to assume that the law of rivers was one of dispersion and not of convergence, and that the best natural type of a river system was to be found, not in the veins of a leaf, but in the body of a spider. Thus the Catalan map of 1375, in some respects the most remarkable geographical production of the Middle Ages, represents all the great rivers of Cathay as radiating from one source to the sea. The misty notions of the great African lakes, early gathered by the Portuguese, condensed themselves into one great sea, that fed the sources not only of the Nile but of the Niger, Congo, Zambesi, and several more. The Hindu myths suggested to mapmakers a great Lake Chimay in Tibet, from which dispersed all the great rivers of Eastern Asia; Ferdinand Mendez Pinto declared, perhaps believed, that he had visited it, and every atlas to the be-

GYON[1] is that which circleth the land of Ethiopia where are now the negroes, and which is called the Land of Prester John. It is indeed believed to be the Nile, which descends into Egypt by a breach made in the place which is called ABASTY. The Christians of St. Matthew the Apostle are there, and the Soldan pays them tribute

ginning of the eighteenth century, if not later, repeated the fiction. A traveller of the seventeenth century, the general of his order and therefore perhaps no vulgar friar, says that *he saw* the Ganges near Goa, where one of its branches entered the sea. And far more recent and distinguished geographers have clung to the like ideas. Ritter more than half accepts the Chinese story of the Dragon Lake of Pamir. Buchanan Hamilton, who did so much for the geography both of India and of Indo-China, not only accepted the stories of the Burmese regarding the radiation of rivers, but himself suggested like theories, such as that of an anastomosis between the Brahmaputra and the Irawadi; whilst the old fancies of the African map-makers have been revived in our own time. (See *Strachey*, in *J. R. G. S.*, vol. xxiii, first paper; *Ritter*, *Erdkunde*, vii, 496; *Burnes*, iii, 180; *Journ. Asiatique*, sér. ii, tom. x, 415; *In.*, xi, 42; *Burton*, in *J. R. G. S.*, xxix, 307; *Blaeu's Atlas*, Amsterdam, 1662, vol. x; *Coronelli*, *Atlante Veneto*, 1691, etc.; *Viaggi di P. Filippo*, etc., p. 230.)

[1] The Septuagint has Γηῶν for the Nile in *Jeremiah* ii, 18, and in *Ecclesiasticus*, xxiv, 37; from the former passage the term was adopted in the Ethiopic books. Many Fathers of the Church thought Gihon passed under ground from Paradise to reappear as the Nile, and the other rivers in like fashion. Ludolf quotes many examples of what he justly calls this foolish story of Gihon and its subterranean wanderings. But such notions were not originated by the Church; for Pomponius Mela supposes the Nile to come under the sea from the antichthonic world, and other heathen writers believed it to be a resurrection of the Euphrates. (*Ludolf*, i. c. 8, § 10–12, and *Comment.*, pp. 119, 120; Note by *Letronne* in *Humboldt's Examen Critique*, etc., iii, 122, 123.) [In the old French poem: *L'entrée d'Espagne*, edited by A. Thomas for the Société des Anciens Textes, 1913, II, p. 214 we have:

Cant ensi ot le duc fornie sa besoigne,
De retorner a Mec et a sun segnors soigne:
Les desert costoient et les vaus de Sandoigne,
Et paserent *Guion* as guez de le Choudoigne.]

["The Tibetans believe that the Titans, or ungodly spirits, were originally gods, but were expelled from heaven, and now occupy a position at the base of Mount Meru, *i.e.*, Mount Kailas, intermediate between heaven and earth....On the summit of Meru is the city of Brahma...the holy river of Ganges issuing from the foot of Vishnu and washing the moon, falls here from the skies, and after encircling the city of Brahma divides into four mighty rivers, flowing in opposite directions. These are (1) on the north the Indus...(2) on the east the Sanpo or Brahmaputra...(3) on the west the Sutlej...(4) on the south the Karnali." C. A. Sherring, *Western Tibet*, 1906, pp. 44–45.]

on account of the river, because they have it in their power to shut off the water, and then Egypt would perish[1].

[1] For *Abasty* in this paragraph the author probably wrote *Abascy* (the *c* and *t* are constantly confounded), the *Abasci* of Polo, from the Arabic name of Abyssinia *Habsh*. Here again in the fourteenth century is Prester John in Africa (see *ante*, p. 26); as the Catalan Map and Sigoli also show him.

This tribute alleged to be paid by the Soldan of Egypt to the King of Ethiopia or Abyssinia is mentioned by Jordanus also (*Mirabilia*, p. 40), and he names the reported amount as five hundred thousand ducats, though he omits the ground of payment. It is also spoken of by Ariosto:

> "Si dice che 'l Soldan, Re dell' Egitto,
> A quel Re dà tributo, e sta suggetto,
> Perch' è in poter di lui dal cammin dritto
> Levare il Nilo, e dargli altro ricetto,
> E per questo lasciar subito afflitto
> Di fame il Cairo e tutto quel distretto.
> Senápo detto è dai sudditti suoi:
> Gli diciam Presto o Preteianni noi."
>
> *Orl. Fur.*, xxxiii, 106.

The question will be found discussed in *Ludolf* (i., c. viii, § 76–92, and *Comment.*, pp. 130–132) *Num Rex Habessinorum Nilum divertere possit ne in Ægyptum fluat?* He refers to the Saracenic history of El Macini, in which we find it related that in the time of Michael, Patriarch of the Jacobites of Alexandria (who was elected in the year 1089, and ruled for nine years), "the Nile became excessively low, wherefore (the Sultan) Mostansir sent him (Michael) up to Ethiopia with costly presents. The king of the country sent out to meet him and received him with reverence, asking wherefore he had come. And he then set forth how the great deficiency of the Nile in Egypt was threatening destruction to that land and its people. The king upon this ordered the cut that had been made to divert the waters to be closed, so that the water might again flow towards Egypt, seeing that the Patriarch had come so far on that account. And the Nile rose three cubits in one night, so that all the fields of Egypt received ample water and could be sown. And the Patriarch returned with much credit to Egypt, and was loaded with gifts and honours by the Prince Mostansir." (*Histor. Saracen. a Georg. Elmacino*, by *Erpenius*, Lug. Bat., 1625, B. iii, c. 8.) The story is (briefly) noticed in Herbelot under the word *Nil*, and is told much as by El Macini from the History of Egypt by Wassaif Shah, who says the famine had lasted seven years when the report reached Egypt of the Nile's having been diverted. (*Notices et Extraits*, viii, p. 47; and also in De Castro's *Voyage of Stephen de Gama.*) He says the thing was much talked of among the Abyssinians, and that it secured that people the privilege of passing through Egypt without paying tribute. (*Astley's Voyages*, i, 114.) Urreta, a Spanish Dominican writer, of whom Ludolf speaks with much contempt, says that the Pope wrote to Menas King of Ethiopia to turn off the Nile, and not to mind about the tribute of three hundred thousand sequins which he got from the Turk to keep it open. A certain Wanzlebius, having been desired by Duke Ernest

The second river is called PHISON, and it goes through India, circling all the land of Evilach, and is said to go down into CATHAY, where, by a change of name, it is called CAROMORAN, i.e. Black Water, and there is found bdellium and the onyx stone. I believe it to be the biggest river of fresh water in the world, and I have crossed it myself. And it has on its banks very great and noble cities, rich above all in gold. And on that river excellent craftsmen have their dwelling, occupying wooden houses, especially weavers of silk and gold brocade, in such numbers (I can bear witness from having seen them), as in my opinion do not exist in the whole of Italy. And they have on the shores of the river an abundance of silk, more indeed than all the rest of the world put together. And they go about on their floating houses with their whole families just as if they were on shore. This I have seen. On the other side of Caffa the river is lost in the sands, but it breaks out again and forms the sea which is called BACUC, beyond THANA[1].

of Saxony to investigate this matter, reported that the Europeans in Egypt looked on the whole story as an Abyssinian rhodomontade, but afterwards in 1677 he claimed to have found a letter from a king of Abyssinia threatening the Sultan with the diversion of the Nile. It is also noticed by Ludolf that Albuquerque is stated by his son to have seriously contemplated this diversion, and to have often urged King Emanuel to send him miners for the job. (*Ludolf*, u.s., and the others quoted above.)

The legend is thus told as a fact also by Simon Sigoli, who travelled to Egypt, Sinai and Palestine with Leonardo Frescobaldi and other Florentines in 1384: "'Tis true that this soldan is obliged to pay a yearly ransom or homage to Prester John. Now this potentate Prester John dwells in India, and is a Christian, and possesses many cities both of Christians and of infidels. And the reason why the Soldan pays him homage is this, that whenever this Prester John chooses to open certain river sluices he can drown Cairo and Alexandria and all that country; and 'tis said that this river is the Nile itself which runs by Cairo. The said sluices stand but little open, and yet the river is enormous. And so it is for this reason, or rather from this apprehension, that the Soldan sends him every year a ball of gold with a cross upon it, worth three thousand gold bezants. And the lands of the Soldan do march with those of this Prester John." (*V. in Terra Santa*, etc., Firenze, 1862, p. 202.)

[1] Dobner has *Chana* (the *c* for *t* again), but the Venice MS. has

The third river is called TYGRIS. It passes over against the land of the Assyrians, and comes down near NYNEVE, that great city of three days' journey, to which Jonas was sent to preach; and his sepulchre is there. I have been there also, and stopped a fortnight in the adjoining towns which were built out of the ruins of the city. There are capital fruits there, especially pomegranates of wonderful size and sweetness, with all the other fruits that we have in Italy. And on the opposite side [of the river] is a city built out of the ruins of Nyneve, which is called MONSOL[1].

Between that river and the fourth, there is a long tract of country bearing these names; viz., *Mesopotamia*, i.e. the land between the waters; *Assyria*, the land of Abraham

the name right, Thana, i.e., Azov. In the confusions of this paragraph Marignolli outdoes himself. He jumbles into one river the Phison, Ganges (or Indus), Volga (or Oxus), Hwang-Ho and Yang-tze-Kiang, and then turns them all topsy-turvy. The *Kara-Muren*, or Black River of the Tartars, as he correctly explains it, is well known to be the Yellow River of the Chinese. But it is not a river whose shores and waters are crowded with the vast population described, and his descriptions here appear to be drawn from his recollections of the Yang-tze-Kiang. The river lost in the sands is perhaps the Oxus, which he would probably pass on his way from Sarai to Almaliq, but he *may* mean the Volga which he saw at Sarai, and which has the best claim to be said to form the Sea of Baku, i.e., the Caspian (*Ethilia...faciens Mare Caspium*, says Roger Bacon). How he connects the Caspian and the Karamuren is puzzling. The Chinese have indeed a notion that the sources of the Hwang-Ho were originally in the mountains near Kashgar, whence their streams flowed into the Lop Nor, and thence diving under ground, issued forth as the Hwang-Ho. There was also an old notion that the waters of the country about Kara-shahr came from the Si-Hai or Caspian (*Timkowsky*, ii, 272); (*Fo-koue-ki*, p. 37; *Julien* in *N. A. des Voyages*, as quoted at p. 213). Something of these legends Marignolli may have heard, without quite digesting.

On this passage, with an amusing sense of his own superior advantages, Dobner observes: "Here Marignola shows himself excessively ignorant of geography; but we must pardon him, for in his day geographical studies had by no means reached that perfection which they have attained now."

[1] The ruins opposite Mosul are those called Nabi Yunus and Kouyunjik, well known from Mr. Layard's excavations and interesting books. A sketch showing the tomb of Jonah mentioned in the text, will be found at p. 131, vol. i, of *Nineveh and its Remains*. Ricold of Montecroce also mentions the traces and ramparts of Nineveh, and a spring which was called the Fount of Jonah.

and Job, where also is the city of King Abagarus, to whom Christ sent a letter written with his own hand, once a most fair and Christian city, but now in the hands of the Saracens. There also I abode four days in no small fear.

We come lastly to the fourth river, by name EUPHRATES, which separates Syria, Assyria, and Mesopotamia from the Holy Land. When we crossed it we were in the Holy Land. In this region are some very great cities, especially ALEP, in which there are many Christians who dress after the Latin fashion, and speak a language very near the French; at any rate like French of Cyprus[1]. Thence you come to Damascus, to Mount Lebanon, to Galilee, to Samaria, Nazareth, Jerusalem, and to the Sepulchre of our Lord Jesus Christ.

Then follows a chapter *Concerning the Trees of Paradise*, from which I extract a few lines.

[The trees] are there still in existence, as the *Pantheon* says[2]; and this is shown by the fruits and leaves which are sometimes carried forth by those rivers, and are known by their medicinal virtue and fragrant odours. Nor is this incredible; for in the adjoining provinces of India likewise there are trees which produce fruit of a marvellous kind every month[3].

[1] "*Loquuntur linguam quasi Gallicam, scilicet quasi de Cipro.*"
"And French she spake both fayre and fetisely,
After the school of Stratford-atte-Bowe,
For French of Paris was to her unknowe."
French no doubt was much spoken at Cyprus under the Lusignans.

[2] The *Pantheon* is the Universal Chronicle, so called, by Godfrey of Viterbo, an ecclesiastical writer who died in 1186. The work is to be seen in "*German. Scriptorum*, etc., *Tomus Alter*, *ex Bibl. Joannis Pistorii Nidarii*, Hanov., 1613." It is a very prolix affair, beginning with *De Divinâ Essentiâ ante omnem creationem*, and is largely interspersed with semi-doggerel hexameters and pentameters.

[3] According to Mas'udi some leaves of Paradise covered Adam's body when cast out. These were scattered by the winds over India, and gave birth to all the perfumes of that country. He also bore with him wheat, and thirty branches of the trees of the Garden, and from these come all our good fruits (*French Trans.*, i, 61). St. Athanasius also accounts for the aromatics of India by the spicy breezes from Paradise adjoining. (*Opera*, Paris, 1698, ii, 279.)

From the chapter *On the Transgression of our First Parents by Temptation of the Serpent.*

And they took the leaves of the fig-tree or plantain[1], and made themselves girdles to hide their shame....Then God pronounced sentence after the confession of their sin, first against the serpent that he should go upon his belly creeping on the earth (but I must say that I have seen many serpents, and very big ones too, that went with half the body quite erect, like women when they walk in the street, and very graceful to look upon, but not to be sure keeping this up for any length of time)....

And he made them coats of skins: so at least we commonly have it, *pelliceas*, "of fur," but we should do better to read *filiceas*, "of fibre"; because they were no doubt of a certain fibrous substance which grows like net-work between the shoots of the coco-palm[2]; I wore one of these myself till I got to Florence, where I left it. And God forbade Adam to eat of the Tree of Life. See, said He to the Angels, that they take not of the Tree of Life, and so live for ever. And straightway the Angel took Adam by the arm and set him down beyond the lake on the Mountain Seyllan, where I stopped for four months. And by chance Adam planted his right foot upon a stone which is there still, and straightway by a divine miracle the form of the sole of his foot was imprinted on the marble, and there it is to this very day. And the size, I mean the length, thereof is two and a half of our palms, or about half a Prague ell. And I was not the only one to measure it, for so did another pilgrim, a Saracen of Spain; for many

[1] "*Ficus seu musarum.*" That the leaves used for girdles by Adam and Eve were *plantain* leaves is a Mahomedan tradition; and it is probably from this that the plantain has been called a *fig* in European languages, a name which seems to have little ground in any resemblance of the fruits, but which misled Milton perhaps to make the banyan the tree of the girdles.

[2] "*Nargillorum,*" from Pers. *Nargil.*

go on pilgrimage to Adam. And the Angel put out Eve on another mountain, some four short days' journey distant. And as the histories of those nations relate (and indeed there is nothing in the relation that contradicts Holy Scripture), they abode apart from one another and mourning for forty days, after which the Angel brought Eve to Adam, who was waxing as it were desperate, and so comforted them both[1].

NARRATIVE CONCERNING THE MOUNTAIN SEYLLAN.

Now, as our subject requires it, and as I deem it both pleasant and for some folks profitable, I propose to insert here an account of Seyllan, provided it please his Imperial Majesty; and if it please him not he has but to score it out.

First, then, it must be told how, and in what fashion I got there, and after that I will speak of what is to be found there.

First, then, when we got our dismissal from the Kaam that mighty Emperor, with splendid presents and allowances from him, and as we proposed to travel by India, because the other overland road was shut up by war and there was no possibility of getting a passage that way, it was the Kaam's order that we should proceed through Manzi, which was formerly known as *India Maxima.*

Now Manzi is a country which has countless cities and nations included in it, past all belief to one who has not seen them, besides great plenty of everything, including fruits quite unknown in our Latin countries. Indeed it has 30,000 great cities, besides towns and boroughs quite

[1] The usual Mussulman tradition runs, that on the violent expulsion of our parents and their tempter from Paradise, Adam fell on the Mountain of Serendib, Eve at Jidda near Mecca, Eblis near Basrah, and the Serpent at Ispahan. Adam after long solitude and penitence was led by Gabriel to Mecca and thence to the Mountain of Arafat (*Recognition*), where he was reunited to Eve after a separation of two hundred years. (*D'Herbelot*; Weil's *Bib. Legends.*)

beyond count. And among the rest is that most famous city of CAMPSAY, the finest, the biggest, the richest, the most populous, and altogether the most marvellous city, the city of the greatest wealth and luxury, of the most splendid buildings (especially idol temples, in some of which there are 1000 and 2000 monks dwelling together) that exists now upon the face of the earth, or mayhap that ever did exist! When authors tell of its ten thousand noble bridges of stone, adorned with sculptures and statues of armed princes, it passes the belief of one who has not been there, and yet peradventure these authors tell no lie[1].

There is ZAYTÚN also, a wondrous fine seaport and a city of incredible size, where our Minor Friars have three very fine churches, passing rich and elegant; and they have a bath also and a *fondaco* which serves as a depôt for all the merchants[2]. They have also some fine bells of

[1] Probably a reference to the accounts of King ssé or Hang chau, by Polo and Odoric, see II, p. 192. But hear what Dobner has to say on Camsay: "In our time *Cambay*, the chief city of Guzerat, which on account of its size, wealth, and splendour, is often called the Indian Cairo. The river Indus flows through the kingdom, so that Marignolli was quite right in a previous passage when he referred the Columns of Alexander to those parts, in imitation of which he put up another himself in the same quarter"!! (p. 95.)

[2] The original (in Dobner) reads: "*habent tres Ecclesias pulcherrimas, optimas et ditissimas*, balneum fundatum, *omnium mercatorum depositorium.*" Meinert and Kunstmann translate "*ein gestiftetes Bad*," but this seems somewhat unmeaning, and I have assumed that *fundatum* should read *Fundacum* (*t* for *c* again) in the sense of the Italian *Fondaco*. This was the word for a mercantile establishment and lodging house in a foreign country, nearly what we should call a factory, and we find it still applied at Venice to the old foreign factories, though the common Italian dictionaries ignore this meaning of the word. In Sicily the word still means *an inn*, especially one where the cattle and goods of traders are put up. It is borrowed from the Arabic *Fanduk*, "a public hostel for traders where they put up along with their wares," and that again comes from the Greek *πανδοχεῖον*.

Pagnini (*Della Decima*, etc., ii, 89) gives a Florentine correspondence about a treaty of commerce with the Sultan of Egypt in the year 1422, in which the chief items of privilege to be demanded for the Florence merchants are under the heads of *Fondaco*, *Church*, *Bath*, *Steelyard*. In the thirteenth century we find the King of Lesser Armenia granting the Venetians at Mamistra "a fondúk to deposit their merchandise and property in." (*Journ. Asiat.*, sér. v, tom. xviii,

the best quality, two of which were made to my order, and set up with all due form in the very middle of the Saracen community[1]. One of these we ordered to be called Johannina, and the other Antonina.

We quitted Zaytún on St. Stephen's day, and on the Wednesday of Holy Week we arrived at Columbum. Wishing then to visit the Shrine of St. Thomas the Apostle, and to sail thence to the Holy Land[2], we embarked on board certain junks, from Lower India[3] which is called Minubar[4]. We encountered so many storms, commencing from St. George's Eve, and were so dashed about by them, that sixty times and more we were all but swamped in the depths of the sea, and it was only by

353.) In a treaty between Abuabdallah Mahomed, King of Granada, and the Genoese, in 1278, it is provided that the latter shall have in all the king's cities *Fundiks* in which to conduct their business, and these shall be allowed to have *churches, baths, oven, and warehouses* (*Not. et Extraits*, xi, 28; see also Amari, *Dipl. Arab.*, pp. xxx, 88, 101). And in a treaty between Michael Palæologus and the Genoese, it is specified that the latter shall have in certain ports and islands *logiam, palatium*, ecclesiam, balneum, *furnum et jardinum* (Ducange, *Hist. de Constantinople*, App., p. 6). These quotations show that the *Ecclesia, Balneum, Fundacum*, and *Depositorium* ran naturally together. It was also the Mahomedan practice to attach a caravanserai (i.e. a *fondaco*) to convents of Kalandars or Darweshes (see Erskine's *Baber*, p. 215).

[1] He has evident glee in mentioning the setting up of the bells in the middle of the Mahomedan quarter of Zaytún; the Mahomedans holding bells in abomination and not allowing them under their rule. Ibn Batuta's account of his terror and dismay, when he first heard bells jangling on all sides of him at Caffa, is amusing (ii, 357).

[2] Meinert suggests that *Terram Sanctam* here is a clerical error for *Terram Sabam*. This is probable, for the first is hardly intelligible.

[3] "*Ascendentes Junkos.*" This is perhaps the oldest item in the Franco-Indian vocabulary. It occurs also in Odoric (see *ante*, p. 131). The Catalan Map gives a drawing and description of these ships called *Inchi* (probably for *Iñchi*) with their bamboo sails. Quoth Dobner: "Vocem hanc in nullo Glossariorum Medii Ævi...reperio. Verosimillime navigia *e juncis texta* intelliguntur, quorum usum Indis esse plures affirmant," etc. (p. 96). It is more singular that the same mistake should have been made by Amerigo Vespucci in his curious letter to one of the Medici giving an account of the voyage of De Gama, whose party he had met at Cape Verde on their return from India. (See *Baldelli Boni, Il Milione*, p. lviii.)

[4] This correct reading is from Venice MS., Dobner having *Nimbar*. See note on Minibar at II p. 74.

divine miracle that we escaped. And such wondrous things we beheld! The sea as if in flames, and fire-spitting dragons flying by[1], and as they passed they slew persons on board the other junks, whilst ours remained untouched, by God's grace, and by virtue of the body of Christ which I carried with me, and through the merits of the glorious Virgin and St. Clare[2]. And having brought all the Christians to penitential mourning, even whilst the gale still blew we made sail, committing ourselves to the Divine guidance, and caring only for the safety of souls. Thus led by the Divine mercy, on the morrow of the Invention of the Holy Cross[3] we found ourselves brought safely into port in a harbour of Seyllan, called PERVILIS[4], over against Paradise. Here a certain tyrant, by name Coya Jaan[5], a eunuch, had the mastery in opposition to the lawful king. He was an accursed Saracen, who by means of his great treasures had gained possession of the greater part of the kingdom.

[1] This is very like Fahian's account of a storm in the same sea, only the Chinese friar's is the more sober (*Fo-koue-ki*, ch. xl).

[2] St. Clara was the townswoman, disciple, and feminine reflexion of St. Francis.

[3] 3rd May.

[4] Meinert and Kunstmann translate *Pervilis* as if it were a Latin adjective. But the name is perfectly Ceylonese in character, e.g. *Padaville* and *Periaville* are names found in Tennent's Map, though not in positions suited to this. From the expression "over against Paradise," and the after mention of Cotta, we may see that it was somewhere not far from Columbo. And a passage in Pridham enables me to identify the port as Barberyn, otherwise called BERUWALA, near Bentotte and the mouth of the Kaluganga. This is now a large fishing village, with a small bay having an anchorage for ships, and a considerable coasting trade. (*Historical*, etc., *View of Ceylon*, pp. 619–20.)

[5] *Coya* or *Coja Jaan* represents, I presume, *Khwája Jahán*. Now this was the title of the Wazir of Delhi; and Ibn Batuta, in reference to a time only a year or two before our author's arrival in Ceylon, mentions as an instance of the arrogance of Nasiruddín the new Sultan of Maabar, that he ordered *his* Wazir and admiral to take the same title of *Khwája Jahán*. Others may have followed the fashion, for it seems probable that our author's accursed Saracen was that "Wazir and Admiral Jálasti" whom Ibn Batuta found in power at Columbo. (*Ibn Batuta*, iv, 185; 204.)

At first he put on a pretence of treating us honourably, but by and by, in the politest manner and under the name of a loan, he took from us 60,000 marks, in gold, silver, silk, cloth of gold, precious stones, pearls, camphor, musk, myrrh, and aromatic spices, gifts from the Great Kaam and other princes to us, or presents sent from them to the Pope. And so we were detained by this man, with all politeness as I said, for four months.

On that very high mountain [of which we have spoken], perhaps after Paradise the highest mountain on the face of the earth, some indeed think that Paradise itself exists. But this is a mistake, for the name shows the contrary. For it is called by the natives *Zindan Baba*; *baba* meaning 'father' (and *mama* 'mother') in every language in the world; whilst *Zindan* is the same as 'Hell,' so that *Zindan Baba* is as much as to say 'the hell of our father,' implying that our first father when placed there on his expulsion from Paradise was as it were in hell[1].

That exceeding high mountain hath a pinnacle of surpassing height, which, on account of the clouds, can rarely be seen. But God, pitying our tears, lighted it up one morning just before the sun rose, so that we beheld it glowing with the brightest flame. In the way down from this same mountain there is a fine level spot, still at a great height, and there you find in order, first the mark of Adam's foot; secondly, a certain statue of a sitting figure

[1] I cannot find any trace of this name in the books about Ceylon. *Zindán* (Pers.) signifies "a dungeon," and seems often applied to buildings of mysterious antiquity. Thus a tower-like building of huge blocks of marble, which exists among those remains north of Persepolis which are supposed to mark the site of Pasargadæ, is called *Zindán-i-Suleiman*, "Solomon's Dungeon." And another relic, described by Sir H. Rawlinson in his paper on the Atropatenian Ecbatana, has the same name. It is very likely that the sepulchre-like building which Marignolli describes below, was called *Zindán-i-Baba* by the Persian visitors. Baba is correctly applied to Adam. Thus Ibn Batuta mentions that of the two roads to the Peak one was *Tarík Baba* (Adam's Road), and the other *Tarík Mama* (Eve's Road) (iv, p. 180).

with the left hand resting on the knee, and the right hand raised and extended towards the west; lastly, there is the house (of Adam) which he made with his own hands. It is of an oblong quadrangular shape like a sepulchre, with a door in the middle, and is formed of great tabular slabs of marble, not cemented, but merely laid one upon another[1].

It is said by the natives, especially by their monks who stay at the foot of the mountain, men of very holy life

[1] It is clear from all this that Marignolli never ascended the Peak. Indeed he does not seem to have dreamt of mounting that "*cacumen supereminens*" as he calls it, but thanks God for a glimpse of it merely. The footmark that he saw therefore was not *the* footmark which has been the object of pilgrimage or curiosity for so many ages. Indeed the length of half an ell which he ascribes to it (*ante*, p. 227) does not agree with that of the peak footstep. The length of the latter is given by Ibn Batuta at eleven spans, by Marshall at five feet six inches, by Tennent at about five feet; all in fair accordance. The "*planities altissima pulchra*" on which Marignolli places the footmark, and apparently also a lake (see *ante*, p. 227), seems to correspond with the "*pulcherrima quædam planities*" and lake of Odoric. I suspect that the place visited by both Franciscans was some Buddhist establishment at one of the stages between the coast and Adam's Peak, where there was a *model* of the sacred footstep, such as is common in Buddhist countries, and such as Tennent states to be shown at the Alu Wihara at Cotta, at Kornegalle, and elsewhere in Ceylon. It is true that there was a second "genuine" footstep shown in Fahian's time (beginning of fifth century), but this was "to the north of the royal city," apparently Anurajapura, and out of Marignolli's way, even if extant in his time. I see from Pridham and Tennent that there appears to be a model of the foot at Palabadulla, one of the resting places in ascending from Ratnapura, which would be the route likely to be followed by Marignolli, considering the position of the port where he landed. Probably the exact site of which our author speaks might still be identified by remains of the ancient building which he calls Adam's Dungeon. Knox also calls the footmark "about two foot long," so that perhaps he was misled in the same manner as Marignolli (p. 3).

For the history of the Peak see Sir J. E. Tennent's *Ceylon*. [Cf. *Marco Polo*, ii, p. 328.] Perhaps he has not noticed that it is represented pictorially in Fra Mauro's Map, with the footstep at the top of it. It must also be added that Tennent quotes from the *Asiatic Journal*, that the first *Englishman* to ascend Adam's Peak was Lieut. Malcolm in 1827. If the date is right, the fact is wrong. For the late Dr. Henry Marshall and Mr. S. Sawers ascended together in 1819, and both published accounts of their ascent. To be sure they were both *Scotchmen!*

The *statua quædam sedens*, etc., is of course a Buddha.

though without the faith[1], that the deluge never mounted to that point, and thus the house has never been disturbed[2]. Herein they put their dreams in opposition to Holy Scripture and the traditions of the saints; but indeed they have some plausible arguments to urge on their side. For they say that they are not descended either from Cain or from Seth, but from other sons of Adam, who [as they allege] begot other sons and daughters. But as this is contrary to Holy Scripture I will say no more about it.

I must remark, however, that these monks never eat flesh, because Adam and his successors till the flood did not do so. They go naked from the loins upwards, and unquestionably they are very well conducted. They have houses of palm-leaves, which you can break through with your finger[3], and these are scattered up and down in the woods, and full of property, and yet they live without the slightest fear of thieves, unless perchance there come vagabonds from foreign parts.

On the same mountain, in the direction of Paradise, is a great fountain[4], the waters of which are clearly visible at a distance of good ten Italian miles. And though it breaks out there, they say that its water is derived from the Fountain of Paradise. And they allege this in proof: that there sometimes turn up from the bottom leaves of unknown species in great quantities, and also lign-aloes,

[1] "*Qui stant ad pedes montis sine fide sanctissimæ vitæ.*" I am doubtful of the meaning.

[2] Tennent mentions that the Samaritan *version* of the Pentateuch, and also an Arabic Pentateuch in the Bodleian, make the Ark rest on the mountains of Serendib or Ceylon (i, 552). Ricold di Montecroce says that the Indians denied that Noah's flood had reached to them, but they lied, for he had noticed as a fact that all the rivers that descended from Ararat flowed towards the Indian Ocean. (*Peregrinat. Quatuor*, p. 122.)

[3] "*Pansala*, 'a dwelling of leaves,' describes the house of a Buddhist priest to the present day." (*Hardy's Eastern Monachism*, p. 129.)

[4] A cascade, I suppose, perhaps the Seetlagunga torrent noticed below.

and precious stones, such as the carbuncle and sapphire, and also certain fruits with healing virtues. They tell also that those gems are formed from Adam's tears, but this seems to be a mere figment[1]. Many other matters I think it best to pass over at present.

CONCERNING ADAM'S GARDEN AND THE FRUITS THEREOF.

The garden of Adam in Seyllan contains in the first place plantain trees which the natives call figs[2]. But the plantain has more the character of a garden plant than of a tree. It is indeed a tree in thickness, having a stem as thick as an oak, but so soft that a strong man can punch a hole in it with his finger, and from such a hole water will flow. The leaves of those plantain trees are most beautiful, immensely long and broad, and of a bright emerald green; in fact, they use them for tablecloths, but serving only for a single dinner. Also new-born children, after being washed and salted, are wrapped up with aloes and roses in these leaves, without any swathing, and so placed in the sand. The leaves are some ten ells in length, more or less, and I do not know to what to compare them (in form) unless it be to elecampane. The tree produces its fruit only from the crown; but on one stem it will bear a good three hundred. At first they are not good to eat, but after they have been kept a while in the house they ripen of themselves, and are then of an excellent odour,

[1] See *Odoric*, p. 171. The Chinese also had this story (*Tennent*, ii, 610).

[2] See note at p. 226. We find from Pridham that "Adam's Garden" is the subject of a genuine legend still existing. At the torrent of Seetlagunga on the way to the Peak, he tells us: "From the circumstance that various fruits have been occasionally carried down the stream, both the Moormen and the Singalese believe, the former that Adam, the latter that Buddha had a fruit garden here, which still teems with the most splendid productions of the East, but that it is now inaccessible, and that its explorer would never return." (*Hist., Polit. and Stat. Acct. of Ceylon*, p. 613.)

and still better taste; and they are about the length of the longest of one's fingers. And this is a thing that I have seen with mine own eyes, that slice it across where you will, you will find on both sides of the cut the figure of a man crucified, as if one had graven it with a needle point[1]. And it was of these leaves that Adam and Eve made themselves girdles to cover their nakedness.

There are also many other trees and wonderful fruits there which we never see in these parts, such as the *Nargil.* Now the Nargil is the Indian Nut. Its tree has a most delicate bark, and very handsome leaves like those of the date-palm. Of these they make baskets and corn measures; they use the wood for joists and rafters in roofing houses; of the husk or rind they make cordage; of the nutshell cups and goblets. They make also from the shell spoons which are antidotes to poison. Inside the shell there is a pulp of some two fingers thick, which is excellent eating, and tastes almost like almonds. It burns also, and both oil and sugar can be made from it. Inside of this there is a liquor which bubbles like new milk and turns to an excellent wine[2].

They have also another tree called *Amburan*[3], having

[1] Mandeville gives a like account of the cross in the plantain or 'apple of Paradise" as he calls it, and so do Frescobaldi and Simon Sigoli in their narratives of their pilgrimage in 1384; who also like Marignolli compare the leaves to elecampane (*Firenze*, 1862, pp. 32, 160). The circumstance is also alluded to by Paludanus in the notes to *Linschoten's Voyages* (p. 101). Padre F. Vincenzo Maria says that the appearance was in India that of a cross merely, but in Phœnicia an express image of the crucifix, on which account the Christians of that country never cut the fruit but broke it (*Viaggio*, etc., p. 350). Old Gerarde observes on this subject: "The Crosse I might perceive, as the form of a Spred-Egle in the root of Ferne, but the Man I leave to be sought for by those that have better eyes and better judgment than myself" (p. 1515). And Rheede: "Transversim secti in carne nota magis fusca seu rufa, velut signo crucis interstincti, ac punctulis hinc inde nigricantibus conspersi." (*Hortus Malabaricus*, i, 19.)

[2] He apparently confounds the coconut milk with the toddy, which is the sap of the tree drawn and fermented; a mistake which later travellers have made.

[3] The Mango (*Am* or *Amba*). I do not know how the word Am-

a fruit of excellent fragrance and flavour, somewhat like a peach.

There is again another wonderful tree called *Chakebaruhe*[1], as big as an oak. Its fruit is produced from the trunk and not from the branches, and is something marvellous to see, being as big as a great lamb, or a child of three years old. It has a hard rind like that of our pine-cones, so that you have to cut it open with an axe; inside it has a pulp of surpassing flavour, with the sweetness of honey and of the best Italian melon; and this also contains some five hundred chestnuts of like flavour, which are capital eating when roasted.

I do not remember to have seen any other fruit trees, such as pears, apples, or figs, or vines, unless it were some that bore leaves only and no grapes. There is an exception, however, at the fine church of St. Thomas the Apostle, at the place where he was Bishop. They have there a little

buranus which he uses is formed. [See *Hobson-Jobson*, s.v. *Mango*.] There is a tree and fruit in Malabar with a considerable resemblance to the mango (perhaps a wild Mango) called *Ambalám* (Rheede, *Hortus Malabar.*, i, 31).

[1] The Jack; a good account of it. *Ciake Baruhe* is the *Shaki Barki* of Ibn Batuta; concerning which see *Jordanus*, p. 13. P. Vincenzo Maria also calls the best kind of Jack *Giacha Barca* (*Viag.*, p. 355). *Baruhe* however comes nearer to *Waracha*, which Knox states to be one Singalese name of the Jack (Ed. 1691, p. 14).

[See on this fruit, I, p. 340, a passage from the Palatine MS. of Florence of the Travels of Odoric thus translated by Yule in *Hobson-Jobson*: "And there be also trees which produce fruits so big that two will be a load for a strong man. And when they are eaten you must oil your hands and your mouth; they are of a fragrant odour and very savoury; the fruit is called *chabassi*." In Baber's *Memoirs* there is an excellent description of the fruit: "Another is the *Kadhil*. This has a very bad look and flavour (odour). It looks like a sheep's stomach stuffed and made into a haggis. It has a sweet sickly taste. Within it are stones like a filbert....The fruit is very adhesive, and on account of this adhesive quality many rub their mouths with oil before eating them. They grow not only from the branches and trunk, but from its root. You would say that the tree was all hung round with haggises." (*Leyden and Erskine's* edition, p. 325.) The Jack is the tree and fruit called *Artocarpus integrifolia*. It is probably derived from the Malayalam name *chăkka* and the Portuguese *jaca*. See *Hobson-Jobson*, s.v.]

vinery which I saw, and which supplies a small quantity of wine. It is related that when he first went thither he used to carry about with him a little wine for masses (as I did myself for the space of nearly two years); and when that was done he went to Paradise, into which he found his way by the help of Angels, and carried away with him some of the grapes, the stones of which he sowed. From these grew the vines which I saw at that place, and from them he made the wine of which he stood in need. Elsewhere there are vines indeed, but they bear no grapes, as I know by experience. The same is the case with melons and cucumbers, and indeed I saw no eatable potherbs there, unless it be an exception that I saw whole thickets of basil.

These then are the trees in Adam's garden. But of what tree was the fruit that he ate I cannot tell; yet might I guess it to be of the citron[1], for it is written,

"*Ipse lignum tunc notavit*
Dampna ligni ut solveret."

Now there were used, it must be observed, in making the cross, palm wood, olive wood, cypress wood, and citron wood, and the last is the only one of the four that can be

[1] "*De cedro.*" This word is ambiguous, but it is evidently the citron and not cedar, from what follows. The quotation is from the hymn PANGE LINGUA GLORIOSI, which is sung in the Roman Church at matins on Passion Sunday, thus:

"*De parentis protoplasti*
Fraude factâ condolens,
Quando pomi noxialis
In necem morsu ruit,
Ipse lignum tunc notavit
Damna ligni ut solveret.

Hoc opus nostræ salutis
Ordo depoposcerat
Multiformis proditoris
Ars ut artem pelleret,
Et medelam ferret inde
Hostis unde læserat."

alleged to bear a fruit which is good to eat and pleasant to the eyes. And these really appear to be the woods of the cross in that which belongs to our Lord the Emperor Charles; whatever people may say about the plantain tree (which is called also a fig tree) and its exhibiting the image of the crucifix; at the same time I don't mean to commit myself to any pre-judgment of the matter. But as regards the fruit before mentioned, there is a certain Hebrew gloss on that proverb of Ezekiel's, "*Patres comederunt uvam acerbam, et dentes filiorum obstupuerunt,*" which needs notice. Where our version has *Patres* the original Hebrew has *Adam*. Now this word is written sometimes one way and sometimes another. For *Adam* is written one way when it signifies *parents*, or *man and woman*, as in Genesis when 'tis said "*Vocavit nomen eorum* Adam" in the plural; and it is written with other letters when it signifies *a man* only. Just as we say on the one hand *hic et hæc homo*, and on the other hand *hic vir* (though I don't mean to say that we use diacritical marks and inherent vowels like the Hebrews), so also *Sem* is written sometimes with a *Zade*, and sometimes with a *Samech*; and *Abram* sometimes with an *Aleph* and sometimes with a *He*, the signification varying accordingly. So then "Adam *comederunt uvam acerbam*" [has been understood of our first father]. But this interpretation is not approved by our divines, for there was no *vinewood* in the cross. The same remark may be made regarding the fig tree for which the sons of Adam in Seyllan stand up, and also regarding the plantain (though it is highly probable that our parents made their aprons of its leaves, seeing that they be so big). As for the olive and the date, though they are "good for food" nobody ever suggested *their* being the forbidden fruit. Yet there *was* palm wood in the cross, as is clearly seen in the reliques belonging to the Emperor; at least that is my opinion. Yet that can hardly be if the story be true that Godfrey of Viterbo tells in his Pantheon[1]. For he says that when Adam was waxing old and infirm, he sent his son Seth to Paradise to seek the promised oil of mercy. The angel warden of Paradise said: "The time is not yet; but take thou these branches of olive, citron, and cypress, and plant them; and when oil shall be got from them thy father shall get up safe and sound." So Seth returned, and found his father dead in Hebron. Wherefore he twisted together those three branches, and planted them above the body of Adam, and straightway they became one tree. And when that tree grew great it was transplanted, first to Mount Lebanon, and afterwards to Jerusalem. And at Jerusalem to this day exists a monastery of the Greeks on the spot where that tree was cut down. The hole whence it was cut is under the altar, and the monastery is called in Hebrew "The Mother of the Cross" from this circumstance. The tree was made known to Solomon by means of the Queen of Saba, and he caused it to be buried under the deep foundations of a tower. But by the earthquake that took place on the birth of Christ, the foundations of the tower were rent, and the tree discovered. It was from it that the pool called *Probatica* acquired its virtues.

CONCERNING THE CLOTHING OF OUR FIRST PARENTS.

And the Lord made for Adam and his wife coats of skins or fur, and clothed them therewith. But if it be asked, whence the skins? the answer usually made is, either that they were expressly created (which savours not of wisdom!); or that an animal was slain for the purpose (and this is not satisfactory, seeing that 'tis believed the animals were at first created only in pairs, and there had

[1] The story here related of Seth is told in some of Godfrey's verses of a "younger son of Noah called Hiontius."

been no time for the multiplication of the species). Now then I say, without however meaning to dogmatize, that for coats of *fur* we should read coats of *fibre.* For among the fronds of the Nargil, of which I have spoken above, there grows a sort of fibrous web forming an open network of coarse dry filaments. Now to this day among the people there and the Indians[1] it is customary to make of those fibres wet weather mantles for those rustics whom they call *camalls*[2], whose business it is to carry burdens, and also to carry men and women on their shoulders in palankins, such as are mentioned in Canticles, "*Ferculum fecit sibi Salomon de lignis Libani,*" whereby is meant a portable litter, such as I used to be carried in at Zaytún and in India. A garment such as I mean, of this *camall* cloth (and not *camel* cloth), I wore till I got to Florence, and I left it in the sacristy of the Minor Friars there. No doubt the raiment of John Baptist was of this kind. For as regards *camel's hair* it is, next to silk, the softest stuff in the world, and never could have been meant. By the way (speaking of camels), I once found myself in company with an infinite multitude of camels and their foals in that immense desert by which you do down from Babylon of the Confusion towards Egypt by way of Damascus; and of Arabs also there was no end! Not that I mean to say there were any camels in Seyllan; but there were innumerable elephants. And these though they be most ferocious monsters seldom hurt a foreigner. I even rode upon one once, that belonged to the Queen of Saba! That beast really did seem to have the use of reason—if it were not contrary to the Faith to think so.

[1] Dobner has *Judeos,* which I take to be an error for *Indos.*

[2] *Hhamál* (Ar.), a porter or bearer. The word is still commonly applied to palankin bearers in Western India.

CONCERNING THE FOOD OF OUR FIRST PARENTS.

Our first parents, then, lived in Seyllan upon the fruits I have mentioned, and for drink had the milk of animals. They used no meat till after the deluge, nor to this day do those men use it who call themselves the children of Adam. Adam, you know, was set down upon the mountain of Seyllan, and began there to build him a house with slabs of marble, etc., as has been already related. At that place dwell certain men under religious vows, and who are of surpassing cleanliness in their habits; yea of such cleanliness that none of them will abide in a house where anyone may have spit; and to spit themselves (though in good sooth they rarely do such a thing) they will retire a long way, as well as for other occasions.

They eat only once a day, and never oftener; they drink nothing but milk or water; they pray with great propriety of manner; they teach boys to form their letters, first by writing with the finger on sand, and afterwards with an iron style upon leaves of paper, or rather I should say upon leaves of a certain tree.

In their cloister they have certain trees that differ in foliage from all others. These are encircled with crowns of gold and jewels, and there are lights placed before them, and these trees they worship[1]. And they pretend

[1] These were doubtless Peepul trees representing the celebrated tree of Buddh-Gaya, of which a shoot has been cherished at Anurajapura for twenty centuries (see *Tennent*, i, 343; ii, 614). Such trees are maintained in the courtyard of nearly every *wihara* or temple in Ceylon as objects of veneration (Hardy's *Eastern Monachism*, p. 212; Knox, p. 18). It is difficult to account for the strange things that Marignolli puts into the mouths of the Buddhists. Probably he communicated with them through Mahomedans, who put things into their own shape. The Buddha's Foot of the Ceylonese monks was the Adam's Foot of the Mahomedans, hence by legitimate algebra Buddha=Adam, and Adam may be substituted for Buddha. The way in which Herodotus makes the Persians, or the Phenicians or Egyptians, give *their* versions of the stories of Io and Europa and other Greek legends, affords quite a parallel case, and probably originated in a like cause, viz., the perversions of *ciceroni*. We may be sure that the Persians knew no more of Io than the Singalese Sramanas did of Adam and Cain. (See *Herod.*, i, 1–5; ii, 54, 55, etc.)

to have received this right by tradition from Adam, saying that they adore those trees because Adam looked for future salvation to come from wood. And this agrees with that verse of David's, "*Dicite in gentibus, quia Dominus regnabit in ligno,*" though for a true rendering it would be better to say *curabit a ligno*[1].

These monks, moreover, never keep any food in their house till the morrow. They sleep on the bare ground; they walk barefoot, carrying a staff; and are contented with a frock like that of one of our Minor Friars (but without a hood), and with a mantle cast in folds over the shoulder *ad modum Apostolorum*[2]. They go about in procession every morning begging rice for their day's dinner. The princes and others go forth to meet them with the greatest reverence, and bestow rice upon them in measure proportioned to their numbers; and this they partake of steeped in water, with coco-nut milk and plantains[3]. These things I speak of as an eye-witness; and indeed

[1] The quotation is from a celebrated reading of Psalm xcvi, 10 (in the Vulgate, xcv, 10), respecting which I have to thank my friend Dr. Kay, of Bishop's College, Calcutta, for the following note:

"The addition *a ligno* (which is not in the Vulgate, i.e. Jerome's 'Gallican Psalter') is from the *old* Vulgate, which was made in Africa in the first or second century, and was used by Tertullian, St. Augustine, etc. It was no doubt through St. Augustine that the rendering was handed down to your friend Marignolli.

"Justin Martyr says (and it was not denied by Trypho) that ἀπὸ ξύλου occurred in the LXX. It is not known I believe in any MS. now existing; and the inference drawn is that Justin had been misled by certain copies in which some pious marginal annotation had been introduced by later copyists into the text." Dr. Kay adds the following quotation by Bellarmine from Fortunatus:

"*Impleta sunt quæ cecinit*
David fideli carmine,
Dicens, De nationibus
Regnavit a ligno Deus."

I may add since writing the above that copious remarks on this reading of the Psalm are to be found in *Notes and Queries*, 2nd series, viii, pp. 470, 516 *seq*.

[2] This use of the phrase satisfactorily illustrates the *alla apostolica* which Varthema so often uses. See Jones and Badger's *Varthema* (HAK. SOC.), pp. 78, 112, etc.

[3] "*Lixam in aqua comedunt cum lacte nargillorum et musis.*"

they made me a *festa* as if I were one of their own order[1].

There follow Chapters *Concerning the Multiplication of the Human Race, The Offerings of Cain and Abel, etc., etc.*, to the end of the first section of his book, which he terms *Thearchos*. These chapters do not contain anything to our purpose except a few slight notices here and there, which I shall now extract. Thus of Cain he says:

If we suppose that he built his city after the murder of Abel there is nothing in this opposed to Scripture, unless so far that it seems to be implied that he never did settle down, but was always a vagabond and a fugitive. This city of his is thought to have been where now is that called KOTA in Seyllan[2], a place where I have been. After he had begotten many sons there he fled towards Damascus, where he was shot by the arrow of Lamech his descendant in the seventh generation; and there, hard by Damascus, his sepulchre is shown to this day[3].

In the next passage also he seems to be speaking of Hebron from personal knowledge:

And the story goes that Adam mourned the death of his son Abel for a hundred years, and desired not to beget any more sons, but dwelt in a certain cave apart from Eve, until by command of an angel he rejoined her, and begat

[1] A most accurate account of the Buddhist monks as they may be seen to-day in Burma, and I presume in Ceylon. What Marignolli saw he describes very correctly; his interpreters are, probably, therefore responsible for the stuff he says he heard.

[2] The author curiously overlooks *Gen.* iv, 17. Kotta, or (Buddhisto-classically) Jáyawardanapúra, near Columbo, is first mentioned as a royal residence about 1314, but it again became the capital of the island in 1410, and continued so about a century and a half. It appears to be represented as such in the great Map of Fra Mauro, under the name of *Cotte Civitas*.

[3] This legend of Lamech shooting the aged Cain in a thicket, by mistake for an animal, and then killing the youth who had pointed out the game to him, seems to have been invented by the Hebrews as an explanation of the saying of Lamech in *Genesis*, iv, 23. It is the subject of a curious fresco in the Campo Santo at Pisa.

Seth. Then he separated himself from the generation of evil doers, and directed his course towards Damascus, and at last he ended his days in EBRON, and there he was buried, some twenty miles from Jerusalem. And the city was called *Arba*, i.e. of the four, because there were buried there Adam the chief, then Abraham, Isaac, Jacob, in the double cave that is in Ebron. And there the Patriarchs and other holy Fathers were afterwards buried, and Joseph also when he was brought up out of Egypt.

To Seth, he says,

Succeeded his son Enoch, who began to call upon the name of the Lord. This is believed to mean that he first instituted the practice of addressing God in audible prayers, and that he founded a religious discipline and peculiar rule of life, such as is followed to this day (they say) by the Bragmans, and by the monks of Seyllan, though these have turned aside to idolatry and to the worship of a tree, as we have related....

. ...And the sons of Adam in Seyllan adduce many proofs that the flood reached not to them. And this is one of the chief, that in the eastern part of the country there are a number of roaming vagabond people whom I have seen myself, and who call themselves the sons of Cain[1]. Their faces are huge, hideous, and frightful enough to terrify anybody. They never can stay more than two days in one place, and if they did they would stink so that nobody could endure them. They seldom show themselves, but yet they are given to trade. Their wives and children, as frightful goblins as themselves, they carry about upon donkeys[2]. Yet St. Augustine and the mass of theologians

[1] Mas'udi says there was a race of Indians descended from Cain in the country of *Kumár* where the aloes wood came from. (*Prairies d'Or*, i, 72.)

[2] Here he speaks of the *Veddahs*, or Aborigines of Ceylon. Compare Tennent's description: "Miserable objects, active but timid, and athletic though deformed, with large heads and misshapen limbs. Their long

deem it absurd to suppose that any should have escaped the Deluge unless in the ark....

...And the ark grounded in the seventh month on a mountain of Armenia, which is near the Iron Gates in the Empire of Uzbek, and is called Ararat in the Lesser Armenia.

Next we come to the *Second Age*, and the beginning of the Second Book which is called *Monarchos*.

From the first chapter, which treats *Of the Distribution of the Earth among the Sons of Noah*, I extract some passages:

Noah therefore under the command of God delivered instructions to his sons about maintaining divine service in the worship of the One God by sacrifices, about the multiplication of offspring, and the division of the earth, that they might replenish it, and live in peace after his death. And he desiring a quiet life for his remaining days, reserved for himself the Isle of Cethym [Chittim] now called Cyprus[1]. Shem the firstborn, as king and priest after his father, obtained half of the world, i.e., all Asia the Great, extending from the White Sea beyond Hungary, where now are the Wallachians[2], in a straight line over all the empire

black hair and beards fell down to the middle in uncombed lumps, they stood with their faces bent towards the ground, and their restless eyes twinkled upwards with an expression of uneasiness and apprehension.... The children were unsightly objects, entirely naked, with misshapen joints, huge heads and protuberant stomachs; the women, who were reluctant to appear, were the most repulsive specimens of humanity I have ever seen in any country" (ii, 450).

[1] Where, says Marignolli in another passage, "he planted a vineyard, which belongs at this day to the Archbishop of Nicosia." (*Dobner*, p. 109.)

[2] "*Olachi*." But what White Sea is meant, that lies beyond Hungary where the Wallachians are? The Caspian, the Sea of Marmora, the Mediterranean, the Baltic, have all claims to the title of the White Sea, but none of these will do, and what *we* call the White Sea seems too remote from Hungary and Wallachia. There was indeed a Great Hungary, and a great Wallachia recognized towards the Ural. (See *Roger Bacon's Opus Majus*, Venice, 1750, p. 173.) Fra Mauro has a *Mar Biancho* represented as a large lake in this quarter; whether it stands for Lake Ladoga, the White Sea, or the Baikal (as Zurla thinks),

of Uzbek, Katay, the Indies, and Ethiopia to the world's end.

The other half was divided between the other two brothers. Cham had Africa (including the Holy Land[1]) by Carthage and Tunis[2] to the world's end. Japhet the younger had Europe where we are now, that is to say, all on this side from Hungary, and all on this side from Rome[3], including Germany, France, Bohemia, Poland and England, and so to the world's end.

The next chapter is *Concerning Worship after the Flood*, a large portion of which is worthy of translation :

would be difficult to say, so compressed is his northern geography; but it is most likely that it means whatever Marignolli means by the same expression. Indeed a glance at Fra Mauro's Map makes Marignolli's division of the earth much more intelligible. There seems to be no doubt that the White Sea of Fra Mauro, and probably, therefore, that of Marignolli, is an exaggeration of the Russian Lake called *Bielo Osero*, which does mean *White Lake*, and out of which flows the R. Szesna, an important feeder of the Volga. The only modification required is that Marignolli conceives Ethiopia as running out eastward, to the south of the Indian Ocean, as remote Africa does in the geography of Edrisi and other Arab writers, as well as that of Ptolemy and the geographer of Ravenna. Make this modification and then you will see how one half of the hemisphere is divided into Europe and Africa, whilst the other is Asia, in which a "a straight line" may be drawn from the White Sea, passing successively through the empire of Uzbek, Cathay, the Indies, Ethiopia, and the World's End !

1 "*Africam ubi est Terra Sancta.*"

2 *Turusium*, which I venture to correct to *Tunisium.*

3 Dobner prints it "*scilicet ab* Ungaria, Cytra, *et* Roma," treating all three as proper names apparently. I suspect it should be "*scilicet ab Ungariâ citrà et* Romaniâ," meaning perhaps from *Hither Hungary*, viz., our modern Hungary as distinguished from the Great Hungary of note (2), p. 246.

Shem was anxious to maintain the worship of the true God, and his history we shall now follow. In the second year after the flood he begat Arfaxat, who in turn begat Elam, from whom the noble race of the Alans in the East is said to have sprung. They form at this day the greatest and noblest nation in the world, the fairest and bravest of men[1]. 'Tis by their aid that the Tartars have won the empire of the east, and without them they have never gained a single important victory. For Chinghiz Caam, the first king of the Tartars, had seventy-two of their princes serving under him when he went forth under God's providence to scourge the world[2]....Arfaxat the son of Shem, at the age of thirty-five begat Sela or Sale, by whom India was peopled and divided into three kingdoms. The first of these is called MANZI, the greatest and noblest province in the world, having no paragon in beauty, pleasantness, and extent. In it is that noble city of CAMPSAY, besides ZAYTÚN, CYNKALAN, JANCI[3], and

[1] "*Major et nobilior natio mundi et homines pulchriores et fortiores.*" Compare with the description by Ammianus Marcellinus of the Alans in his time: "Proceri autem Alani paene sunt omnes et pulchri, crinibus mediocriter flavis, oculorum temperatâ torvitate terribiles, et armorum levitate veloces" (xxxi, 2).

[2] [This is a mistake; the Alans entered the service of the Mongols only after the conquest of their country by Okkodai. "The Mongols, when they had passed the Caucasus in 1223, found the Alans living on the northern skirts of the Caucasus. Fifteen years later the Alans became subject to Batu Khan, after they had made a stout resistance to the Mongols. The Mohammedan historians who record the expeditions against the Alans call them indiscriminately *Alans* or *Asi* (d'Ohsson, ii, 619, 620)." (Bretschneider, *Med. Res.*, ii, p. 85.) "We learn from the *Yüan shi* that in the Mongol period the Alans were not only well known in China, but their nation furnished many able officers to the Mongol-Chinese empire. Several of them held high offices or distinguished themselves as valiant captains. Among the biographies in the *Yüan shi*, more than twenty meritorious Alans, some of them of royal blood, have been immortalised, and besides these the names of many others are found there. The Alans are generally termed there *A-su*, sometimes also *A-sze*. The name *A-lan* occurs there only once, viz., in the list of the Si pei ti, where it is coupled with A-su. The *Yüan shi* mentions the *A-su* first *s.a.* 1223." (Bretschneider, *Med. Res.*, ii, pp. 87–88.) See p. 186 *n.*]

[3] [Dobner has *Janu.*] Janci is doubtless Yang chau, see note to *Odoric*, p. 210.

many other cities. Manzi was formerly called CYN, and it has to this day the noble port and city called Cynkalan, i.e. "Great India" [Great China], for *kalan* signifies *great*. And in the Second India, which is called MYNIBAR there is CYNKALI, which signifieth "Little India" [Little China], for kali is *Little*[1].

The second kingdom of India is called Mynibar[2], and 'tis of that country that St. Augustine speaketh in treating of the Canine Philosophers, who had this name of Canine because they used to teach people to do as dogs do, e.g. that a man should never be ashamed of anything that was natural to him[3]. They did not, however, succeed in persuading these people even that sons might without shame bathe before their fathers, or let their nakedness be seen by them[4].

It is in this country that lies the city of Columbum, where the pepper grows, of which we have already spoken.

The third province of India is called Maabar, and the church of St. Thomas which he built with his own hands is there, besides another which he built by the agency of

[1] On *Cynkalan* or Canton and *Cynkali* or Cranganore, see notes to *Odoric*, pp. 179 and 133. As regards Cranganore it may be added that it seems to have been one of the most ancient capitals of Malabar, and in some of the ancient copper deeds appears to be called Muyiri-Kodu, which a writer in the *Madras Journal* indicates as perhaps identifying it with the classical *Muziris* (?). It is now almost a deserted place, but the ancient line of its Rajas still exists (*Day*, p. 11). In connexion with Marignolli's interpretation of Cynkali it is somewhat curious that Abdurrazzak tells us the people of the neighbouring city of Calicut were known by the name of *Chini-Bachagán*, "Sons of the Chinese" or "Chinese Young Ones." There is no Persian word *kali*, "little." The nearest explanation that I can find for Marignolli's etymology is the Arabic *kalíl*, "little, small, moderate" (*Richardson*).

[2] Here and where it occurs just before, Dobner has *Nymbar*, but the Venice MS. has correctly *Mynibar*. See note at p. 132.

[3] See Augustine, *De Civitate Dei*, xiv, 20.

[4] Here the author refers to the remarkable decency of the Hindus in such matters, which may well rebuke some who call them "niggers." "Among the Lydians," says Herodotus, "and indeed among the barbarians generally, it is reckoned a deep disgrace, even to a man, to be seen naked" (i, 10).

workmen. These he paid with certain very great stones which I have seen there, and with a log cut down on Adam's Mount in Seyllan, which he caused to be sawn up, and from its sawdust other trees were sown. Now that log, huge as it was, was cut down by two slaves of his and drawn to the seaside by the saint's own girdle. When the log reached the sea he said to it, "Go now and tarry for us in the haven of the city of Mirapolis[1]." It arrived there accordingly, whereupon the king of that place with his whole army endeavoured to draw it ashore, but ten thousand men were not able to make it stir. Then St. Thomas the Apostle himself came on the ground, riding on an ass, wearing a shirt, a stole, and a mantle of peacock's feathers, and attended by those two slaves and by two great lions, just as he is painted, and called out "Touch not the log, for it is mine!" "How," quoth the king, "dost thou make it out to be thine?" So the Apostle loosing the cord wherewith he was girt, ordered his slaves to tie it to the log and draw it ashore. And this being accomplished with the greatest ease, the king was converted, and bestowed upon the saint as much land as he could ride round upon his ass. So during the day-time he used to go on building his churches in the city, but at night he retired to a distance of three Italian miles, where there were numberless peacocks[2]...and thus being shot in the side with an arrow such as is called *friccia*[3], (so that

[1] Mirapolis is a Grecized form of Mailapúr, Meliapur, or, as the Catalan Map has it, Mirapor, the place since called San Thomé, near the modern Madras. *Mailapúram* means or may mean *Peacock-Town*. A suburb still retains the name Mailapúr. It is near the shore, about three miles and a half south of Fort St. George, at the mouth of the Sydrapetta River. [*Marco Polo*, ii, p. 355 *n.*]

[2] There is an evident hiatus here, though not indicated as such in the copies. Marignolli probably meant to relate, as Polo does (iii, 22), how the saint being engaged in prayer in the middle of the peafowl, a native aiming at one of them shot him.

[3] Meinert has here "*mit einem Pfeile, indisch* Friccia *genannt.*" But it is no *Indisch*, only the Italian *Freccia*=*Flèche*. I do not know why the word is introduced.

his wound was like that in the side of Christ into which he had thrust his hand), he lay there before his oratory from the hour of complines, continuing throughout the night to preach, whilst all his blessed blood was welling from his side; and in the morning he gave up his soul to God. The priests gathered up the earth with which his blood had mingled, and buried it with him. By means of this I experienced a distinct miracle twice over in my own person, which I shall relate elsewhere[1].

Standing miracles are, however, to be seen there, in respect both of the opening of the sea, and of the peacocks[2]. Moreover whatever quantity of that earth be removed from the grave one day, just as much is replaced spontaneously against the next. And when this earth is taken in a potion it cures diseases, and in this manner open miracles are wrought both among Christians and among Tartars and Pagans[3].

[1] He does not in this work.

[2] "*Tam de apertione maris quam de pavonibus.*" There is nothing before about this opening of the sea, and the meaning is dark. John of Hese has a foolish story about St. Thomas's tomb being on an island in the sea, and that every year a path was laid dry for fifteen days for the pilgrims to pass through the sea. But Marignolli who had been at the place could not mean such stuff as this. Maffei however mentions that St. Thomas, in erecting a cross at Meliapor, which was then ten leagues from the sea (!), prophesied that when the sea should reach that vicinity white men should come from the world's end and restore the law which he had taught. Perhaps there is an allusion to such a tradition here. There is also a curious Tamul legend bearing upon this which is cited in Taylor's *Catalogue Raisonné of Or. MSS.* (Madras, vol. iii, p. 372). Mailapur was anciently inhabited by Jainas. One had a dream that in a few days the town would be overwhelmed by the sea. Their holy image was removed further inland, and three days later the old town was swallowed up. The temples were then reestablished in a town called Mailamanagara, where exactly the same thing happened again. It is added that tradition runs in reference to the whole coast from San Thomé to the Seven Pagodas, that extensive ruins exist beneath the sea and are sometimes visible.

[3] The mention of Tartars here is curious, and probably indicates that the Chinese ships occasionally visited Mailapur. The Chinese are constantly regarded as Tartars at this time.

The Roman Catholic ecclesiastical travellers and hagiologists seem to have striven who should most expand the missionary travels of

That king also gave St. Thomas a perpetual grant of the public steelyard for pepper and all aromatic spices,

Thomas the Apostle. According to an abstract given by Padre Vincenzo his preaching began in Mesopotamia, extended through Bactria, etc., to China, "the States of the Great Mogul" (!) and Siam: he then revisited his first converts, and passed into Germany, and thence to Brazil, "as relates the P. Emanuel de Nobrega," and from that to Ethiopia. After thus bringing light to Asia, Europe, America, and Africa, the indefatigable Apostle retook his way to India, converting Socotra by the way, and then preached in Malabar and on the Coromandel coast, where he died as here related.

It is a somewhat remarkable circumstance in relation to the alleged mission of Thomas to India, that whilst the Apocryphal Acts of the Apostles, ascribed to Abdias, Bishop of Babylonia, relate that before he visited that part of India where he was killed, he had in another region of India converted a king called Gundopharus, a king's name nearly identical with this (Gondophares) has in recent times become known from the Indo-Scythian coins discovered in N. W. India. The strange legend ran that this king Gundopharus sent to the West a certain merchant named Abban to seek a skilled architect to build him a palace. Whereupon the Lord sold Thomas to him as a slave of His who was expert in such work. After leaving Gundopharus Thomas went to the country of a certain King Meodeus (*Mahadeva?*), where he was eventually put to death by lances. The story which Marignolli tells of the great log survived for many generations, and is related in much the same way by Maffei and by Linschoten towards the end of the sixteenth century, and again by the Carmelite Padre Vincenzo late in the seventeenth. It was supposed to be alluded to among other things in the mystic inscription which surrounded the miraculous cross on St. Thomas's Mount. And strange to say Gasparo Balbi relates something like a duplicate of the miracle which he declares he witnessed, and which occurred for the benefit of the Jesuits when in sore need of long beams for a new church at San Thomé.

The spot where Thomas is believed to have been slain is, according to Heber, at the "Little Mount," a small rocky knoll with a Roman Catholic church upon it (now "Church of the Resurrection"), and where a footmark of the Apostle in the rock is I believe still exhibited, close to Marmalong Bridge, on the Sydrapetta river, adjoining the suburb still called Mailapur. The "Great Mount" is an insulated hill of granite some two miles further up on the south side of the river, with an old church on its summit, built by the Portuguese in 1651, but now the property of the Catholic Armenians. I believe it is or was under the altar of a church on the latter site that the miraculous cross existed which was believed to have been cut in the rock by Thomas himself, and to exhibit various annual phenomena, sometimes sweating blood, which betokened grievous calamities. "These wonders began," says P. Vincenzo, with *sancta simplicitas*, "some years after the arrival of the Portuguese in India." Alexander Hamilton however says that tradition assigned the Great Mount as the scene of the martyrdom.

The Padre Vincenzo "would not wonder if that were true" which John, Patriarch of the Indies, was said to have declared to Pope Calixtus, viz., that St. Thomas every year appeared visibly and ad-

and no one dares take this privilege from the Christians

ministered the sacrament to his Indian Christians. John of Hese has got a story of this kind too.

[Mr. W. R. Philipps has a valuable paper on *The Connection of St. Thomas the Apostle with India* in the *Indian Antiquary*, xxxii, 1903, pp. 1–15, 145–160; he has come to the following conclusions: "(1) There is good early evidence that St. Thomas was the apostle of the Parthian empire; and also evidence that he was the apostle of 'India' in some limited sense,—probably an 'India' which included the Indus Valley, but nothing to the east or south of it. (2) According to the Acts, the scene of the martyrdom of St. Thomas was in the territory of a king named, according to the Syriac version, Mazdai, to which he had proceeded after a visit to the city of a king named, according to the same version, Gūdnaphar or Gūndaphar. (3) There is no evidence at all that the place where St. Thomas was martyred was in Southern India; and all the indications point to another direction. (4) We have no indication whatever, earlier than that given by Marco Polo, who died 1324, that there ever was even a tradition that St. Thomas was buried in Southern India."]

[In a recent and learned work (*Die Thomas-Legende*, 1912, 8vo.) Father J. Dahlmann has tried to prove that the story of the travels of St. Thomas in India has an historical basis. If there is some possibility of admitting a voyage of the Apostle to N.W. India (and the flourishing state of Buddhism in this part of India is not in favour of Christian Evangelization) it is impossible to accept the theory of the martyrdom of Thomas in Southern India.]

In the beginning of the sixteenth century Barbosa found the church of St. Thomas half in ruins and grown round with jungle. A Mahomedan fakir kept it and maintained a lamp. Yet in 1504, which is several years earlier than Barbosa's voyage, the Syrian Bishop Jaballaha, who had been sent by the Patriarch to take charge of the Indian Christians, reported that the House of St. Thomas had begun to be inhabited by some Christians, who were engaged in restoring it. [See Marco Polo, ii, pp. 355 *n. seq.*]

The Portuguese have a curious history of the search for the bones of St. Thomas by a deputation sent by the Viceroy Duarte Menezes in 1522, under orders from King John III. The narrative states circumstantially that the Apostle's bones were found, besides those of the king whom he had converted, and an inscription commemorating the building of the church by St. Thomas, etc. The bones were eventually removed to Goa. Yet older tradition in the West asserted positively that Thomas was buried at Edessa.

There are numbers of poor native Christians at Madras now. Most of the men who man the *masúla* or surf-boats are such. Have they come down from St. Thomas's time, or who are they? Does anybody know? (See *P. Vincenzo Maria, Viaggi*, pp. 132–136; *Assemani*, pp. 32 and 450; *Linschoten*, p. 28; *Gasparo Balbi*, f. 86; *Kircher, China Illustrata*, p. 53; *Heber's Journal*; *Barbosa* in *Ramusio*, i, f. 315; *Hamilton's New Account of the E. Indies*, 1744, i, 359; *Fabricius*, Collection of Apocryphal books of New Testament (*proper title mislaid*), pp. 691, 699; *Reinaud* in *Mém. de l'Acad. des Insc.* (1849) xviii, p. 95; *Maffei*, *Historia Indica*, l. viii; *Faria y Sousa's Portuguese Asia*, pt. iii, c. 7.)

but at the peril of death[1]. I spent four days there; there is an excellent pearl fishery at the place.

. . . .

Now to say something of the monstrous creatures which histories or romances have limned or lied about, and have represented to exist in India. Such be those that St. Augustine speaks of in the Sixteenth Book *De Civitate Dei*; as, for example, that there be some folks who have but one eye in the forehead; some who have their feet turned the wrong way; some alleged to partake of the nature of both sexes, and to have the right breast like a man's, the left breast like a woman's; others who have neither head nor mouth, but only a hole in the breast. Then there are some who are said to subsist only by the breath of their nostrils; others a cubit in height who war with cranes. Of some 'tis told that they live not beyond eight years, but conceive and bear five times. Some have no joints; others lie ever on their backs holding up the sole of the only foot they have to shade them; others again have dog's heads. And then poets have invented ypotamuses and plenty of other monsters.

Concerning all these St. Augustine concludeth either that they exist not at all, or if they do exist they have the use of reason, or are capable of it. All men come from Adam, and even if they be natural monstrosities still they are from Adam. Such monstrosities are indeed born among ourselves from time to time, and a few also in those regions; but then they amount to a good many if you take what are born from the whole family of man[2]. Such

[1] One of the old copper grants, which are claimed by the Malabar Christians as the charters of their ancient privileges, contains a passage thus interpreted in the *Madras Journal* for 1844, p. 119: "We have given as eternal possession to Iravi Corttan, the lord of the town, the brokerage and due customs of all that may be measured by the *para*, weighed by the balance, stretched by the line, of all that may be counted or carried,...salt, sugar musk, and lamp-oil, or whatever it be, namely within the river mouth of Codangulor" (Cranganore), etc.

[2] St. Augustine's chapter is headed: "*An ex propagine Adam vel*

is the case (as he exemplifies the matter) with the different sorts of hunchbacks, with men who have six fingers, and many others of like character[1]. So the most noble Emperor Charles IV brought from Tuscany a girl whose face, as well as her whole body, was covered with hair, so that she looked like the daughter of a fox[2]! Yet is there no such race of hairy folk in Tuscany: nor was her own mother even, nor her mother's other children so, but like the rest of us[3]. Such too was that monster whom we saw in Tuscany, in the district of Florence, in our own time and which a pretty woman gave birth to. It had two heads perfectly formed, four arms, two busts, perfect as far as the navel, but there running into one. There was one imperfect leg sticking out of the side, and only two legs below, yet it was baptized as two persons. It survived for a week. I saw also at Bologna, when I was lecturing there, a ewe which bore a monstrous lamb of like character, with two heads and seven feet. Yet we do not suppose that such creatures exist as a species, but regard them as

filiorum Noe quædam genera hominum monstrosa prodierint?" After mentioning a number of the alleged monsters, such as are detailed here, and some of which he says were painted in mosaic in the *Maritima Platea* at Carthage, he comes to the conclusion cited by Marignolli. (*De Civitate Dei*, xvi, 8.)

[1] According to Ricci in Trigault (*De Christiana Exped. apud Sinas*, 1617, p. 94) many in the southern provinces of China "had two nails upon the little toe of either foot, a thing noticed in all the people of Cochin China, their neighbours, and perhaps an indication that they had all formerly six toes." These six-toed men occur also in India occasionally. I had a servant with this wealth of toes, and his name (Changa) was a sort of punning allusion to the peculiarity. [Cf. *Kiao-chi*, "crossed toes," in *Marco Polo*, ii, p. 119 *n.*]

[2] This is mentioned by Matteo Villani, who says that when the emperor was at Pietra Santa, on his return from his coronation at Rome, there was presented to him a female child of seven, all woolly like a sheep, as if with a wool badly dyed of a red colour, and covered with this to the extremities of the lips and eyelids. The empress, marvelling at such a phenomenon, entrusted the child to her damsels and took her to Germany (*Chron.*, bk. v, ch. 53).

[3] See portrait of the "Hairy Woman" in the *Mission to Ava* in 1855. In that case the phenomenon had appeared in at least three generations. [See II, 168.]

natural monstrosities. So doth God choose to show forth His power among men, that we may render thanks to Him that He hath not created us with such deformities, and that we may fear Him!

But I, who have travelled in all the regions of the Indians, and have always been most inquisitive, with a mind indeed too often addicted more to curious inquiries than to virtuous acquirements, (for I wanted if possible to know everything)—I have taken more pains, I conceive, than another who is generally read or at least well known[1], in investigating the marvels of the world; I have travelled in all the chief countries of the earth, and in particular to places where merchants from all parts of the world do come together, such as the Island of Ormes, and yet I never could ascertain as a fact that such races of men really do exist, whilst the persons whom I met used to question me in turn where such were to be found. The truth is that no such people *do* exist as nations, though there may be an individual monster here and there. Nor is there any people at all such as has been invented, who have but one foot which they use to shade themselves withal. But as all the Indians commonly go naked, they are in the habit of carrying a thing like a little tent-roof on a cane handle, which they open out at will as a protection against sun or rain. This they call a *chatyr*[2]; I brought one to Florence with me. And this it is which the poets have converted into a foot.

[1] "*Qui plus dedi operam, ut puto, quam alius qui legatur vel sciatur.*" Does this point at Odoric?

[2] *Chatr* (Pers.), an umbrella. It is strange that he should require to give so roundabout a description, for Ibn Batuta says that everybody, gentle and simple, at Constantinople used parasols at this time. I observe that a gilt umbrella is a part of the insignia of high church dignitaries in Italy, as it is in Burma and other Buddhistic countries. When did this originate? [Dobner has *Cyatyr.*]

ANECDOTE CONCERNING A CERTAIN INDIAN WHO WAS BAPTISED.

Here I must relate how when I was staying at Columbum with those Christian chiefs who are called *Modilial*[1], and are the owners of the pepper, one morning there came to me in front of the church a man of majestic stature and snowy white beard, naked from the loins upwards with only a mantle thrown about him, and a knotted cord [crossing his shoulder] like the stole of a deacon. He prostrated himself in reverence at full length upon the sand, knocking his head three times against the ground. Then he raised himself, and seizing my naked feet wanted to kiss them; but when I forbade him he stood up. After a while he sat down on the ground and told us the whole story of his life through an interpreter. This interpreter [strange to say] was his own son, who having been taken by pirates and sold to a certain Genoese merchant, had been baptized, and as it so chanced was then with us, and recognized his father by what he related.

The old man had never eaten flesh, had never but once been in the way of begetting offspring, habitually fasted four months in the year, ate only a little rice boiled in water, with fruit and herbs, and that late in the evening, used to spend his nights in prayer, and before he entered his place of prayer washed his whole body, and put on a dress of spotless linen reserved for this only. He then would go in and worship the devil in his image, with the most single-minded devotion. He was the priest of the whole of his island, which was situated in the remotest region of the Indies.

Now God seeing his purity enlightened him first with

[1] *Mudiliar* (Tamul), a head man. The word is in abundant and technical use in Ceylon, and probably in the south of India also.

wisdom from within; and afterwards the demon was constrained to address him through the idol's mouth, speaking thus: "Thou art not in the path of salvation! God therefore enjoineth thee to proceed to Columbum, a distance of two years voyage by sea, and there shalt thou find the messenger of God who shall teach thee the way of salvation!" "Now, therefore," said he to me, "here am I, come to thy feet and ready to obey thee in all things; and what is more, it was thy face that I saw in my dreams, as now I recognize." Then having prayed with tears, and strengthened him in his intent, we assigned his baptized son as his teacher and interpreter. And after three months' instruction I baptized him by the name of Michael, and blessed him, and sent him away, whilst he promised to preach to others the faith that he had acquired[1].

This story serves to exemplify that God (as St. Peter said of Cornelius the centurion) is no respecter of persons, but whosoever keepeth the law that is written in the heart (For the light of Thy countenance hath shone upon us, O Lord!) is accepted of Him, and is taught the way of salvation.

But I did not fail to inquire whether this man, who had for two years been sailing about the unexplored seas and islands of the Indies, had seen or even heard anything of those monsters of which we have been speaking; but he knew nothing whatever about them. Nor could I learn more when I was with the Queen of Saba; though there the sun rises just the opposite of here, and at noon the shadow of a man passes from left to right, instead of from

[1] The old man was evidently a Brahman, accurately described, and it is almost too great a stretch of charity to suppose that he came truly in search of instruction. For certainly the interpreter at least was playing on Marignolli's simplicity and vanity with the stories of the two years voyage, of the miraculous admonition, etc., to make him think he was enacting Peter to this new Cornelius. In fact it looks as if the whole was got up as a trick, in the spirit of those which the Duke and Duchess played on Don Quixote.

right to left, as it does here[1]. The north pole there was six degrees below the horizon, and the south pole as much elevated above it, as has been pointed out to me by Master Lemon of Genoa, a very noble astronomer, besides many other wonderful things in regard to the stars.

Giants do exist, undoubtedly; and I have seen one so tall that my head did not reach above his girdle; he had a hideous and disgusting countenance. There are also wild men, naked and hairy, who have wives and children, but abide in the woods. They do not show themselves among men, and I was seldom able to catch sight of one; for they hide themselves in the forest when they perceive any one coming. Yet they do a great deal of work, sowing and reaping corn and other things; and when traders go to them, as I have myself witnessed, they put out what they have to sell in the middle of the path, and run and hide. Then the purchasers go forward and deposit the price, and take what has been set down[2].

It is a fact also that monstrous serpents exist [in the east], and very like that which our lord the Emperor Charles hath in his park at Prague. There are also certain animals with countenances almost like a man's; more particularly in the possession of the Queen of Saba,

[1] "*Oritur sol modo opposito nobis, et in meridie transit umbra viri ad dextrum, sicut hic ad sinistrum, et occultatur ibi Polus Articus nobis gradibus sex, et antarticus totidem elevatur.*" [Dobner, p. 114.] I presume the man is supposed to be looking at his shadow with his back to the sun. The account is then intelligible.

[2] He may here refer either to the Veddahs of Ceylon (see *ante*, p. 245), or to the Poliars and like tribes of the continent, whom he may have seen during his long stay at Columbum, for both practise this dumb trade. Regarding the Veddahs, and the many authorities for their trading in this fashion from FaHian downwards, see *Tennent*, i, 592, etc.; and regarding the Poliars, see *Markham's Travels in Peru and India*, p. 404. A like fashion of trade is ascribed by Pliny (probably through some mistake) to the Seres; by Ibn Batuta to the dwellers in the Dark Lands of the North (ii, 400, 401); and by Cosmas to the gold-sellers near the Sea of Zingium or Zanzibar (*Montfaucon*, ii, 139). See also *Cadamosto* in *Ramusio*, i, and *Herodotus*, iv, 196, with Rawlinson's note thereon.

and in the cloister at Campsay in that most famous monastery where they keep so many monstrous animals, which they believe to be the souls of the departed[1]. [Not that they really are so] for I ascertained by irrefragable proof that they are irrational animals, except, of course, in so far as the devil may make use of them as he once did of the serpent's tongue. [Such delusions] those unbelievers may deserve to bring upon themselves because of their unbelief. But otherwise I must say that their rigid attention to prayer and fasting and other religious duties, if they but held the true faith, would far surpass any strictness and self-denial that we practise[2]. However [as I was going to say] those animals at Campsay usually come to be fed at a given signal, but I observed that they never would come when a cross was present, though as soon as it was removed they would come. Hence I conclude that these monsters are not men, although they may seem to have some of the properties of men, but are merely of the character of apes[3]; (indeed if we had never seen apes before we should be apt to look upon *them* as men!); unless forsooth they be monsters such as I have been speaking of before, which come of Adam's race indeed, but are exceptional and unusual births.

Nor can we conceive (and so says St. Augustine likewise) that there be any *antipodes*, i.e. men having the soles

[1] This is a very curious and unexceptional corroboration of Odoric's quaint story of the convent garden at King ssé (see, I, p. 202).

[2] So Ricold of Montecroce, who frequented the Mahomedan monastic institutions to study their law with the view of refuting it (he afterwards published a translation of the Koran and an argument against it), expresses his astonishment at finding *in lege tantæ perfidiæ opera tantæ perfectionis*. Who would not be astonished, he goes on, "to see the zeal of the Saracens in study, their devoutness in prayer, their charity to the poor, their reverence for the name of God, for the prophets and the holy places, the gravity of their manners, their affability to foreigners, their loving and peaceable conduct towards each other?" (*Peregrin. Quatuor*, etc., p. 131.)

[3] The argument of the cross would seem to cut the other way!

of their feet opposite to ours. Certainly not[1]. For the earth is founded upon the waters. And I have learned by sure experience that if you suppose the ocean divided by two lines forming a cross, two of the quadrants so formed are navigable, and the two others not navigable at all. For God willed not that men should be able to sail round the whole world.

I *have*, however, seen an hermaphrodite, but it was not able to propagate others like itself. Nor indeed does a mule propagate. Now let us go back to our subject.

The next chapter is one *Concerning the Multiplication of the Human Race, and the Division of the Earth, and the Tower of Babel.* I extract the following:

And they came to the plain of Senaar in the Greater Asia, near to the great River Euphrates. There indeed we find a vast level of seemingly boundless extent, in which, as I have seen, there is abundance of all kinds of fruits, and especially of dates, but also olives and vines in great plenty; so also of all field and garden produce, pumpkins, melons, and watermelons.

Then of Babel and Nimrod:

So he began and taught them to bake bricks to serve instead of stone, and, as there are many wells of bitumen there, they had bricks for stone, and bitumen for mortar. And this bitumen is a kind of pitch, very black and liquid, mixt with oil; and when it is used with bricks in building

[1] See *De Civitate Dei*, xvi, 9. Cosmas also rejects the notion of Antipodes with great scorn. "Scripture says that God made of one (blood) all nations of men for to dwell on the *whole* face of the earth, and not upon EVERY face of the earth" (not ἐπὶ παντὶ προσώπῳ, but ἐπὶ παντὸς προσώπου). But his clinching argument is, "How could rain at the Antipodes be said to *fall*? Why it would *come up* instead of falling" (pp. 121, 157, 191 of *Montfaucon*). I remember hearing that the Astronomer Royal, on finding fault with an engraver who had prepared the plates for a treatise of his wrongside upward, was met by the argument, "Why, sir, I thought there was no up or down in space!"

it solidifies and sets so hard that it is scarcely possible by any art to separate the joints, as I have myself seen and felt when I was on that Tower; and some of that hardened bitumen I carried away with me. The people of the country are continually demolishing the Tower, in order to get hold of the bricks. And the foundations of the city were laid upon the most extensive scale, so that every side of the square was, they say, eight Italian miles; and from what one sees this seems highly probable. They set the Tower at the extremity of the walls next the river, as if for a citadel, and as they built up the walls they filled the interior with earth, so that the whole was formed into a round and solid mass. In the morning when the sun is rising it casts an immensely long shadow across that wide plain[1].

[1] The ruin here identified by Marignolli with the Tower of Babel appears to be that called by Rich *Mujelibé*, and by Layard *Babel*. It is about half a mile from the present channel of the river. Layard speaks of "a line of walls which, leaving the foot of Babel, stretch inland about two miles and a half from the present bed of the Euphrates." It is generally admitted however that these cannot be the real ramparts of old Babylon, though Rich thought they might be the interior enclosure of the palaces; whilst Rennell took them to be the walls of some more recent city. Layard mentions that the excavation of bricks from the remains is still a trade, and they are sold as far as Baghdad. A like trade has thriven for years at Agra in India, where bricks are never made, but *dug for*.

The excavations at the Mujelibé or Babel showed that the structure was much as Marignolli describes, viz. an exterior of burnt bricks laid in bitumen enclosing the unburnt bricks which form the interior mass. So Nebuchadnezzar himself says in the Birs Nimrud inscription as rendered by Oppert: "The earthquake and the thunder had dispersed its sun-dried clay; the bricks of the casing had been split, and the earth of the interior had been scattered in heaps....In a fortunate month, in an auspicious day, I undertook to build porticoes around the crude brick masses, and the casing of burnt bricks." (*English Cyclop.*, article *Babylon*; *Rich's Memoir on Bab. and Persepolis*, 1839; *Smith's Dict. of the Bible* quoted in *Quarterly Review*, Oct. 1864; *Rawlinson's Herodotus*, with a clear plan in vol. ii.) It seems impossible, from his mention of the river and ramparts, etc., that Marignolli should here speak of the Birs Nimrud. (See also next note.) In later times Cæsar Federici, and again Tavernier, describe yet another ruin, that called *Akkerkuf* much nearer Baghdad, as the Tower of Babel.

CONCERNING THE DIVISION OF TONGUES.

Having related that history, and how the greatest part of the Tower was destroyed by lightning, he goes on:

And they attempted, it seems, to build similar towers elsewhere, but were not able. Insomuch that even when a certain soldan erected a great building upon the foundation of such a tower, it was struck down by lightning, and on his several times renewing the attempt it was always struck down. So he took his departure into Egypt, and there built the city of Babylon, and is still called the Soldan of Babylon[1].

. . . .

The second son of Nimrod was Belus, and had his residence in Babel after him....Now *Bagbel*, as it is called in their language, is different from Babylon. For the latter means *confusion*, whilst *bag* with the letter *g* means a *garden* or *paradise*. [*Bagbel* therefore means the Garden] of Bel, and it is called also *Bagdag*[2].

[1] This quaint statement of the supposed reason for the removal of the Caliphate to Egypt refers perhaps to the Birs Nimrud. Its lightning-rent aspect has struck all who have seen it, and is referred to even in the inscription quoted in the preceding note.

Babylon of Egypt is close to Old Cairo, and is still known as *Babul*. The name comes down from classic times, being mentioned by several writers from Ctesias to Ptolemy, and Babylon of Egypt was the headquarters of the Roman garrison in the time of Augustus. Cairo and Babylon existed together in the middle ages as two distinct cities; the merchants and artificers chiefly residing at Babylon; the Sultan, his amirs and men-at-arms in Cairo and the *Castrum*, which was, I suppose, the present citadel. But the city of the Egyptian Soldan is very commonly called in those days simply *Babylon*. Edrisi mentions that the city of Misr (which now means Cairo) was called in Greek *Bamblunah*. Pegolotti uses the term *Cairo de Bambillonia*. Mandeville, after carefully distinguishing between the two Babylons, puts the Furnace of the Three Children at the Egyptian Babylon; and yet he had served the Soldan in Egypt. (*Smith's Dict. of Gr. and Rom. Geog.*; *Marini Sanutii Torselli*, *Lib. Secret. Fid.*, etc., i, c. 6; *Edrisi*, i, 302; *Pegolotti*, cap. xv; *Mandeville*, p. 144.)

[2] Marignolli gets into a muddle in trying to connect *Babel* and *Baghdad*, building on the Persian *Bágh*, garden.

He then relates how Belus originated idolatry, and finishes with this singular passage:

The Jews however, the Tartars, and the Saracens, consider us to be the worst of idolaters, and this opinion is not confined to Pagans only, but is held also by some of the Christians. For although those Christians show devotion to pictures, they hold in abomination images, carved faces, and alarmingly life-like sculptures such as there are in our churches[1]; as for example on the sepulchre of St. Adalbert at Prague.

Then follow chapters *Concerning Nynus*, and *Concerning the Wife of Nynus.*

Semiramis, the wife of Nynus, the glory of womankind, hearing that her husband was slain, and fearing to entrust the government to her son, who was yet a child, kept him closely concealed. Meanwhile she adopted a dress made after the Tartar fashion, with large folds in front to disguise her bust, long sleeves to hide her lady's hands, long skirts to cover her feet, breeches to maintain her disguise when she mounted on horseback, her head well covered up, and so gave herself out for the son of Nynus, ruled in his name, and ordered that style of dress to be generally followed. She then ordered warlike armaments, and invaded India and conquered it....In India she clandestinely gave birth to a daughter, whom she made when grown up Queen of the finest island in the world, SABA[2] by name. In that

[1] "*Abhominantur larvas, facies, et horrendas sculpturas sicut sunt in ecclesiis.*" [Dobner, p. 118.] Not only the Oriental Christians, but even Jewish Doctors, distinguished between paintings and figures in relief, considering the former to be lawful (*Ludolf.*, *Comment.*, p. 372).

[2] Respecting Saba, see Introductory Notices. In this odd story of Semiramis and her daughter the Queen of Saba, we may perhaps trace the Arab traditions about the birth of Belkis (as they call her), Queen of Sheba or Saba in the time of Solomon. Her mother was said to be a daughter of the *jinns*, called *Umeira*, who falling in love with the Wazir of the tyrant King of Saba, *carried him to the island where she lived*, and married him. Within a year's time she bore

island women always, or for the most part, have held the government in preference to men. And in the palace there I have seen historical pictures representing women seated on the throne, with men on bended knees adoring before them. And so also I saw that actually in that country the women sat in the chariots or on the elephant-chairs, whilst the men drove the oxen or the elephants.

The only points worth noticing in his next chapter *Concerning Abraham*, are his derivation, often repeated, of *Saracen* from *Sarah*; and the remark regarding the Dead Sea, that it can be seen from the dormitory of the Minor Friars on Mount Zion[1].

The following chapter headed *Concerning the Kingdom of the Argives*, ends with a discussion *whether tithes are obligatory on Christians*, and this leads to an anecdote:

As long as the Church and its ministers are provided for in some other way, it may be doubted whether the law of tithe should be imposed; as it certainly was not by the Apostles or by the Fathers for many a day after their time. And a case occurred in my own experience at KAMUL[2], when many Tartars and people of other nations, on their first conversion, refused to be baptized unless we would

him Belkis, with whom the Wazir eventually returned to Saba, and the tyrant father being slain for his misdeeds, Belkis became the wise and glorious Queen who visited Solomon (*Weil's Biblical Legends*, pp. 195–197). Is it accidental that this story of Marignolli's associates Semiramis with the Queen of Sheba, the *Belkis* of the Arabs, whilst from modern researches *Beltis* the chief female deity of the Assyrians, appearing sometimes as the *wife of Nin*, becomes identified with the ancient stories of Semiramis? (see *Rawlinson's Herodotus*, i, 484, 495, 513).

[1] This is remarked also by Mas'udi.

[2] Kamul, Komul, Qomul, or Kamil, the Hami of the Chinese, and the station at which the routes eastward from the north and the south sides of the T'ien Shan converge, and from which travellers generally start to cross the desert before entering China (see *Polo*, ii, 36; and Benedict Goës, *infra*). The people of Kamil were all Buddhists in Marco Polo's time. In 1419 Shah Rúkh's envoys found there the mosque and Buddhist temple side by side.

swear that after their baptism we should exact no temporalities from them; nay, on the contrary, that we should provide for their poor out of our own means. This we did, and a multitude of both sexes in that city did then most gladly receive baptism. 'Tis a doubtful question, but with submission to the Church's better judgment I would use no compulsion.

After sundry chapters about the *Foundation of Rome* and the like, we come at last to the *Prologue or Preface* (!) viz., to the actual Bohemian history. 'Tis a wonderful specimen of rigmarole, addressed to the emperor, in which the author shows the reluctance of a man entering a shower-bath in January to commit himself to the essential part of his task. The history affords none of the reminiscences which we seek for extract: a few notices of interest remain however to be gathered from his third book, which he calls *Jerarticus*.

Thus, in speaking of circumcision, he says:

Talking on this matter with some of the more intelligent Jews who were friends of mine (at least as far as Jews can be friends with a Christian), they observed to me that the general law in question could never be fulfilled except with a very sharp razor, either of steel or of some nobler metal, such as bronze or gold. And they agreed with the dictum of Aristotle in his book of Problems, when he expressly asserts that cuts made with a knife of bronze or gold are healed more quickly than such as are made with a steel instrument. And this accords with the practice of the surgeons of Cathay, as I have seen.

From the chapter *Concerning Jehoiada* [*Yoyada*] *the Priest*.

At this time God pitying his people caused Elias to appear, who had been kept by God, it is not known where. That may be true which the Hebrews allege (as Jerome mentions in his comment on I Chronicles, xxi), viz., that he is the same as Phineas the son of Eleazar[1]. But it is asserted both by the Hebrews and the Sabæans, i.e., the people of the kingdom of the Queen of Saba, that he had his place of abode in a very lofty mountain of that land which is called Mount Gybeit, meaning the Blessed Mountain. In this mountain also they say that the Magi were praying on the night of Christ's nativity when they saw the Star. It is in a manner inaccessible, for from the middle of the mountain upwards the air is said to be so thin and pure that none, or at least very few, have been able to ascend it, and that only by keeping a sponge filled with water over the mouth. They say however that Elias by the will of God remained hidden there until the period in question.

The people of Saba say also that he still sometimes shows himself there. And there is a spring at the foot of that mountain where they say he used to drink, and I have drunk from that spring myself. But I was unable to ascend that Blessed Mountain, being weighed down with infirmities, the result of a very powerful poison that I had

[1] The Hebrew notions about the identity of Phineas and Elias have been adopted and expanded by the Mahomedans, who also identify in some way with them their mysterious prophet Khidhr. Hermitages or chapels dedicated to Khidhr and Elias appear to have been very numerous in Mussulman countries, especially on *hill-tops* (see *Ibn Batuta* passim). And the oriental Christians and semi-Christians also always associate Elias with mountain tops. There seems to be scarcely a prominent peak in the Greek Archipelago with which the name of Elias is not connected.

I do not know what *Gybeit* is, which he interprets as *Beatus*. *Kubeis* is the name of one of the holy mountains at Mecca of which wonderful things are related, but I find no meaning assigned to the name. There are many mountains in Java (if Java be the Saba of our author) which might in vast height and sublimity of aspect answer to the suggestions of Marignolli's description; none better perhaps than the Tjerimai, rising in isolated majesty to a height greater than Etna's, in the immediate vicinity of the coast, and close to Cheribon, the earliest seat of Mahomedanism in the island. Little less striking, and still more lofty, though not so isolated, is the Great S'lámat, a little further eastward, and by a singular coincidence its name (from the Arabic *Saláמat*, Peace or Salvation) might fairly be translated *Mons Beatus*.

swallowed in Columbum, administered by those who wished to plunder my property. Although I was passing pieces of flesh from my intestines with a vast amount of blood, and suffered from an incurable dysentery of the third species for something like eleven months, a disease such as they say no one ever escaped from with life, yet God had compassion on me and spared me to relate what I had seen. For I did recover, by the aid of a certain female physician of that Queen's, who cured me simply by certain juices of herbs and an abstinent diet.

I frequently saw the Queen, and gave her my solemn benediction. I rode also upon her elephant, and was present at a magnificent banquet of hers. And whilst I was seated on a chair of state in presence of the whole city she honoured me with splendid presents. For she bestowed on me a golden girdle, such as she was accustomed to confer upon those who were created princes or chiefs. This was afterwards stolen from me by those brigands in Seyllan. She also bestowed raiment upon me, that is to say one hundred and fifty whole pieces[1] of very delicate and costly stuff. Of these I took nine for our lord the Pope, five for myself, gave three apiece to each of the chief among my companions, with two apiece to the subordinates, and all the rest I distributed in the Queen's own presence among her servants who stood around; that so they might perceive I was not greedy. And this thing was highly commended, and spoken of as very generous. I trust this little anecdote will not displease [His Majesty].

This and the following chapters contain a few incidental allusions to his homeward journey through the Holy Land. Thus he speaks of the entire destruction of the Temple and of the existence of a Mosque of the Saracens upon its site;

1 "*Pecias integras.*"

he gives a slight description of Bethlehem, with the Fountain of David, and the Cave of the Nativity, and alludes to having visited the Wilderness of the Temptation.

In one passage he quotes as the favourable testimony of an enemy, how

Machomet the accursed, in his Alcoran, in the third *Zora*, speaketh thus: O Mary, God hath purified thee and made thee holy above all women! etc.

The last extract that I shall make is from the same chapter.

Also all the philosophers and astrologers of Babylon and Egypt and Chaldea calculated that in the conjunction of Mercury with Saturn a girl should be born, who as a virgin, without knowledge of men, should bear a son in the land of Israel. And the image of this Virgin is kept in great state in a temple in Kampsay, and on the first appearance of the moon of the first month[1] (that is of February, which is the first month among the Cathayers) that new year's feast is celebrated with great magnificence, and with illuminations kept up all the night.

1 "*Prima lumina mensis primi*"; perhaps he means up to the full moon of the first month? The Chinese year commences from the new moon nearest to the middle point of Aquarius. The sun would enter Aquarius, according to the calendar in Marignolli's time, about the 28th of January, so that the Chinese first month would correspond in a partial way to February. The feast to which he alludes is the celebrated Feast of Lanterns, which is kept through the first fifteen days of the moon, but especially on the full moon. The image of which he speaks is doubtless that of the Buddhist personage whom the Chinese call *Kwan yin*, and to whom they give the name of "the Virgin" in conversing with Europeans, whilst conversely they apply the name of Kwan yin to the Romish images of the Virgin Mary (see *Davis's Chinese*, ii, 177). It does not appear however, that the Feast of Lanterns is connected with the worship of Kwan yin. Her birth is celebrated on the 19th day of the second moon, and another feast in her honour on the 16th day of the eleventh moon (*Chine Mod.*, ii, 649, 652). [Kwan yin (Avalōkitêçvara) is the Chinese Goddess of Mercy; her chief shrine is at Poo too in the Chusan Archipelago; in the Dalai Lama, of Tibet, the bodhisattwa Avalokiteçvara is believed to appear on earth. The Feast of Lanterns, *Shang yuen tsié*, celebrated on the fifteenth day of the first moon of the year, has nothing to do with Kwan yin.]